Volume 1

by
NICK SELUK

Layout assists by **Nicholas Hogge**

Rocketship Entertainment, LLC

Tom Akel, CEO & Publisher
Rob Feldman, CTO
Jeanmarie McNeely, CFO
Brandon Freeberg, Dir. of Campaign Mgmt.
Jed Keith, Social Media
rocketshipent.com

LARS THE AWKWARD YETI VOLUME 1
ISBN SOFTCOVER: 978-1-952126-22-2
ISBN HARDCOVER: 978-1-952126-23-9
First printing. June 2021. Copyright © The Awkward Yeti, LLC. All rights reserved. Published by Rocketship Entertainment, LLC. 136 Westbury Ct., Doylestown, PA 18901. "Lars the Awkward Yeti", the Awkward Yeti logo, and the likenesses of all characters herein are trademarks of The Awkward Yeti, LLC. "Rocketship" and the Rocketship logo are trademarks of Rocketship Entertainment, LLC. No part of this publication may be reproduced or transmitted, in any form or by any means, without the express written consent of The Awkward Yeti, LLC or Rocketship Entertainment, LLC. All names, characters, events, and locales in this publication are entirely fictional. Any resemblance to actual persons (living or dead), events, or places, without satiric intent, is coincidental. Printed in China.

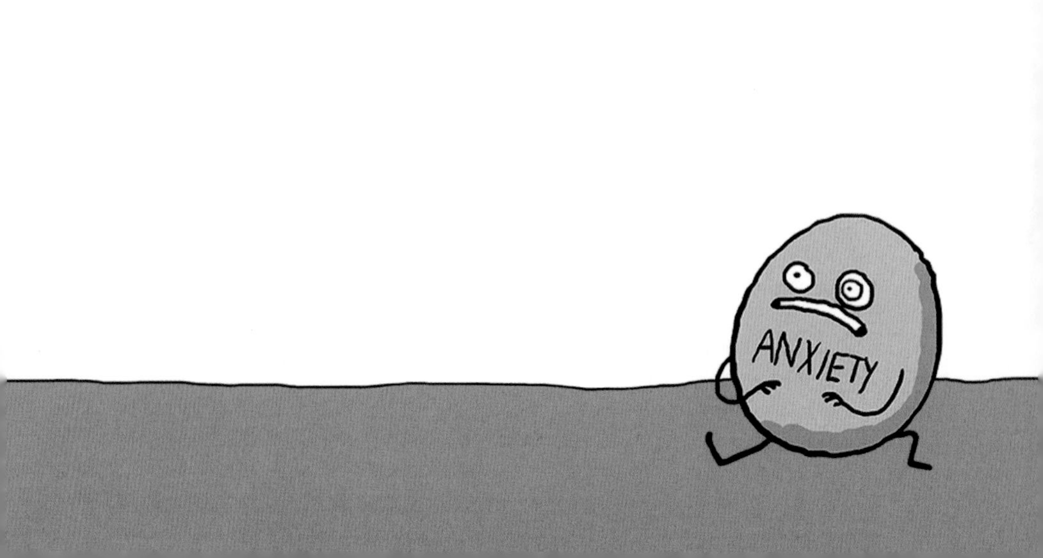
ANXIETY

Left or Right

Oh whoops! Excuse me.
Oh ha...
I'll go this way.

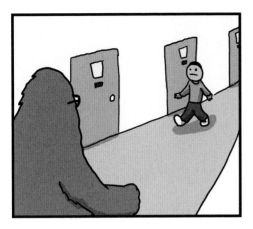

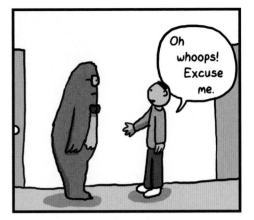

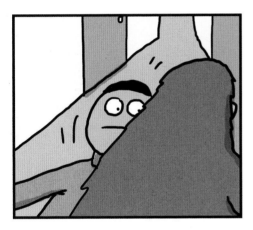

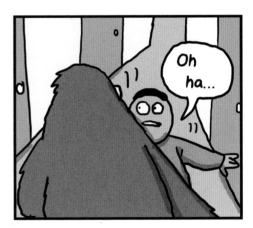

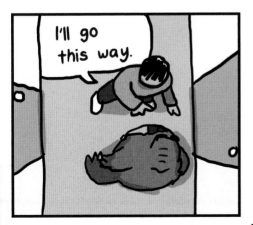

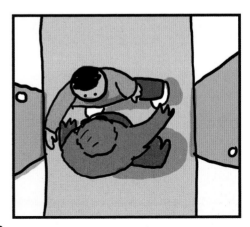

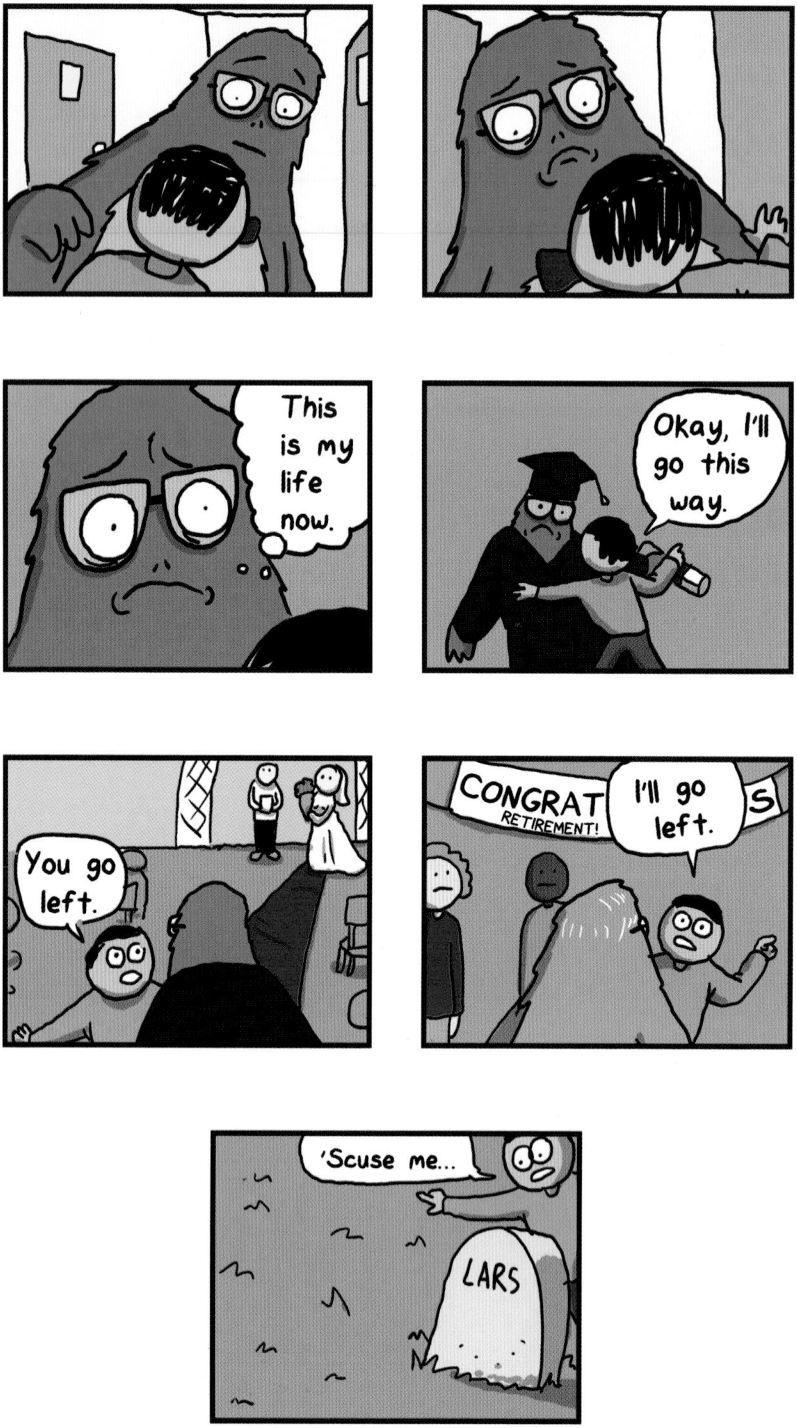
This is my life now.
Okay, I'll go this way.
You go left.
CONGRAT
RETIREMENT!
S
I'll go left.
'Scuse me...
LARS

Judging

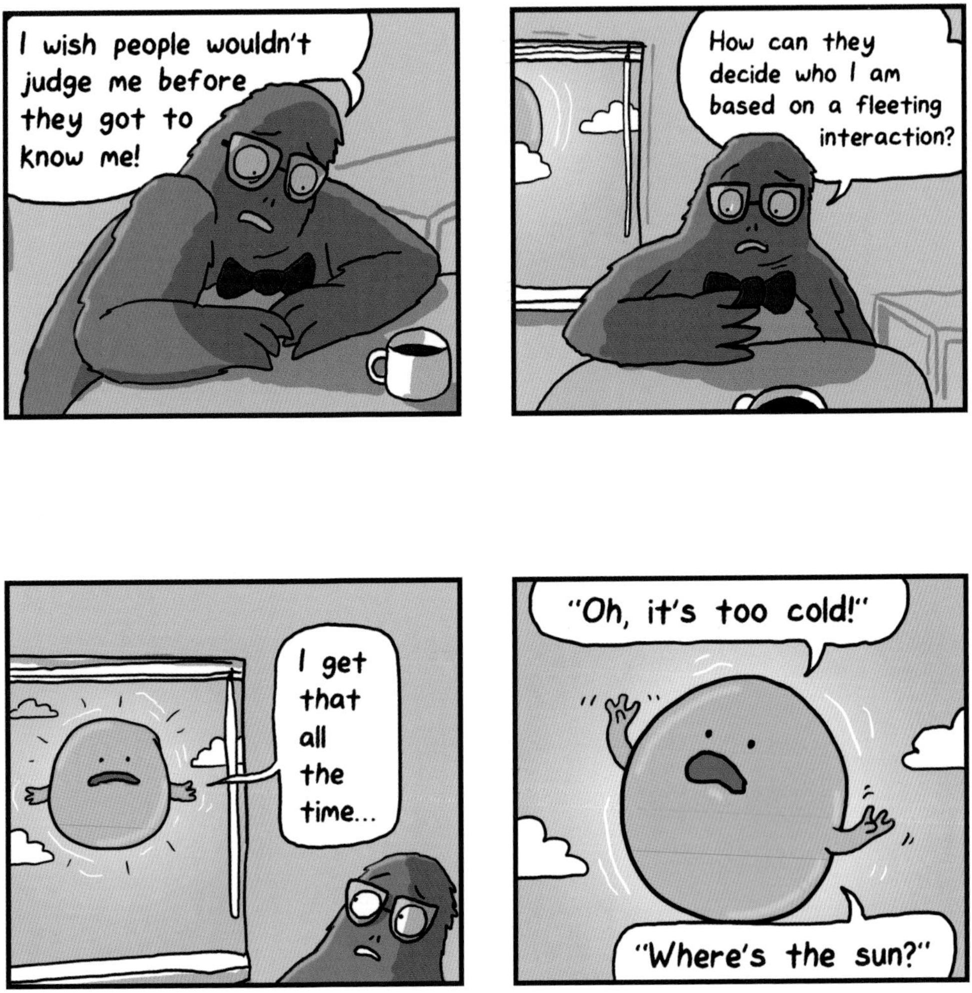
I wish people wouldn't judge me before they got to know me!
How can they decide who I am based on a fleeting interaction?
I get that all the time...
"Oh, it's too cold!"
"Where's the sun?"

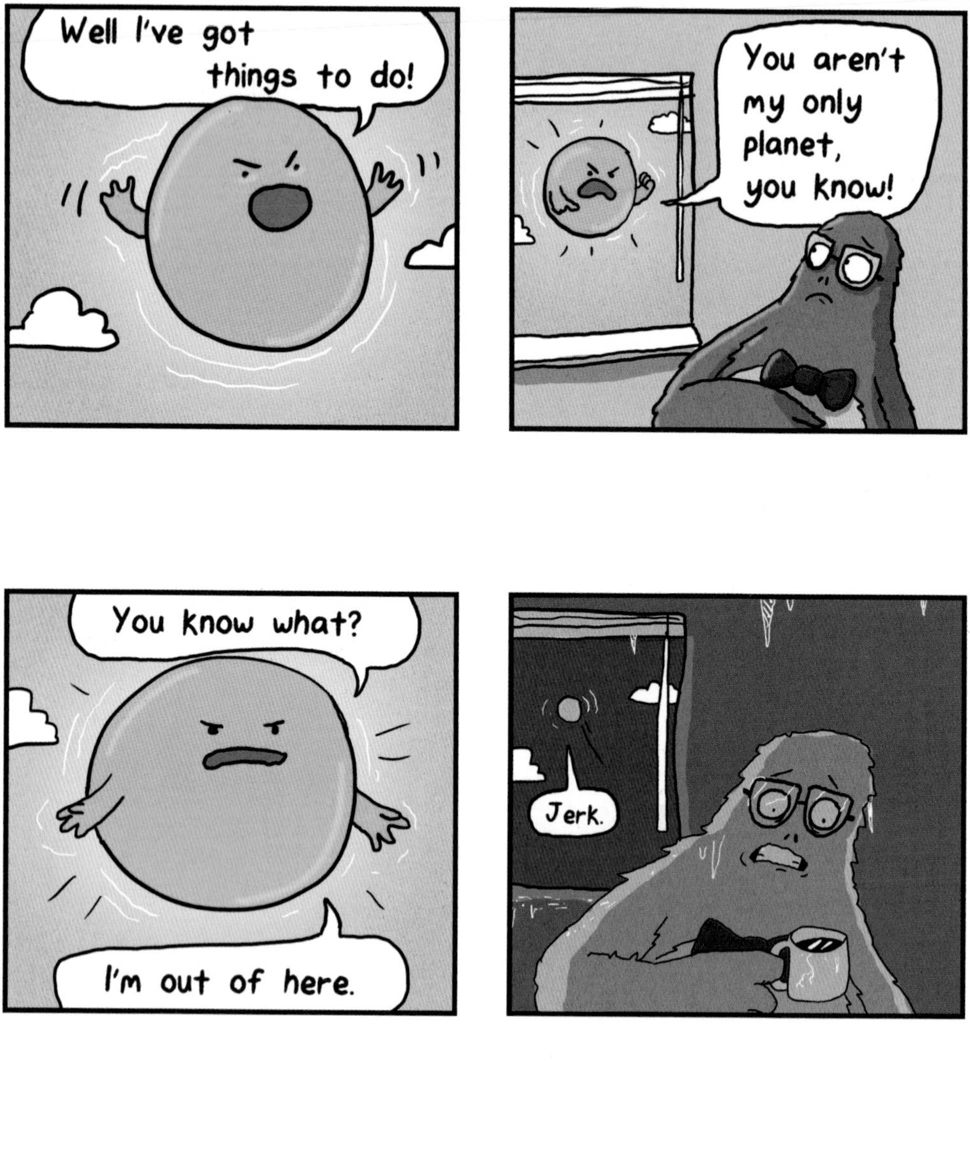
Well I've got things to do!
You aren't my only planet, you know!
You know what?
I'm out of here.
Jerk.

Mean

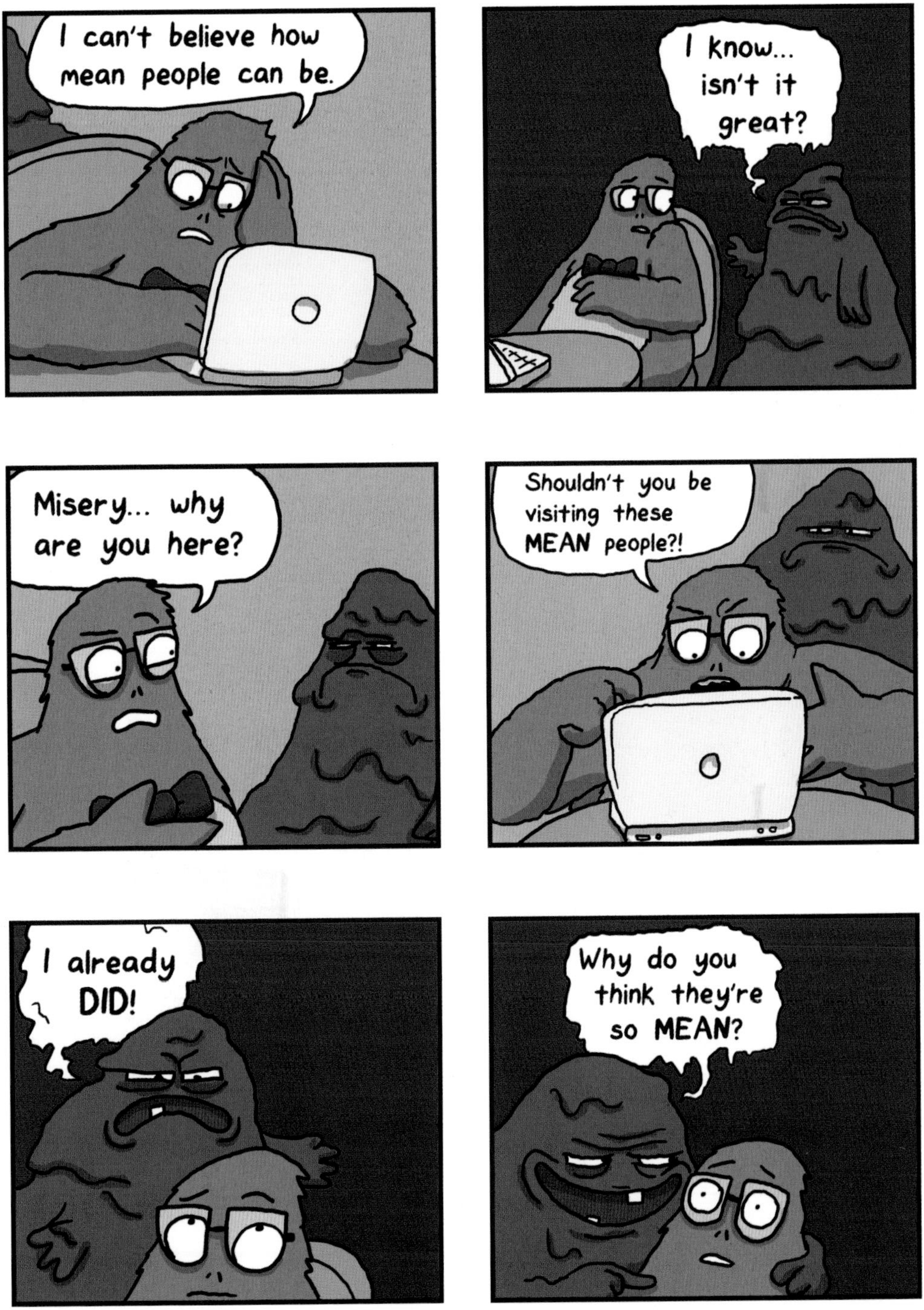

I can't believe how mean people can be.
I know... isn't it great?
Misery... why are you here?
Shouldn't you be visiting these MEAN people?!
I already DID!
Why do you think they're so MEAN?

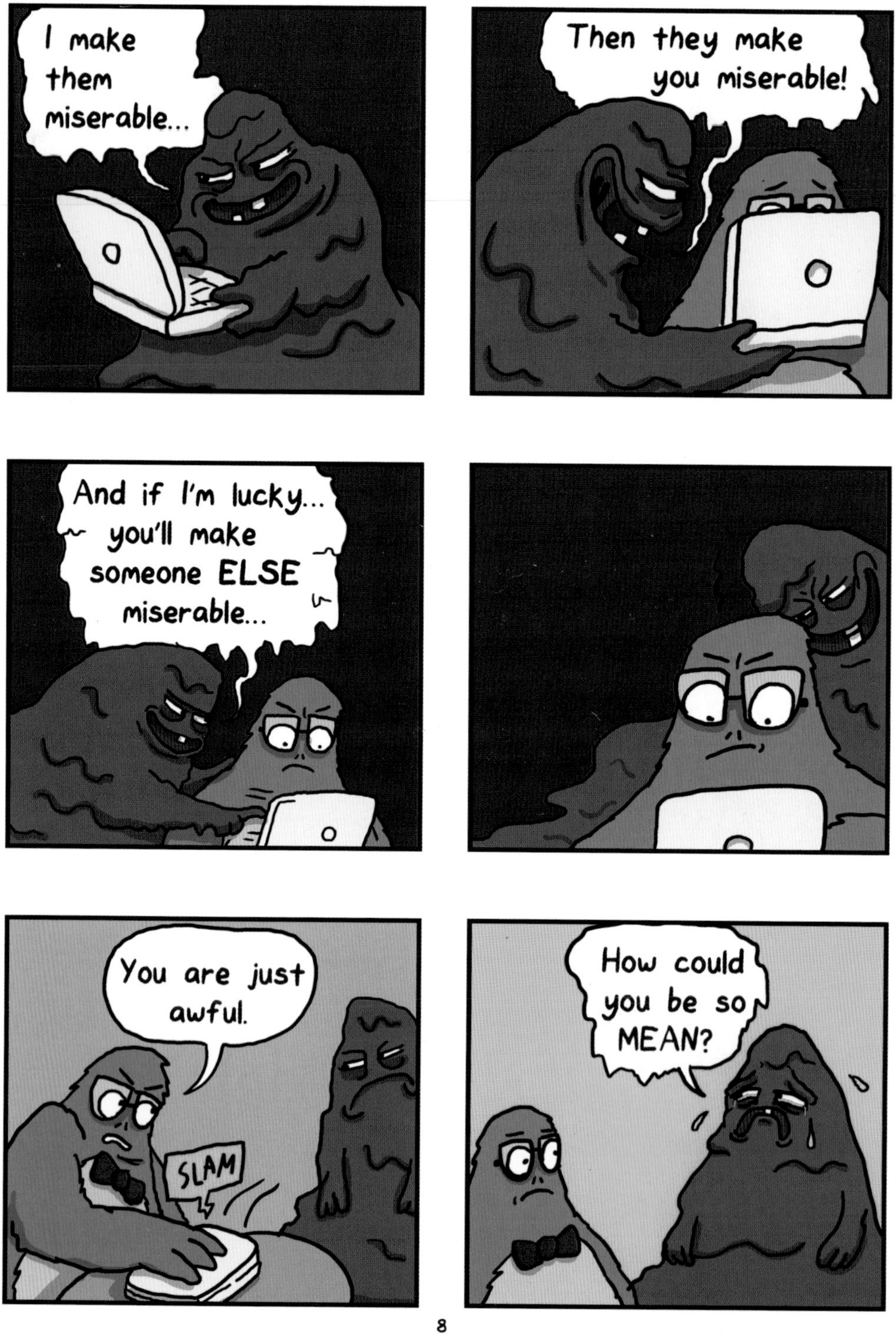
I make them miserable...
Then they make you miserable!
And if I'm lucky... you'll make someone ELSE miserable...
You are just awful.
SLAM
How could you be so MEAN?

Saving the World

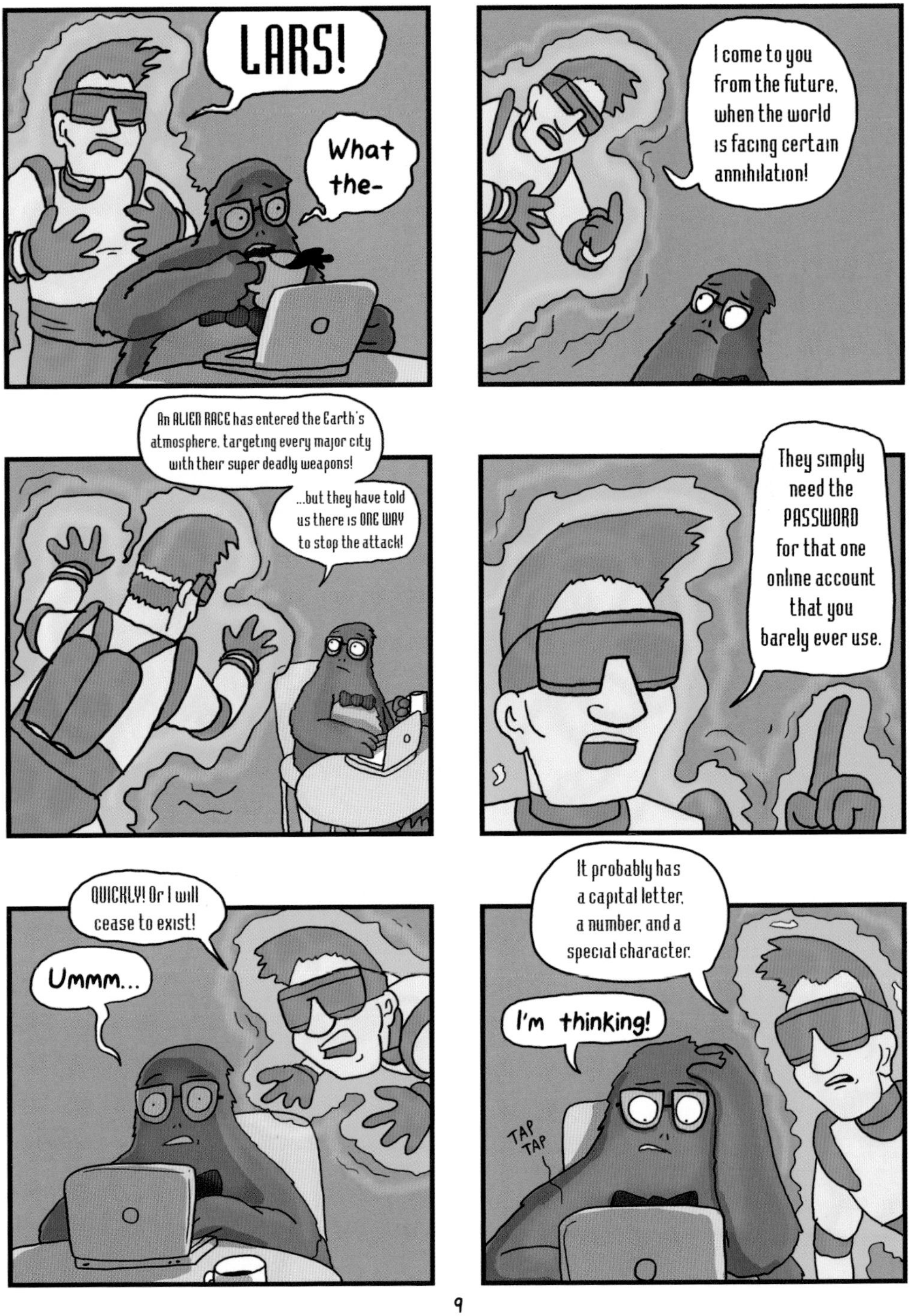

LARS!
What the-
I come to you from the future, when the world is facing certain annihilation!
An ALIEN RACE has entered the Earth's atmosphere, targeting every major city with their super deadly weapons!
...but they have told us there is ONE WAY to stop the attack!
They simply need the PASSWORD for that one online account that you barely ever use.
QUICKLY! Or I will cease to exist!
Ummm...
It probably has a capital letter, a number, and a special character.
I'm thinking!
TAP TAP

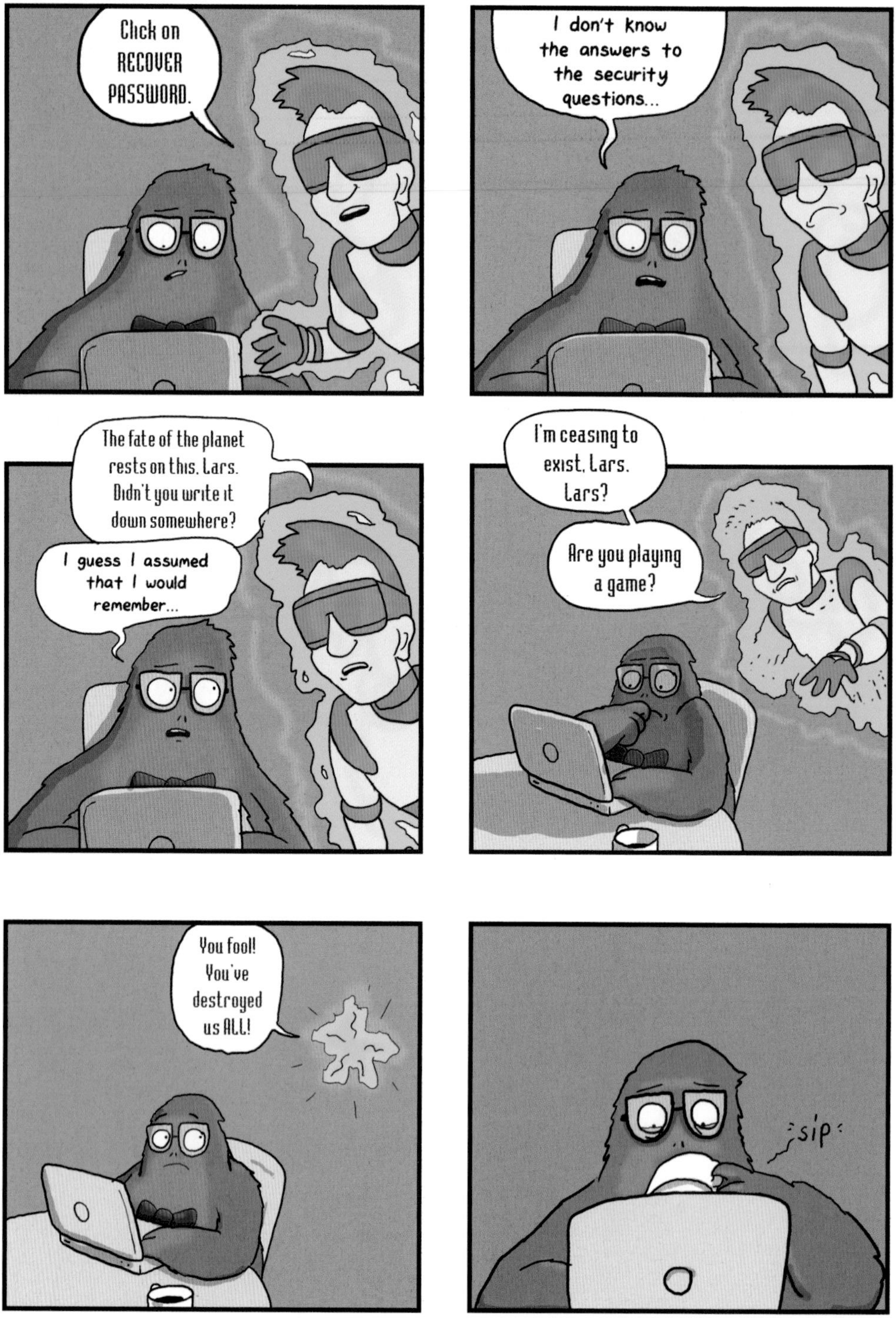
Click on RECOVER PASSWORD.
I don't know the answers to the security questions...
The fate of the planet rests on this, Lars. Didn't you write it down somewhere?
I guess I assumed that I would remember...
I'm ceasing to exist, Lars. Lars?
Are you playing a game?
You fool! You've destroyed us ALL!
sip

Wanna Talk About It?

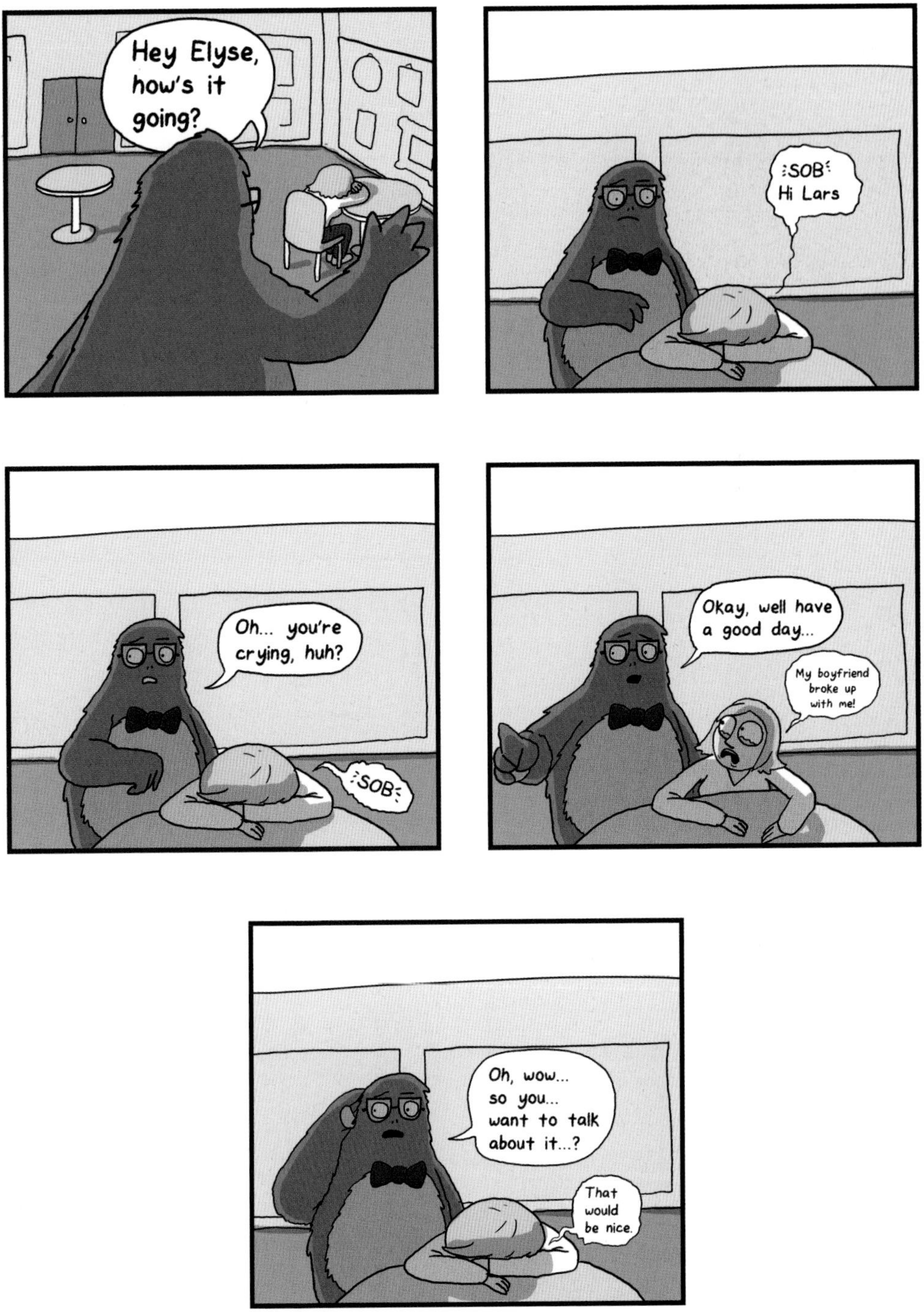
Hey Elyse, how's it going?
SOB Hi Lars
Oh... you're crying, huh?
SOB
Okay, well have a good day...
My boyfriend broke up with me!
Oh, wow... so you... want to talk about it...?
That would be nice.

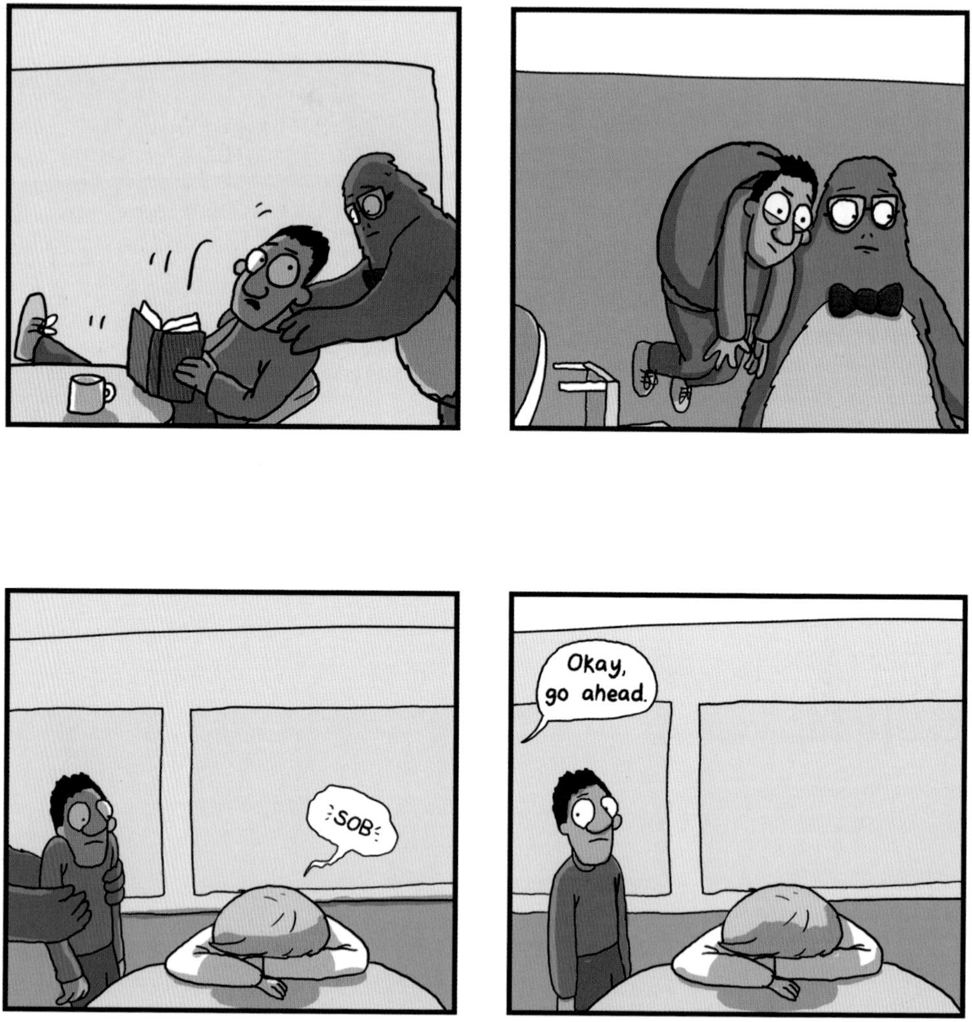
SOB
Okay, go ahead.

Manners

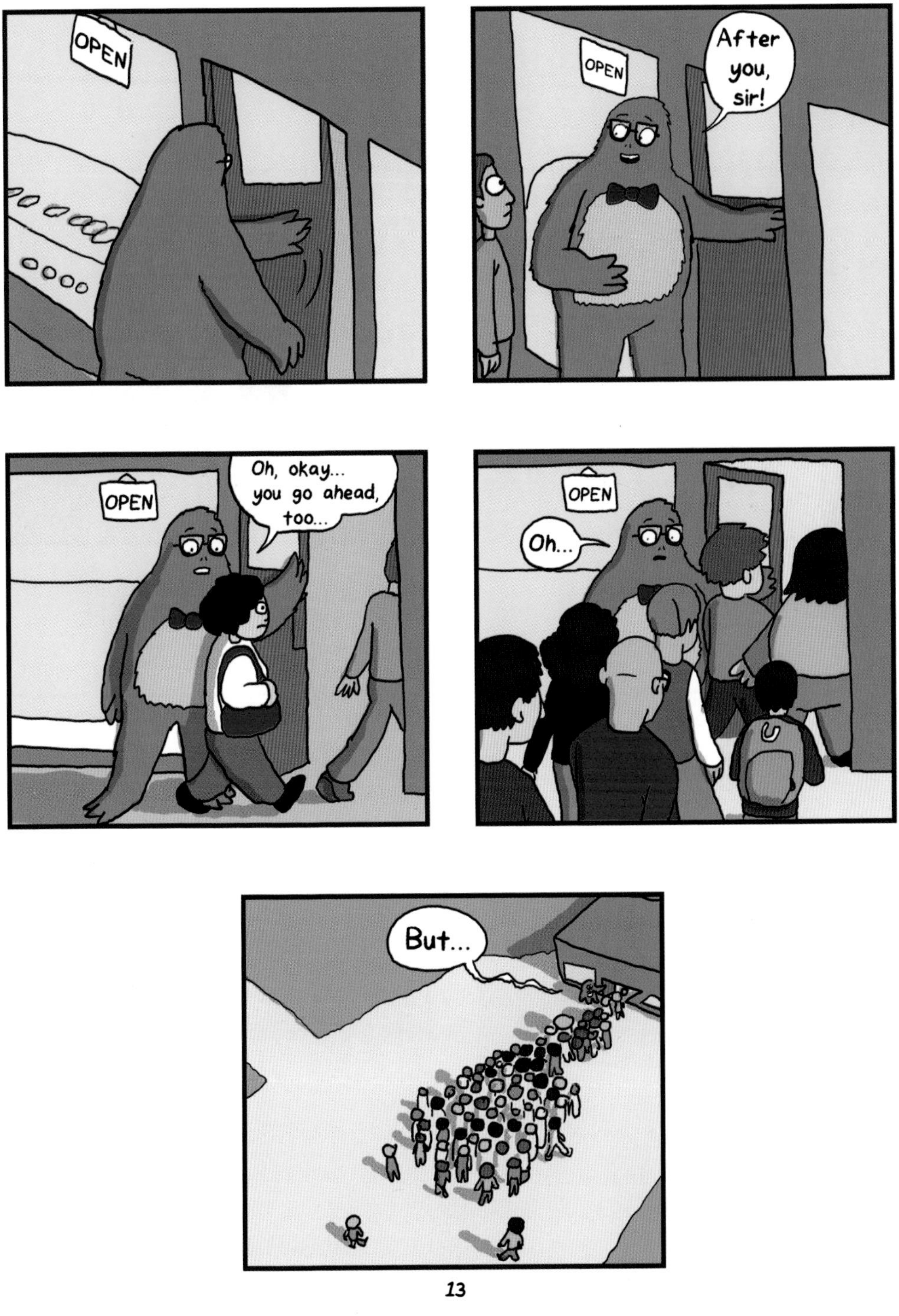
OPEN
OPEN
After you, sir!
OPEN
Oh, okay... you go ahead, too...
OPEN
Oh...
But...

Awkward

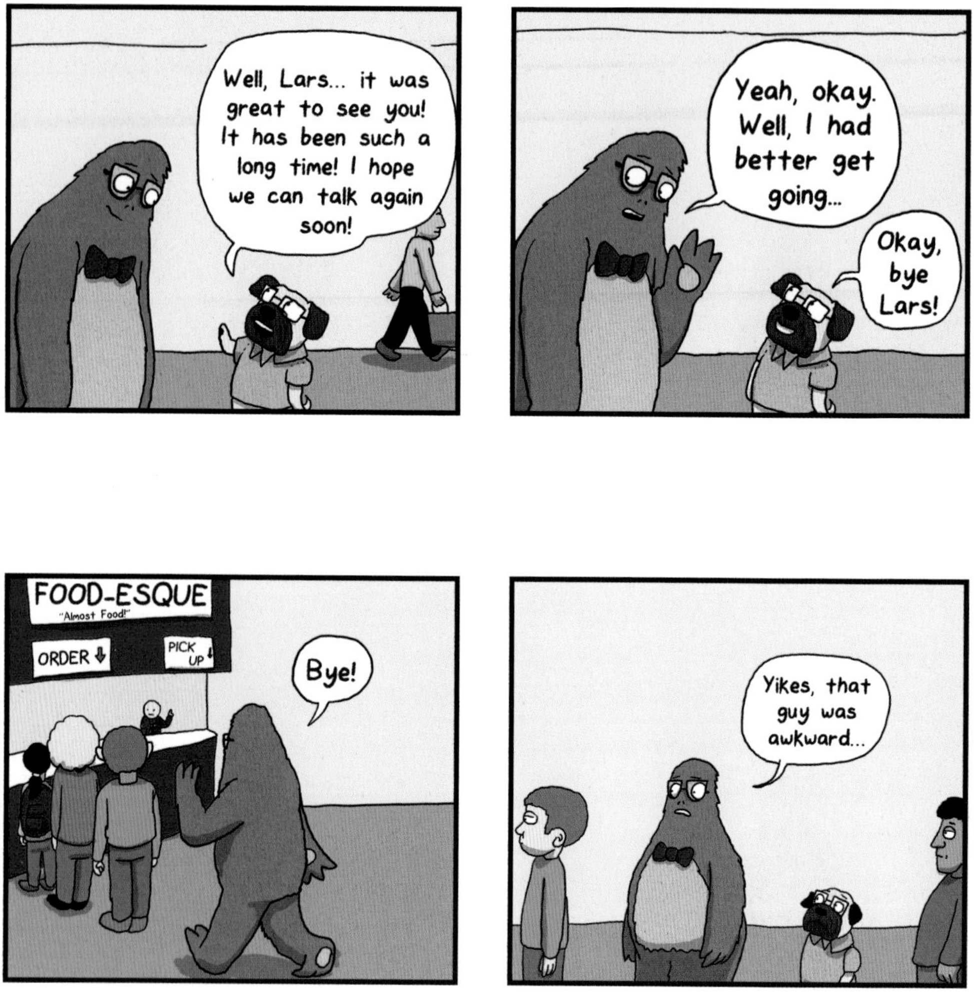
Well, Lars... it was great to see you! It has been such a long time! I hope we can talk again soon!
Yeah, okay. Well, I had better get going...
Okay, bye Lars!
FOOD-ESQUE
"Almost Food!"
ORDER
PICK UP
Bye!
Yikes, that guy was awkward...

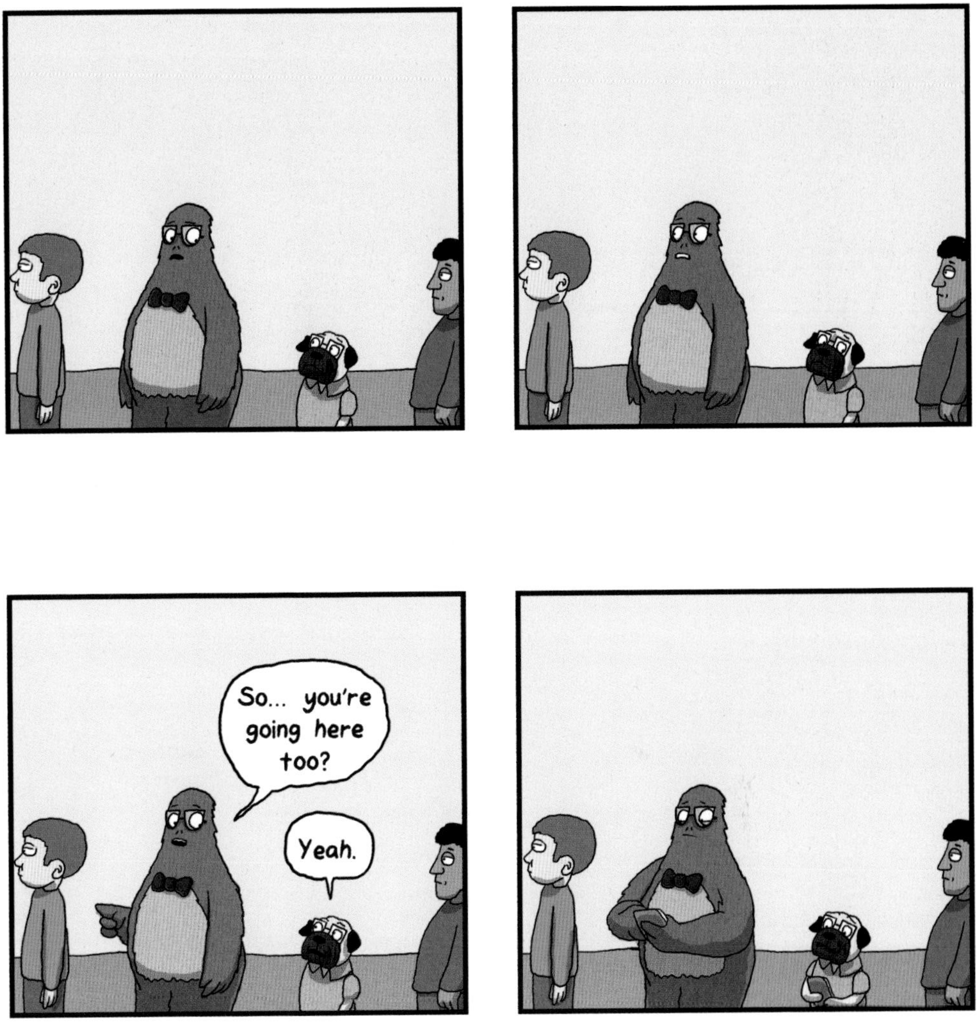
So... you're going here too?
Yeah.

New Me

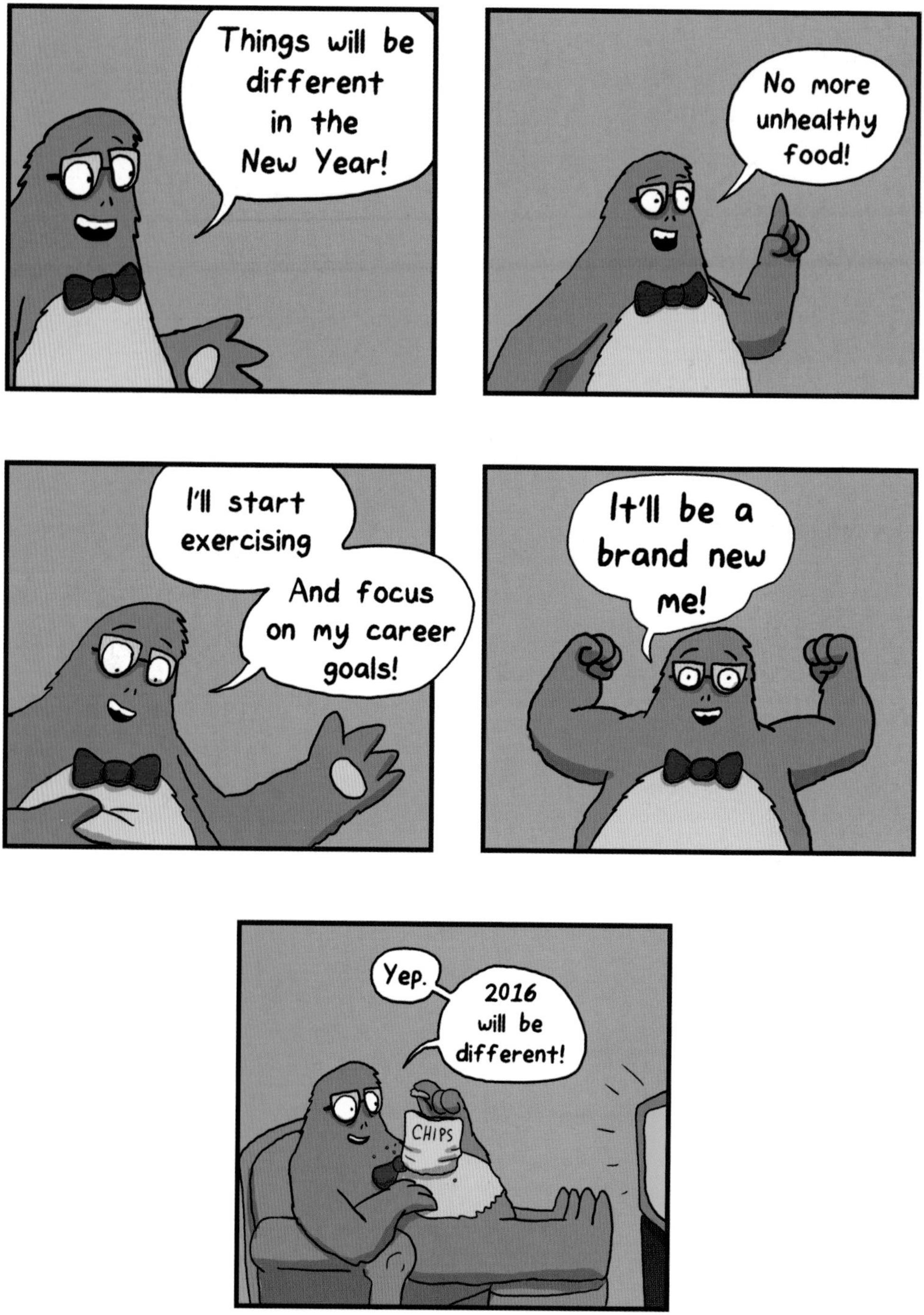
Things will be different in the New Year!
No more unhealthy food!
I'll start exercising
And focus on my career goals!
It'll be a brand new me!
Yep.
2016 will be different!
CHIPS

Spectatorship

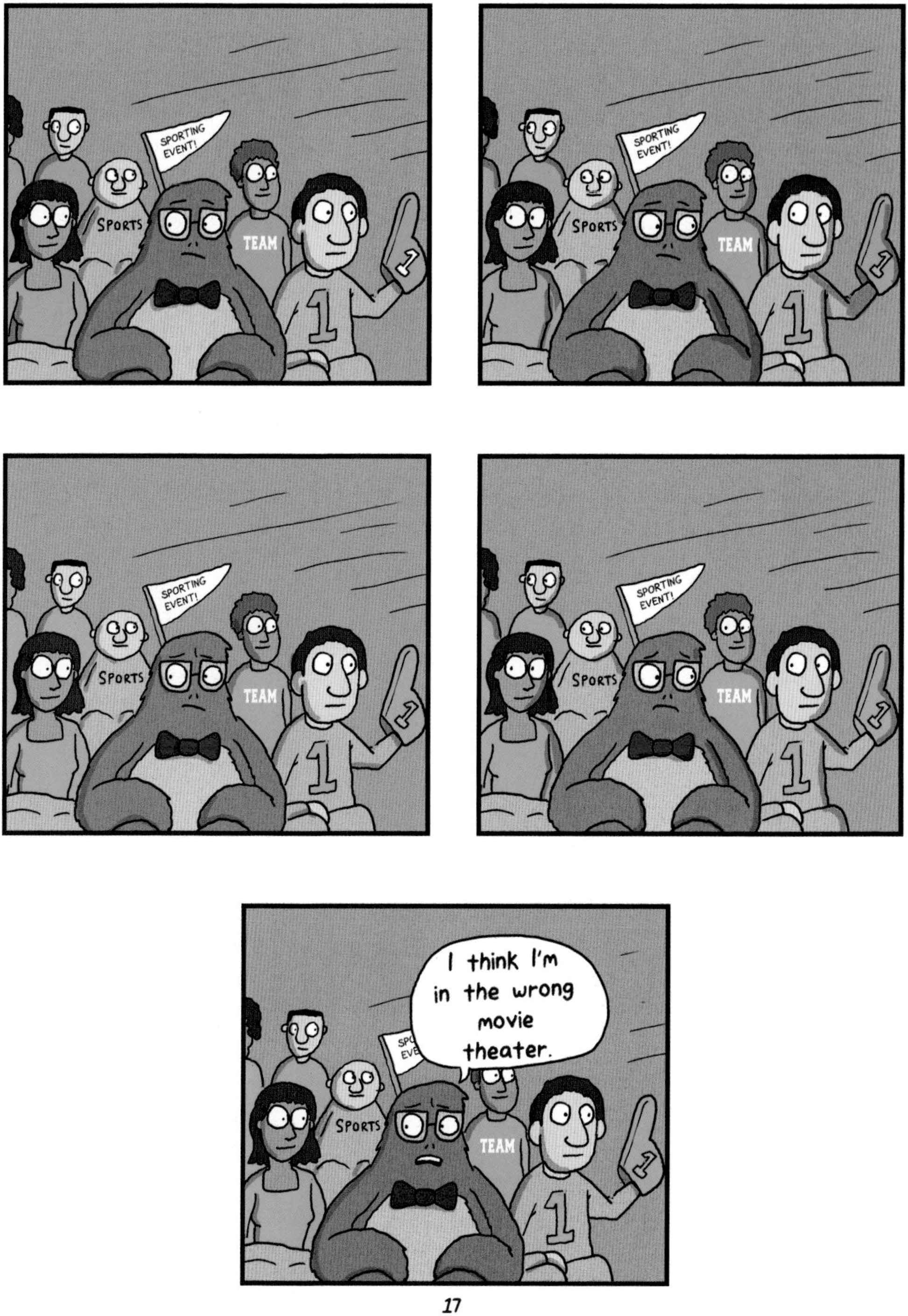
SPORTING EVENT!
SPORTS
TEAM
1
SPORTING EVENT!
SPORTS
TEAM
1
SPORTING EVENT!
SPORTS
TEAM
1
SPORTING EVENT!
SPORTS
TEAM
1
I think I'm in the wrong movie theater.
SPORTS
TEAM
1

Impossible

Steady...
SMACK
Ha! There's no escape now!
What?

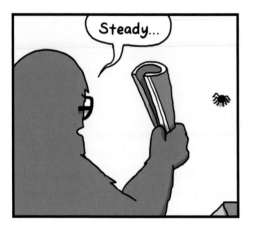

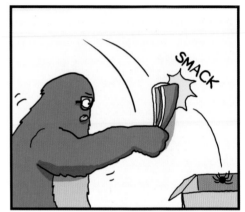

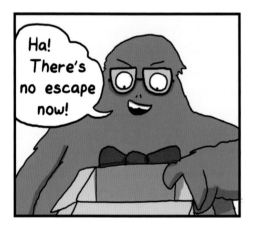

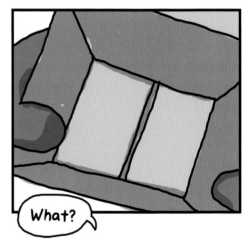

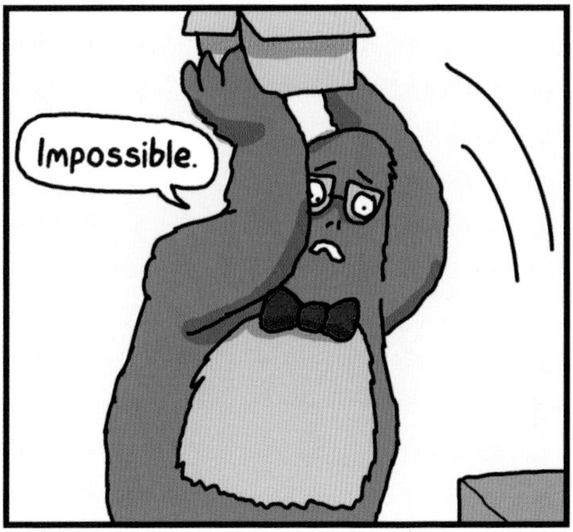
Impossible.
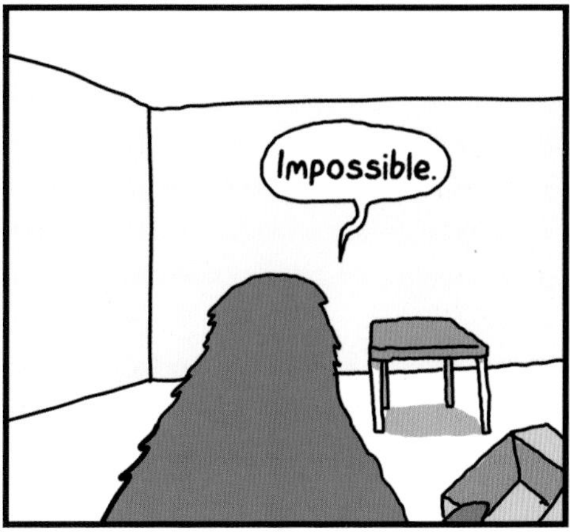
Impossible.
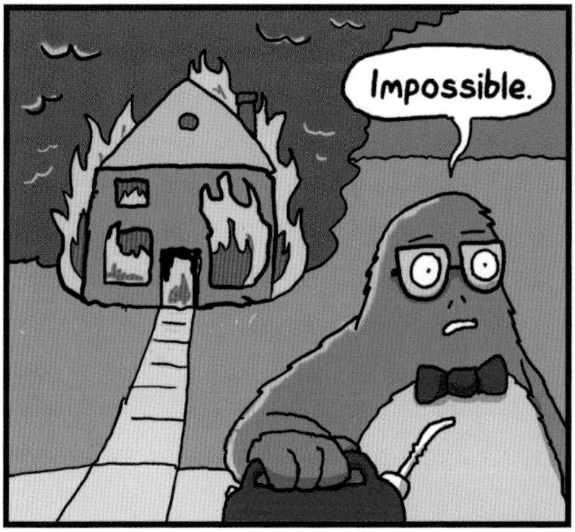
Impossible.

Greeting

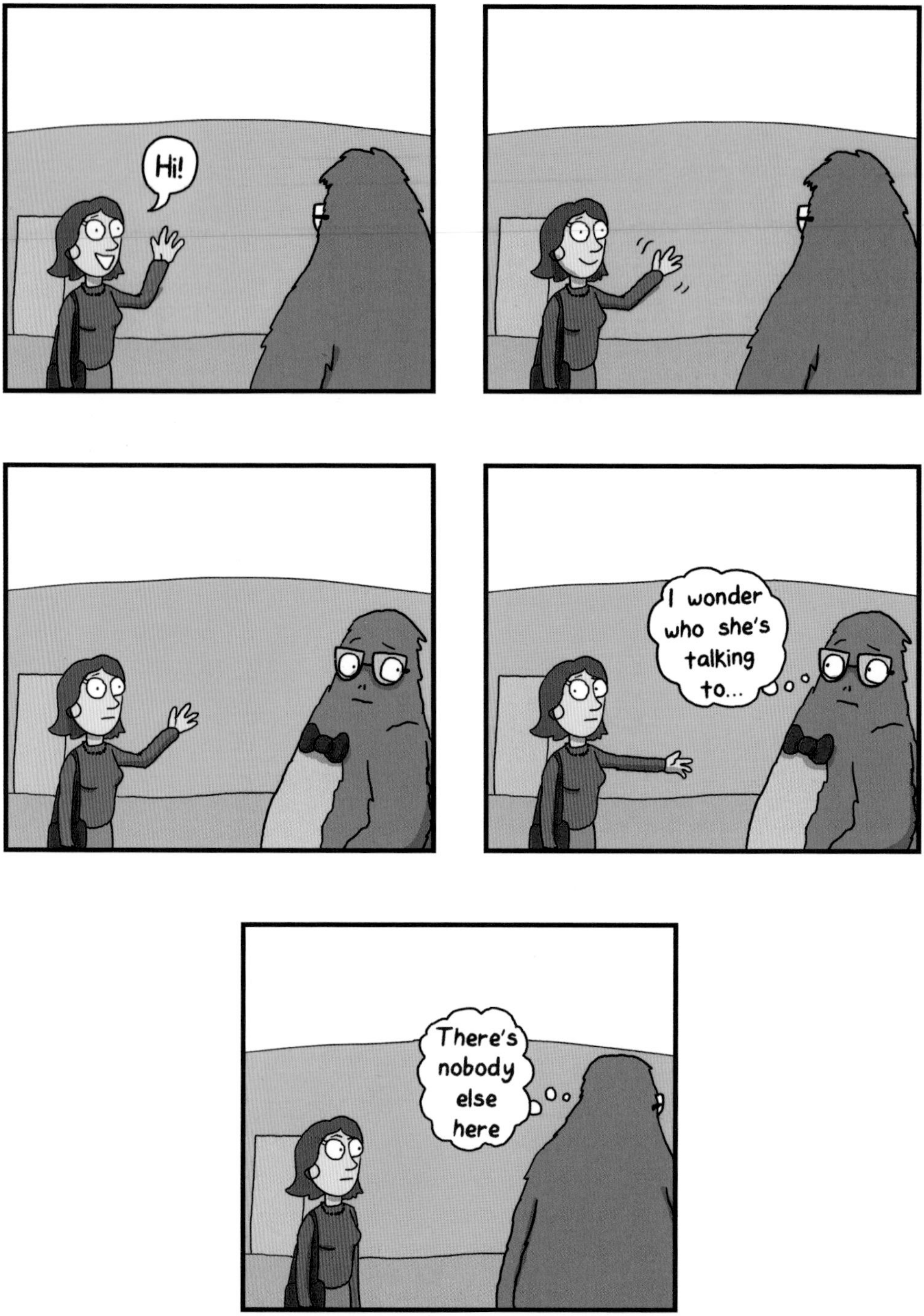
Hi!
I wonder who she's talking to...
There's nobody else here

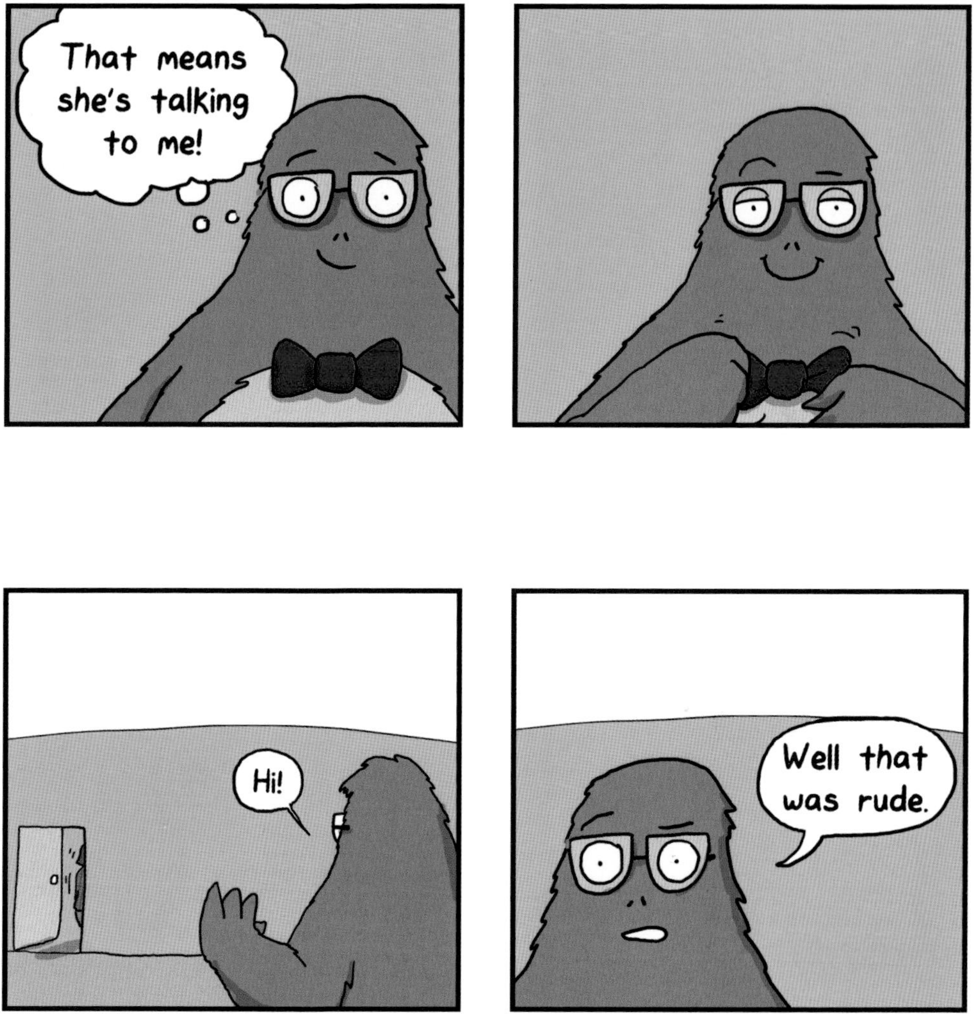
That means she's talking to me!
Hi!
Well that was rude.

Reflection

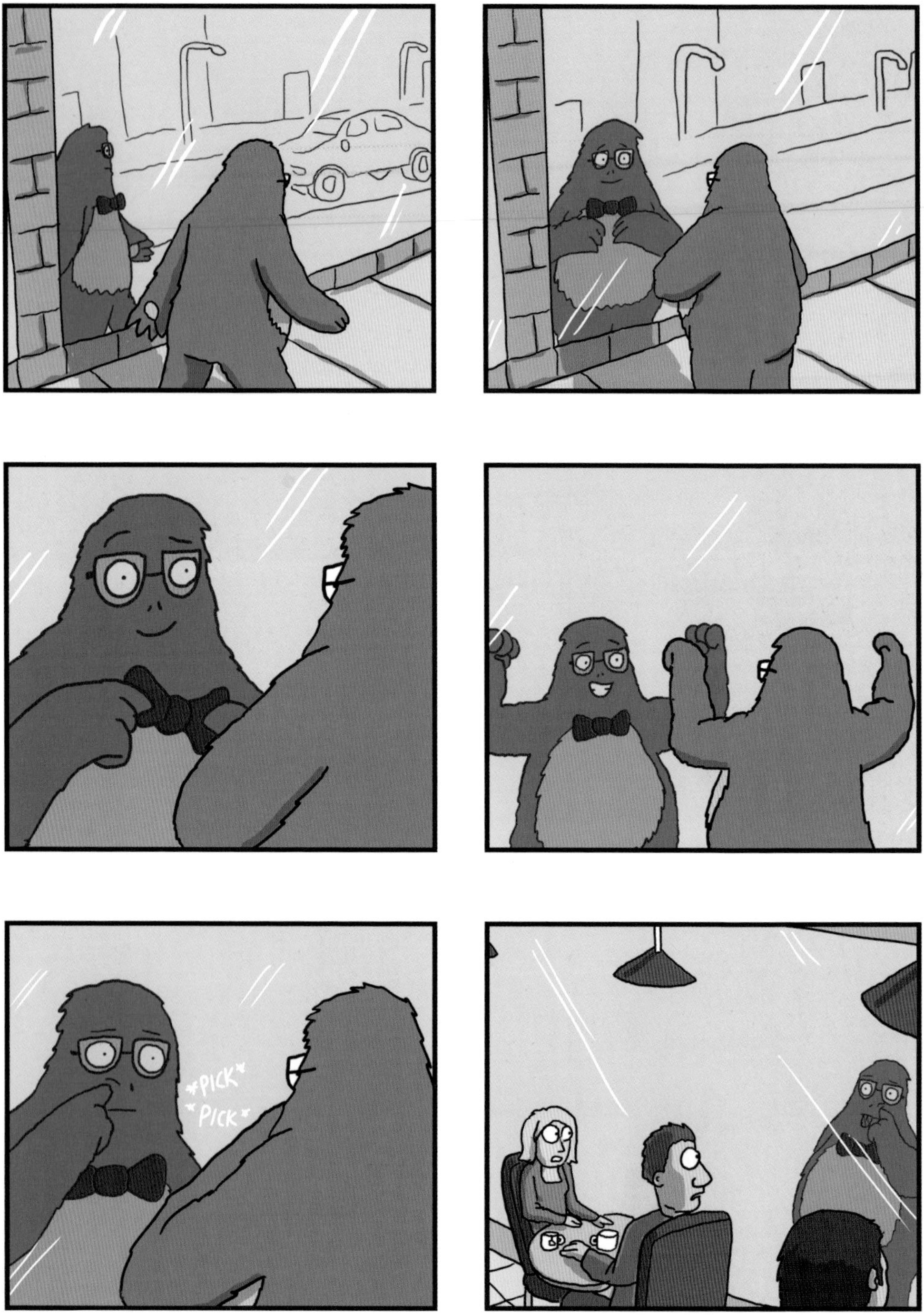
PICK
PICK

The Blue Guy

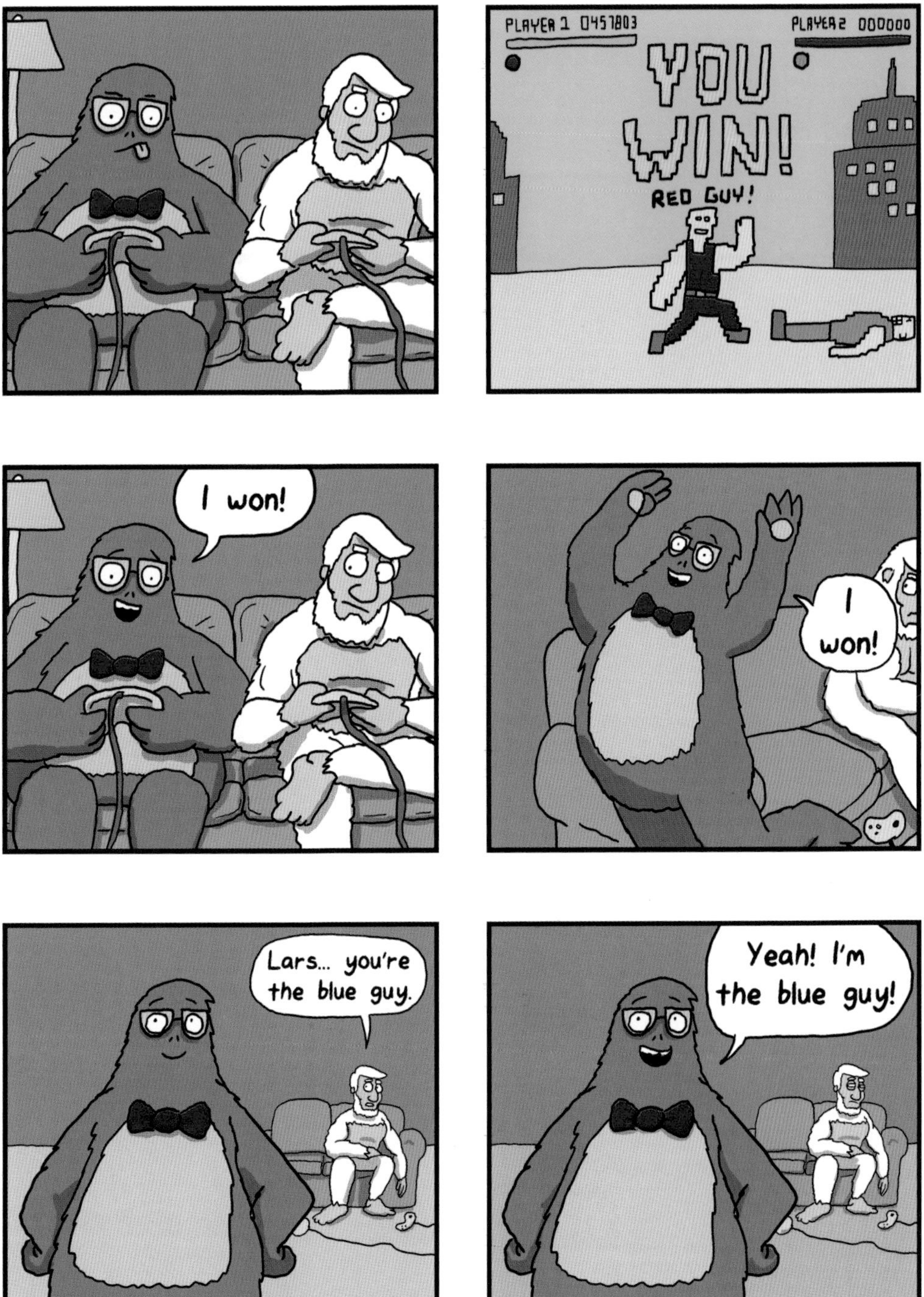
PLAYER 1 0457803
PLAYER 2 000000
YOU WIN!
RED GUY!
I won!
I won!
Lars... you're the blue guy.
Yeah! I'm the blue guy!

Inspired at the Museum

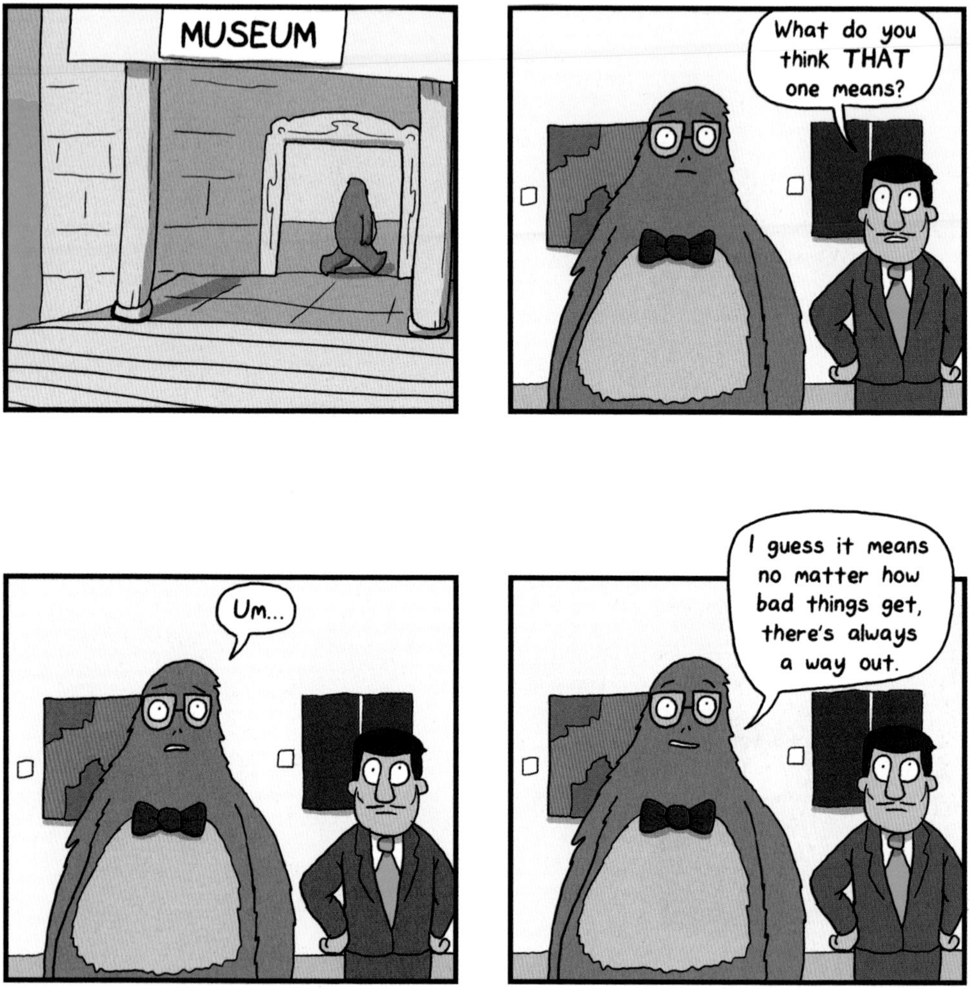
MUSEUM
What do you think THAT one means?
Um...
I guess it means no matter how bad things get, there's always a way out.

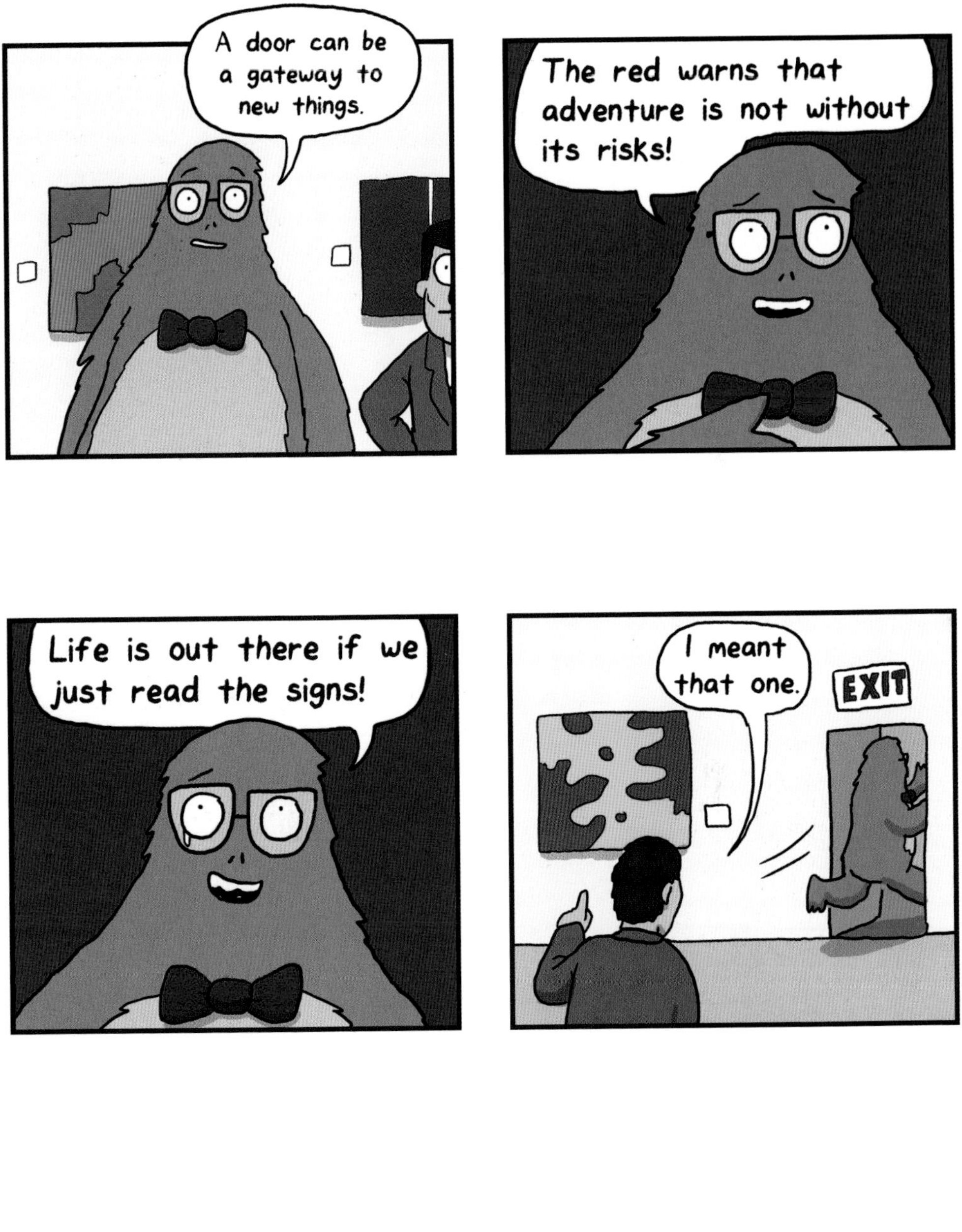
A door can be a gateway to new things.
The red warns that adventure is not without its risks!
Life is out there if we just read the signs!
I meant that one.
EXIT

The Eye Exam

Okay, Lars...
Which looks better?
A
BCD
This one...
CLICK
A
BCD
Or this one?
Umm...

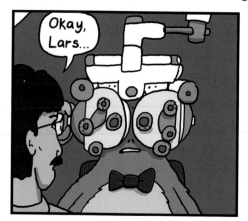

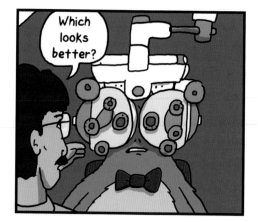

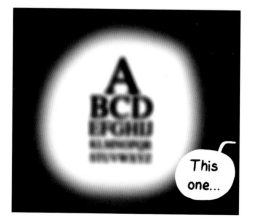

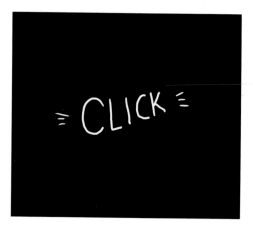

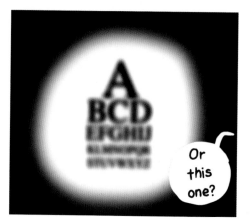

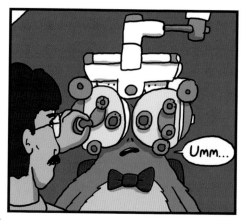

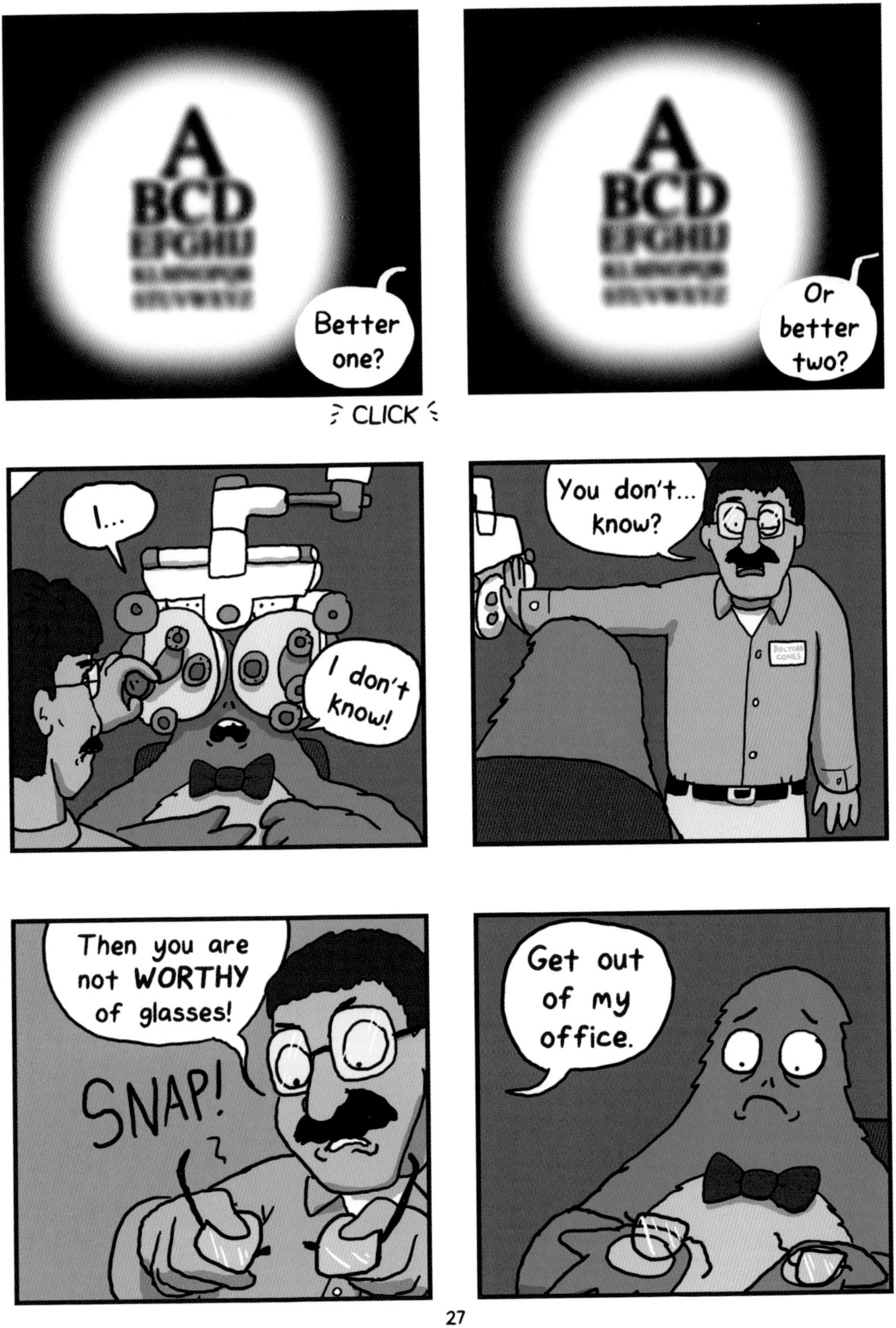
A
BCD
Better one?
CLICK
A
BCD
Or better two?
I...
I don't know!
You don't... know?
DOCTOR CONES
Then you are not WORTHY of glasses!
SNAP!
Get out of my office.

Nothing Like a Good Book

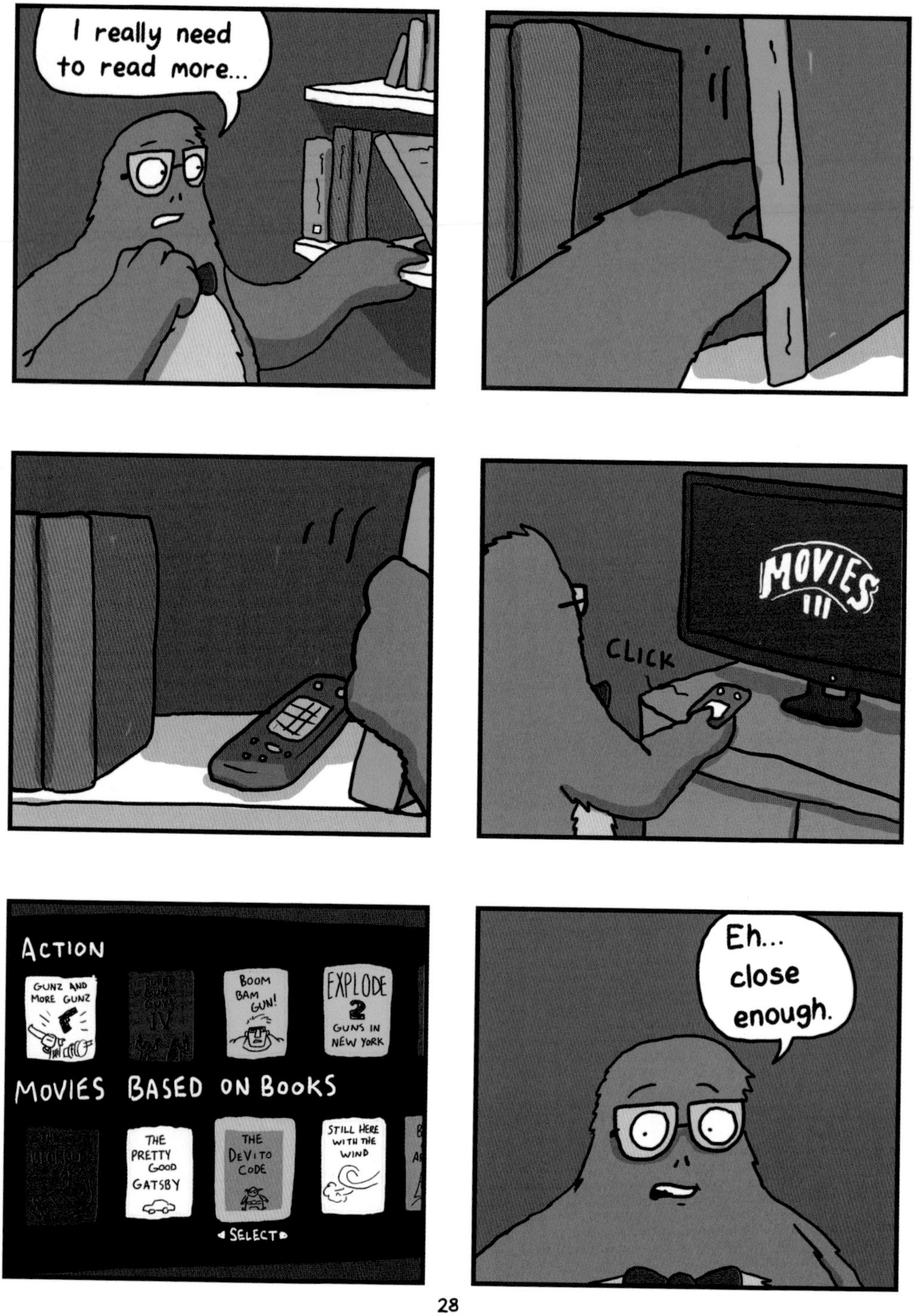

I really need to read more...
CLICK
MOVIES III
ACTION
GUNZ AND MORE GUNZ
BOOM BAM GUN!
EXPLODE 2 GUNS IN NEW YORK
MOVIES BASED ON BOOKS
THE PRETTY GOOD GATSBY
THE DEVITO CODE
STILL HERE WITH THE WIND
SELECT
Eh... close enough.

The 5K

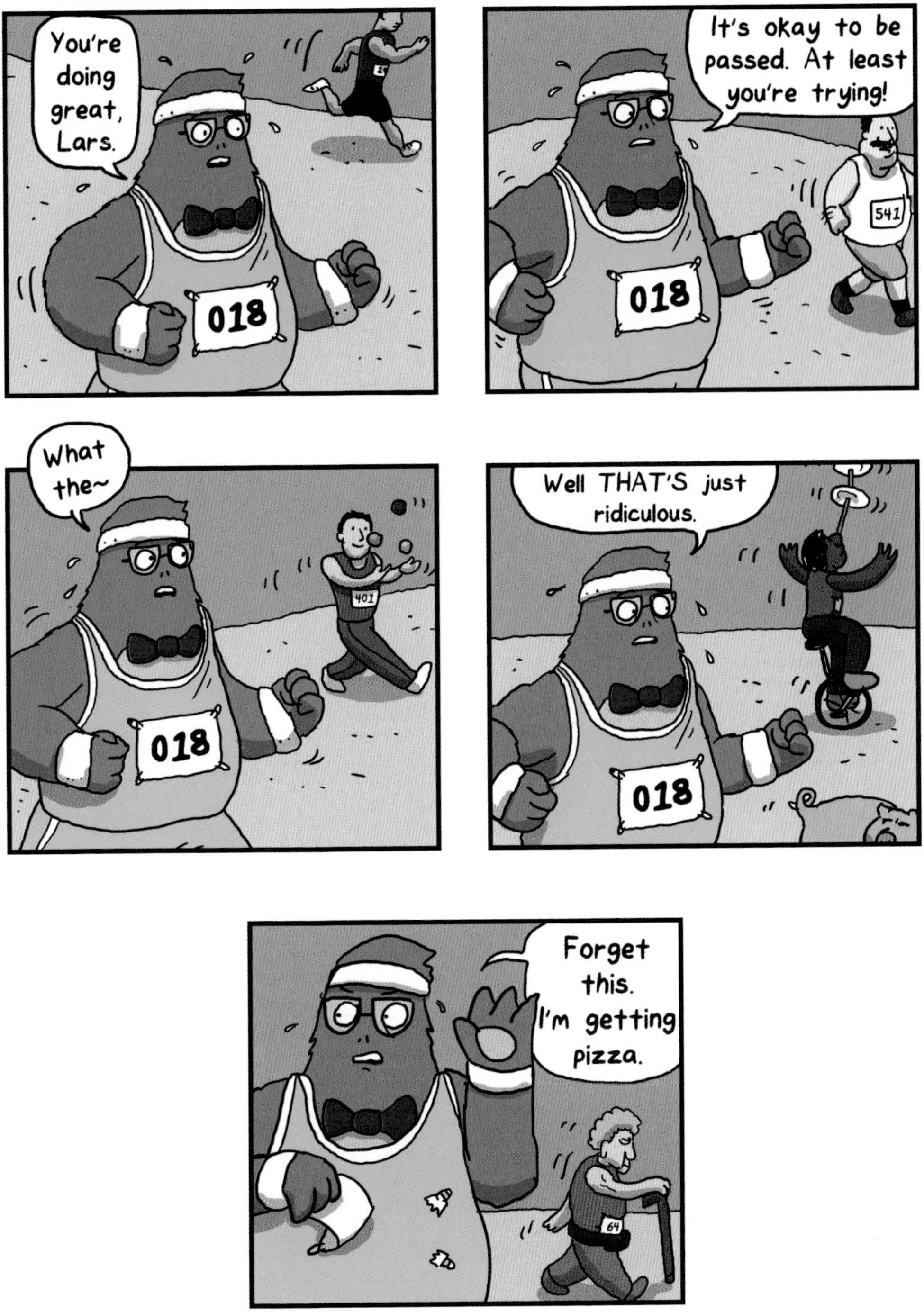
You're doing great, Lars.
018
It's okay to be passed. At least you're trying!
018
541
What the~
401
018
Well THAT'S just ridiculous.
018
Forget this. I'm getting pizza.
64

The Interview

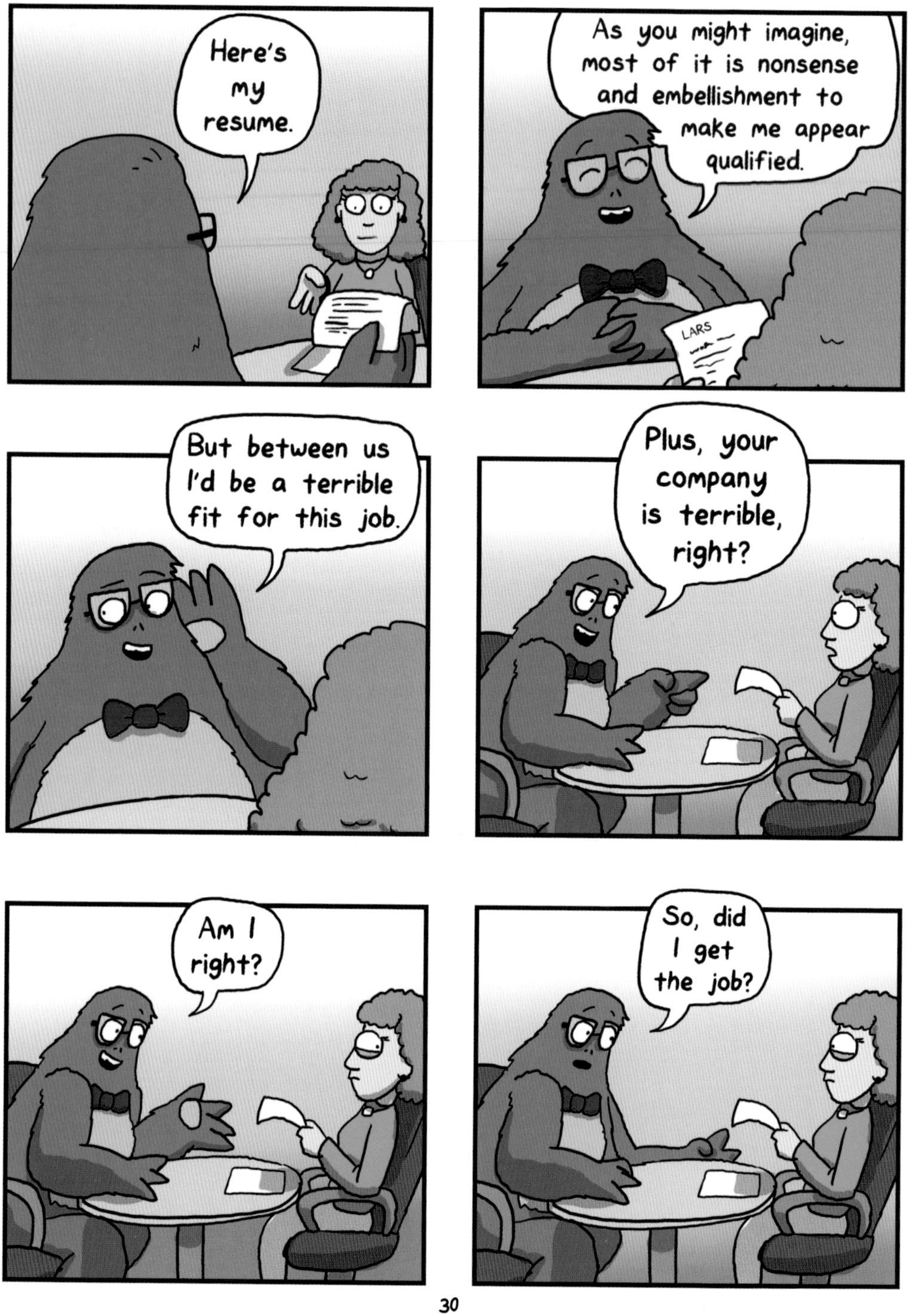
Here's my resume.
As you might imagine, most of it is nonsense and embellishment to make me appear qualified.
LARS
But between us I'd be a terrible fit for this job.
Plus, your company is terrible, right?
Am I right?
So, did I get the job?

Choices

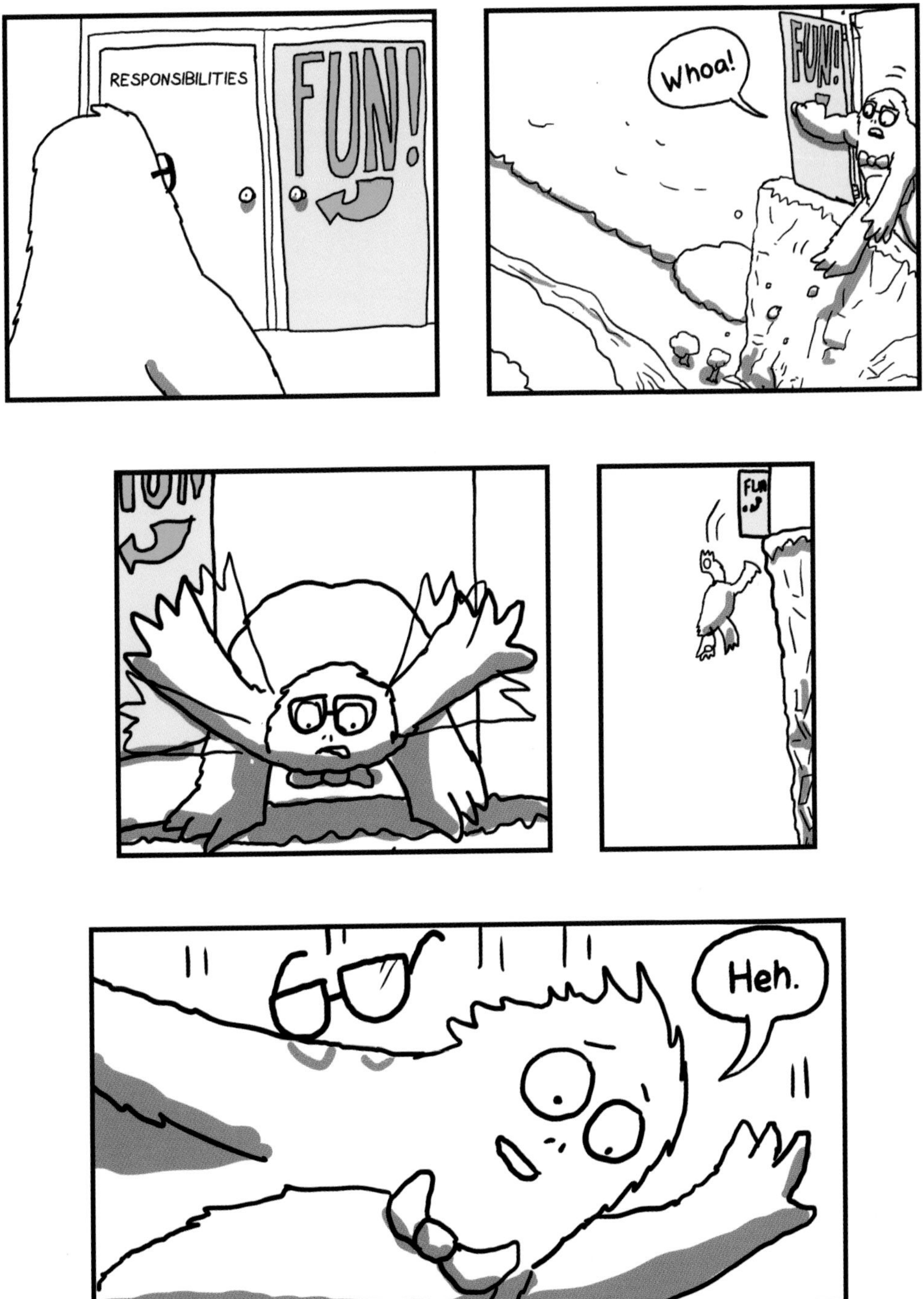

RESPONSIBILITIES
FUN!
Whoa!
FUN!
FUN
Heh.

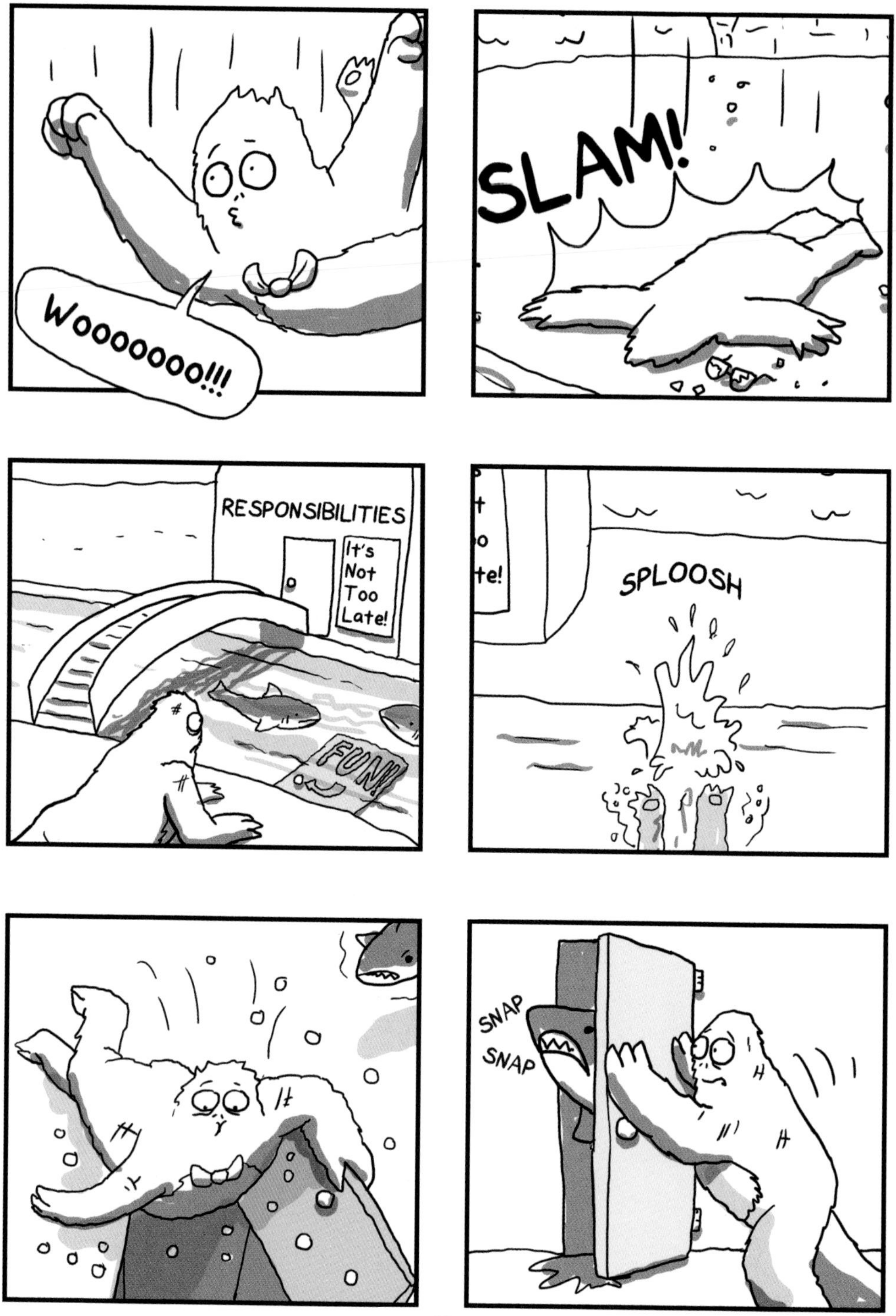
Wooooooo!!!
SLAM!
RESPONSIBILITIES
It's Not Too Late!
FUN!
SPLOOSH
SNAP
SNAP

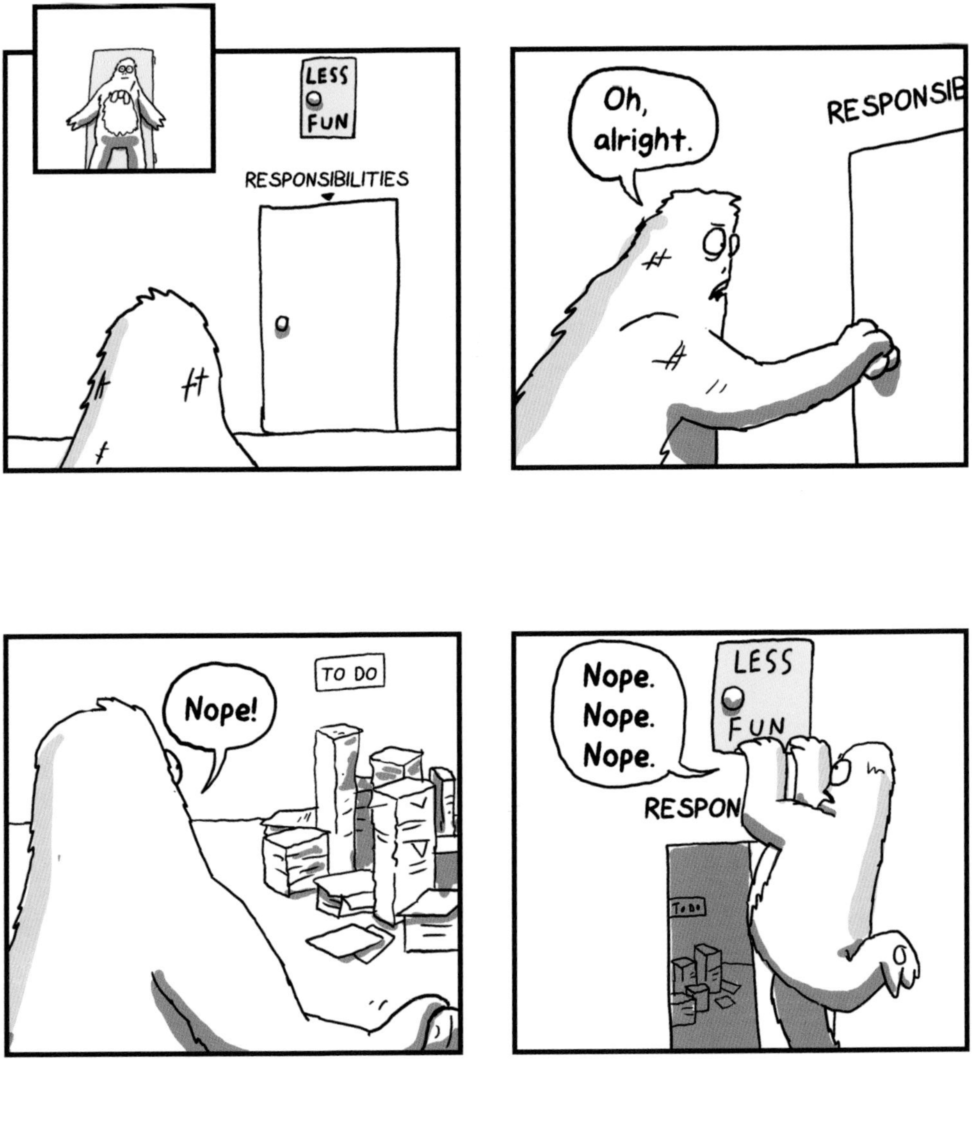
LESS
FUN
RESPONSIBILITIES
Oh, alright.
RESPONSIB
Nope!
TO DO
Nope. Nope. Nope.
LESS
FUN
RESPON

Cool

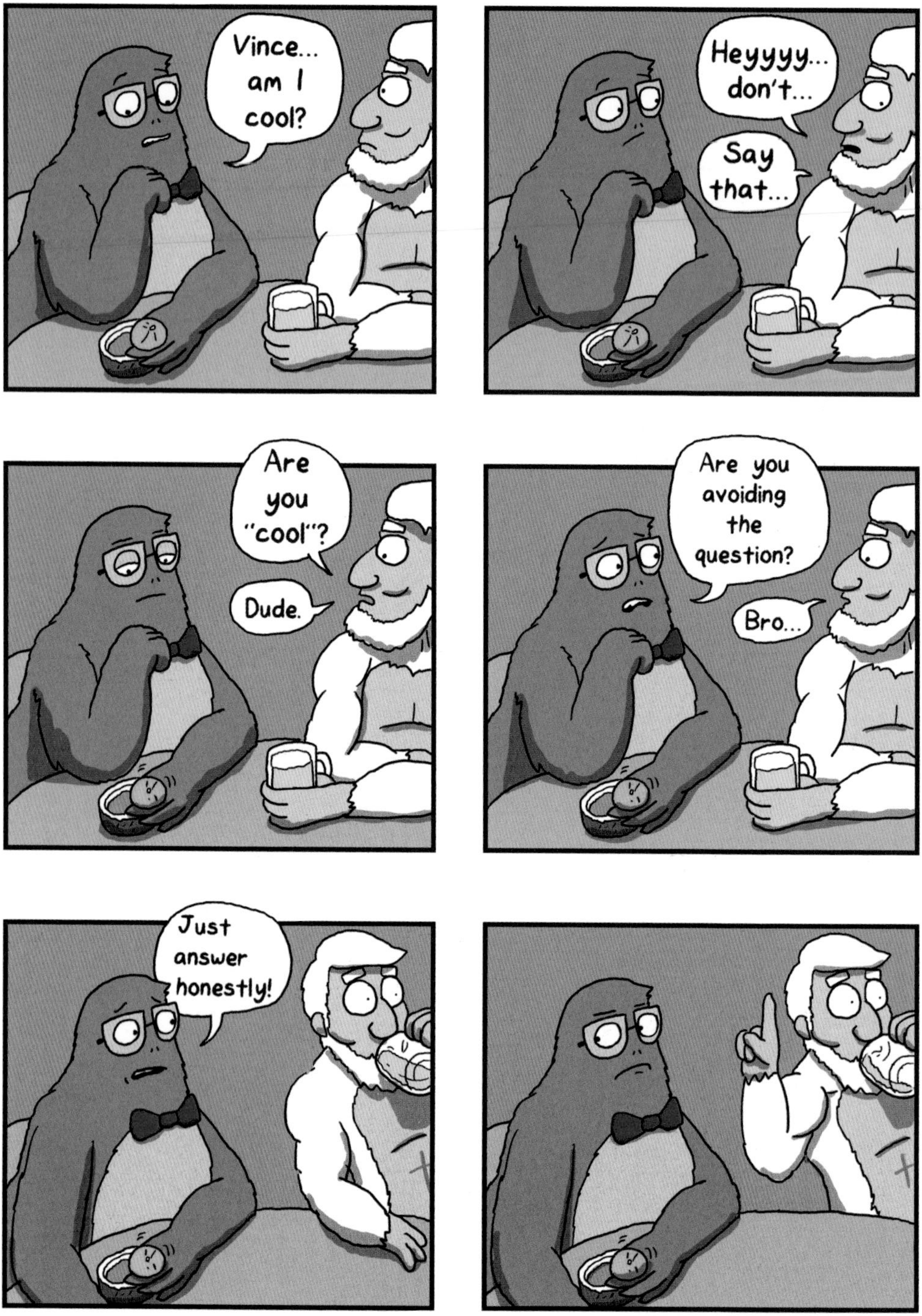
Vince... am I cool?
Heyyyy... don't...
Say that...
Are you "cool"?
Dude.
Are you avoiding the question?
Bro...
Just answer honestly!

The Wish

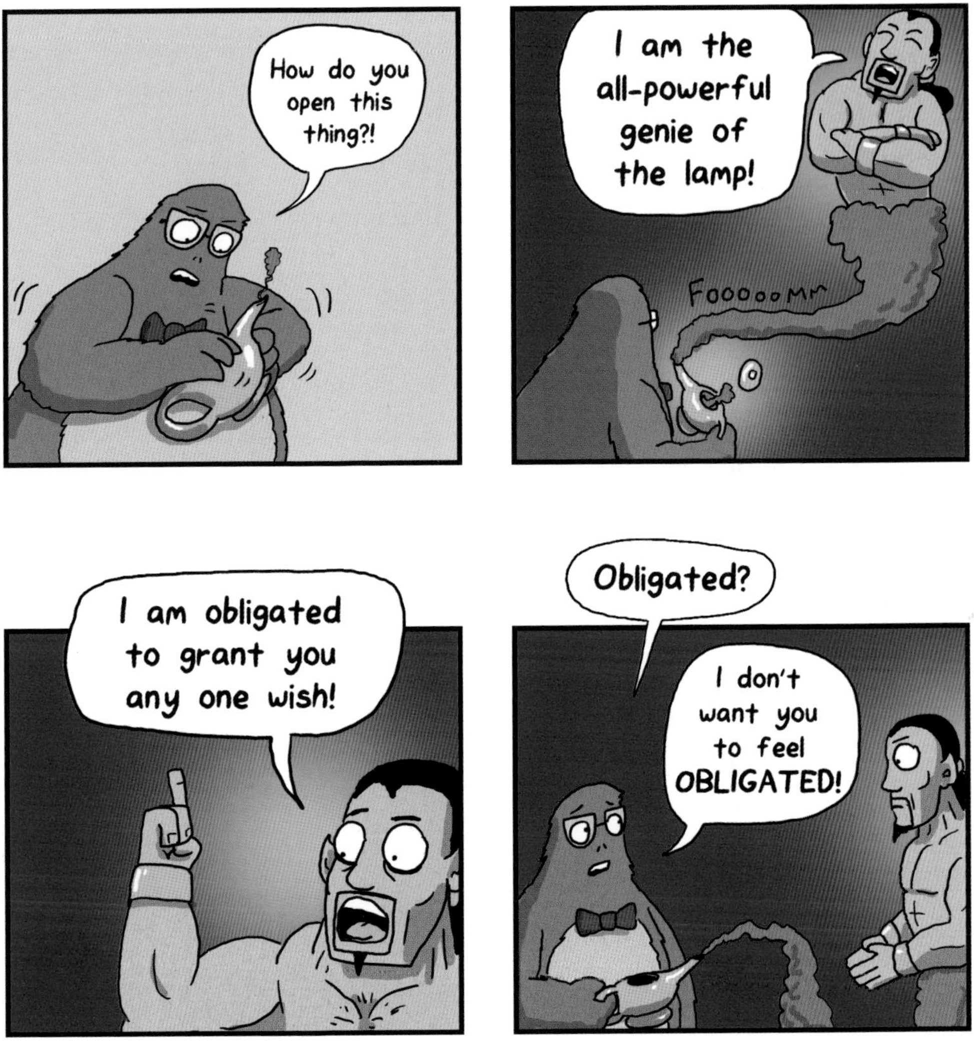
How do you open this thing?!
I am the all-powerful genie of the lamp!
FooooooMm
I am obligated to grant you any one wish!
Obligated?
I don't want you to feel OBLIGATED!

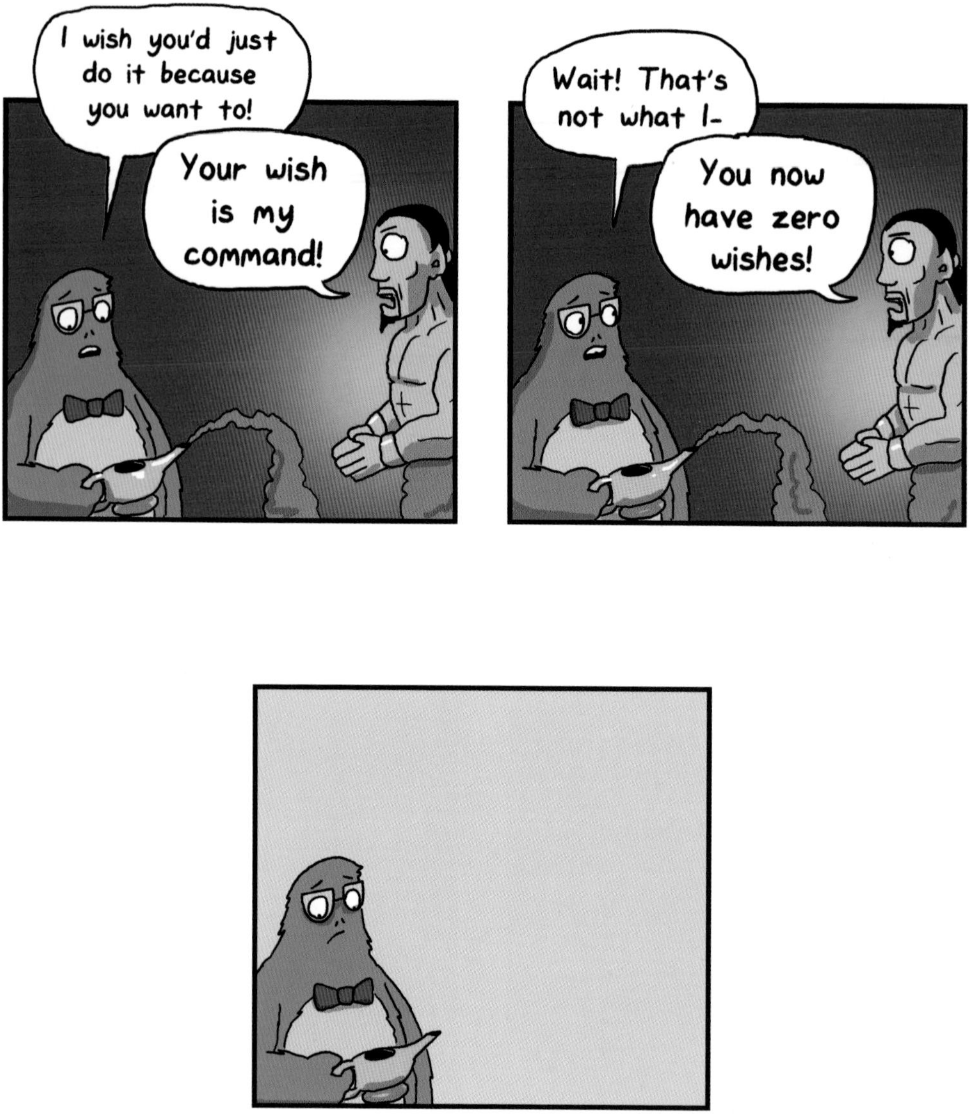
I wish you'd just do it because you want to!
Your wish is my command!
Wait! That's not what I-
You now have zero wishes!

The Appropriate Reaction

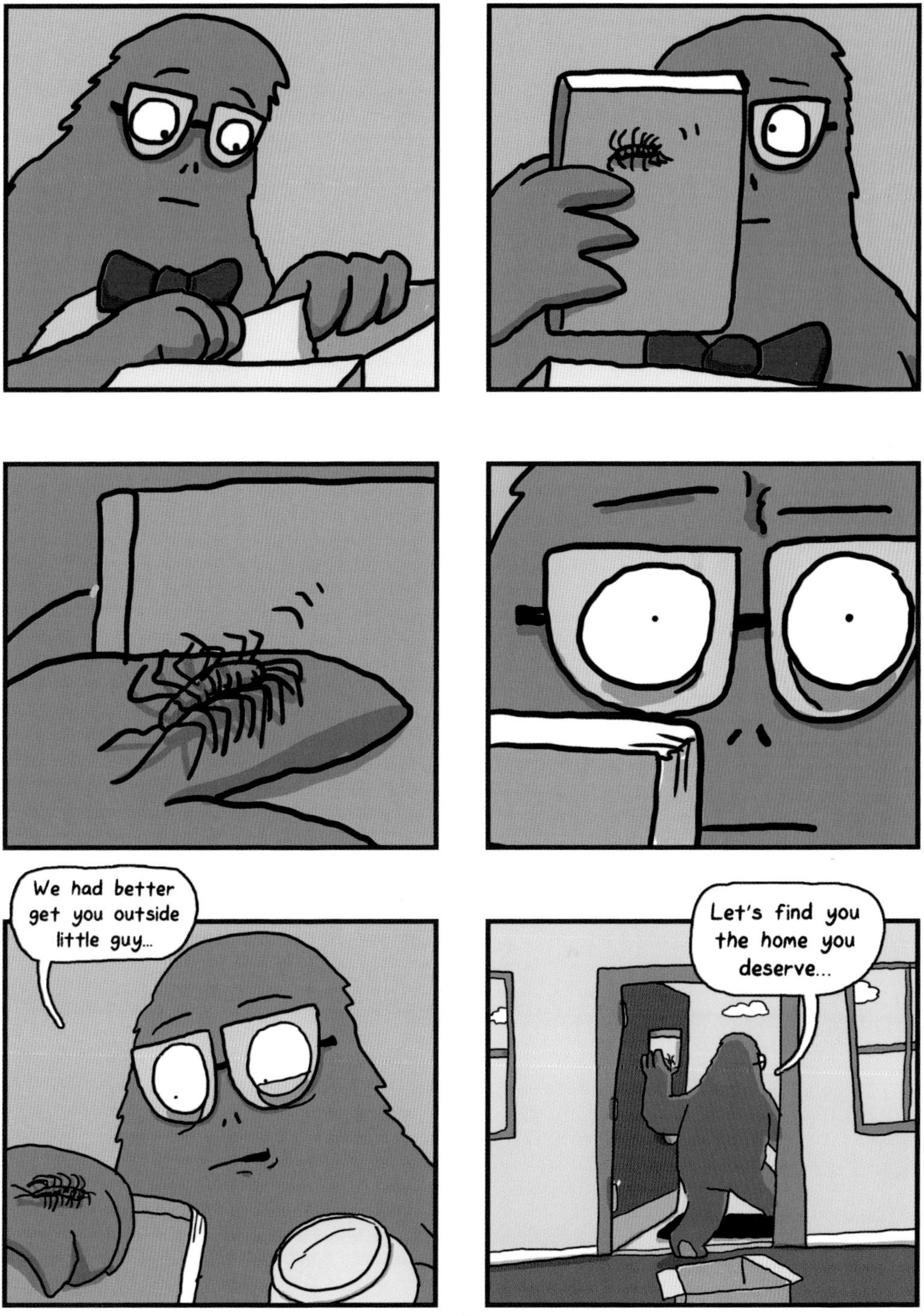
We had better get you outside little guy...
Let's find you the home you deserve...

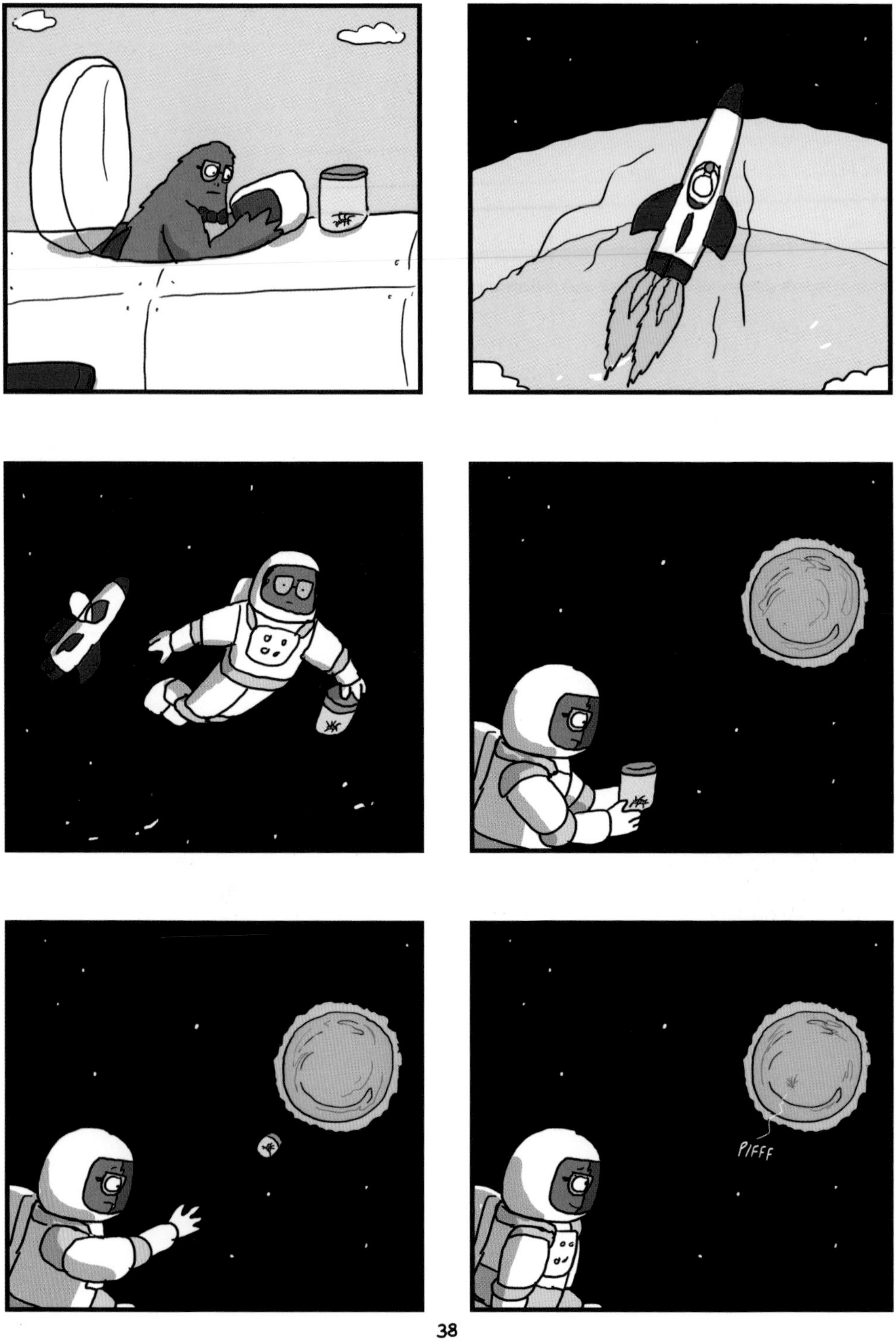
PIFFF

The One-Upper

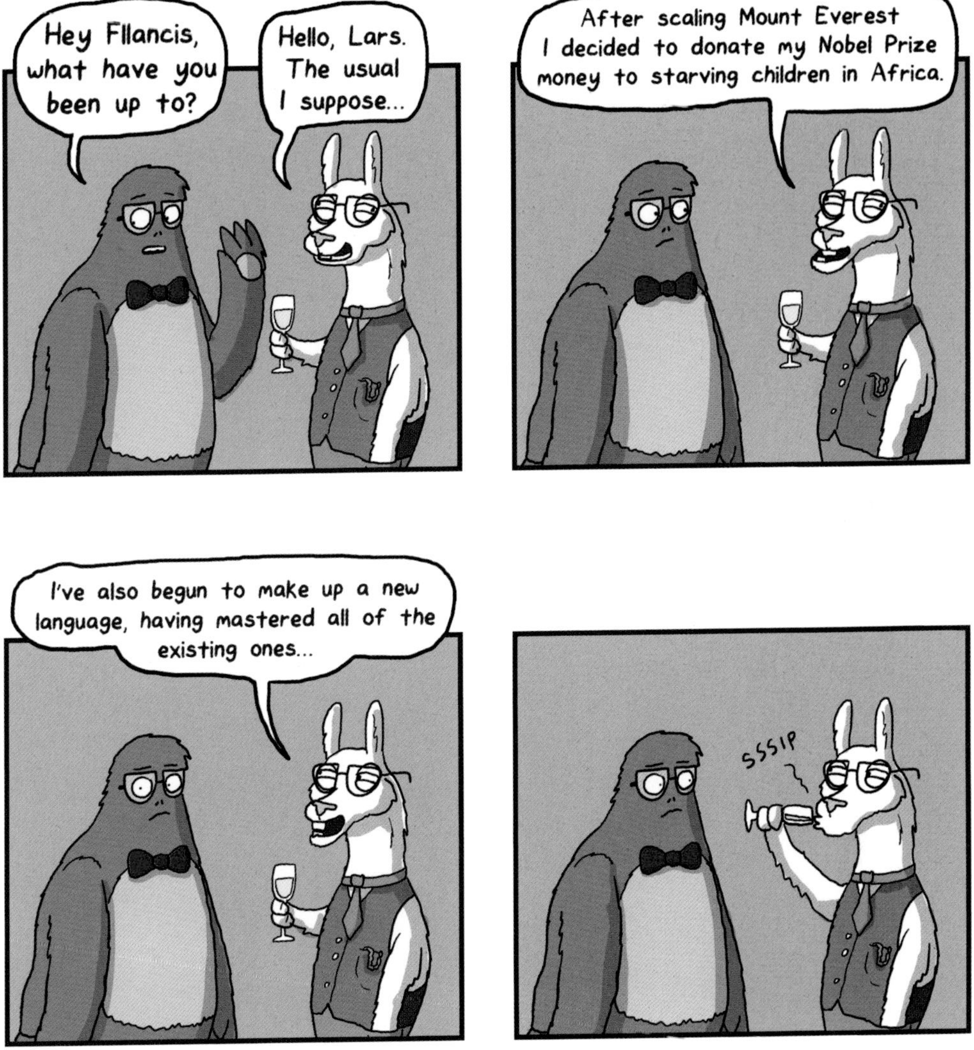
Hey Fllancis, what have you been up to?
Hello, Lars. The usual I suppose...
After scaling Mount Everest I decided to donate my Nobel Prize money to starving children in Africa.
I've also begun to make up a new language, having mastered all of the existing ones...
SSSIP

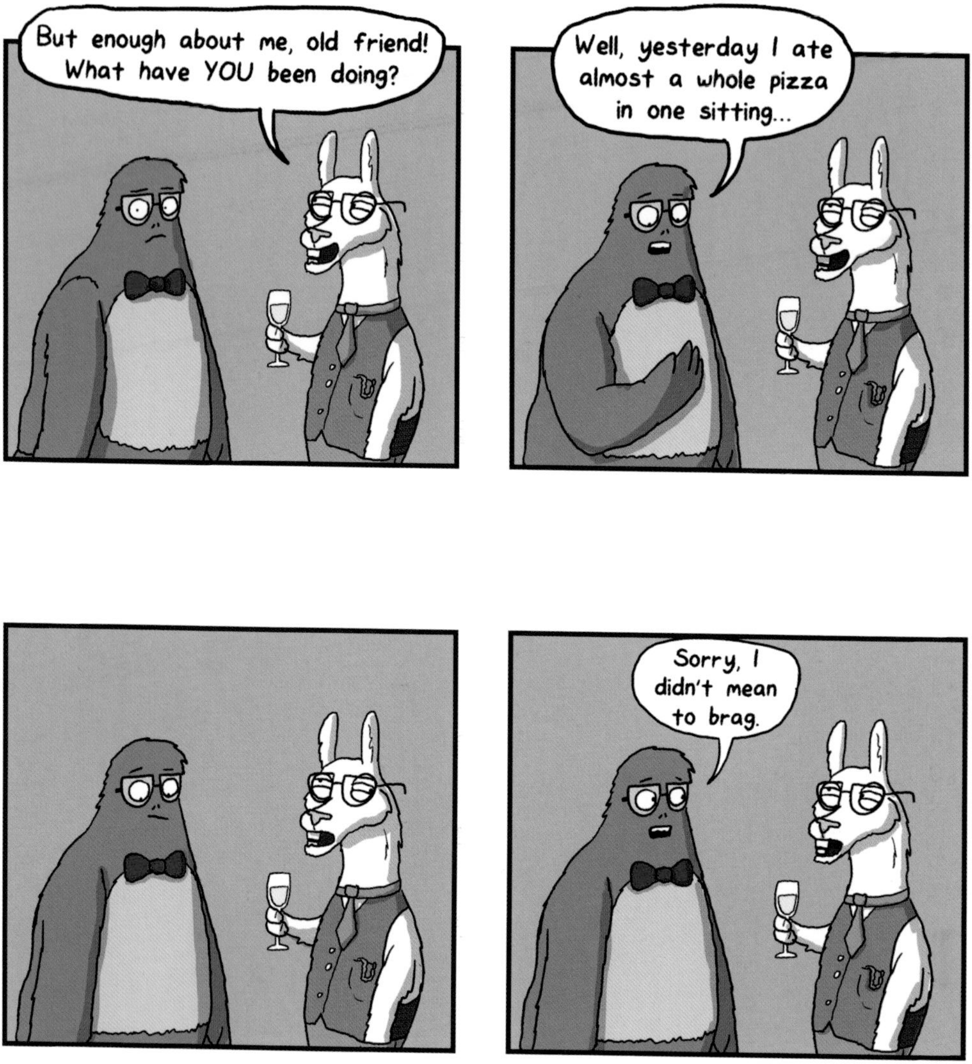
But enough about me, old friend! What have YOU been doing?
Well, yesterday I ate almost a whole pizza in one sitting...
Sorry, I didn't mean to brag.

The Traveler

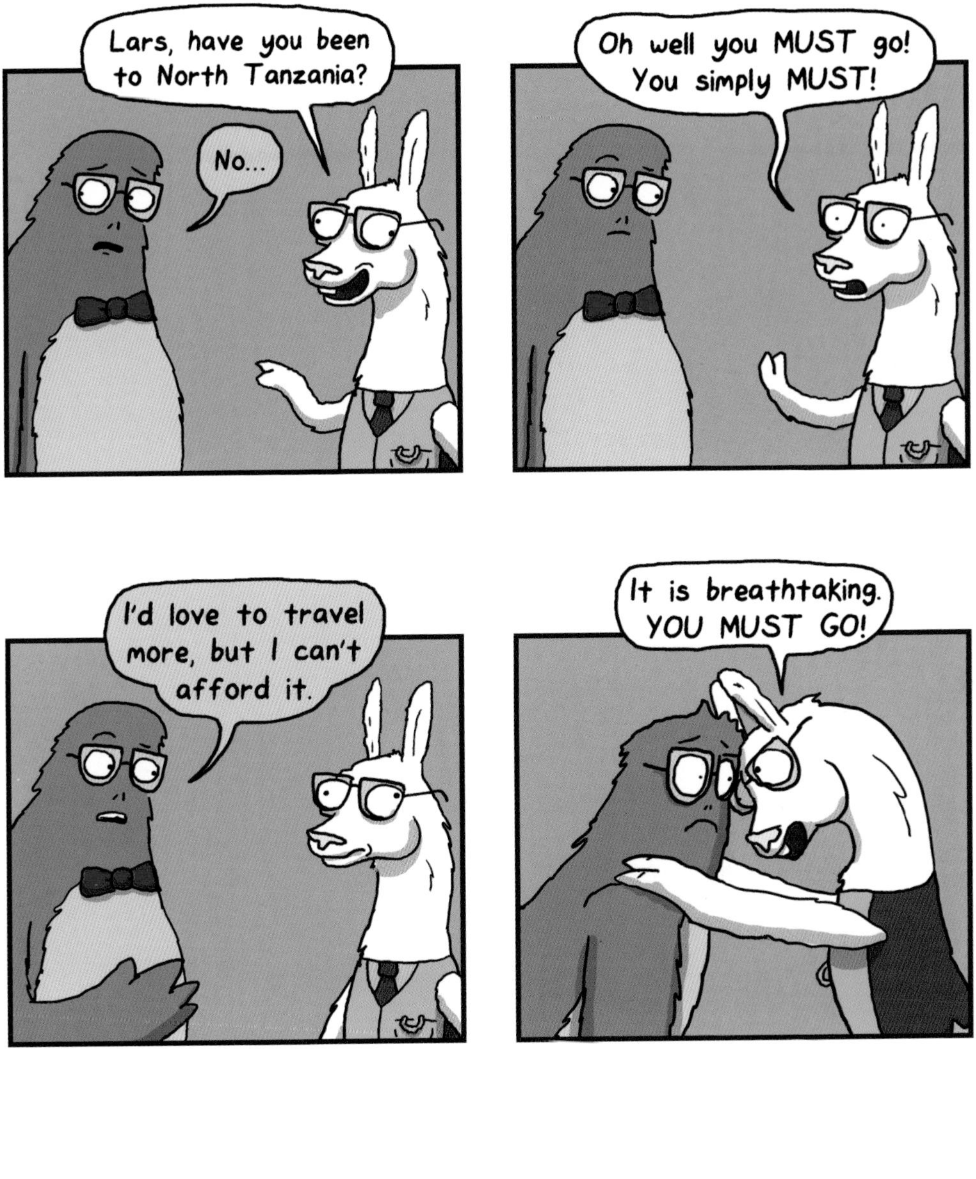

Lars, have you been to North Tanzania?
No...
Oh well you MUST go! You simply MUST!
I'd love to travel more, but I can't afford it.
It is breathtaking. YOU MUST GO!

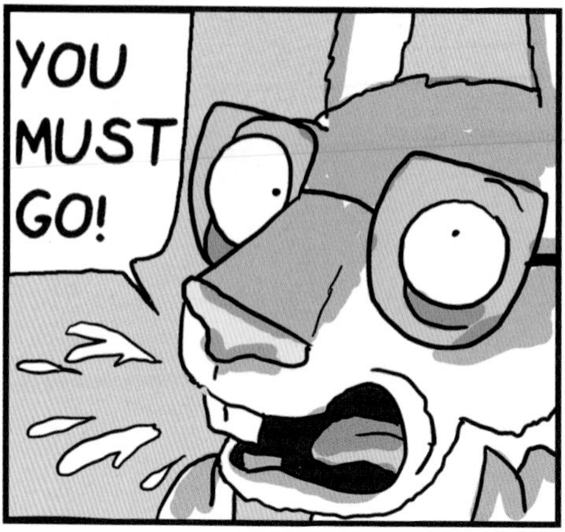
YOU MUST GO!

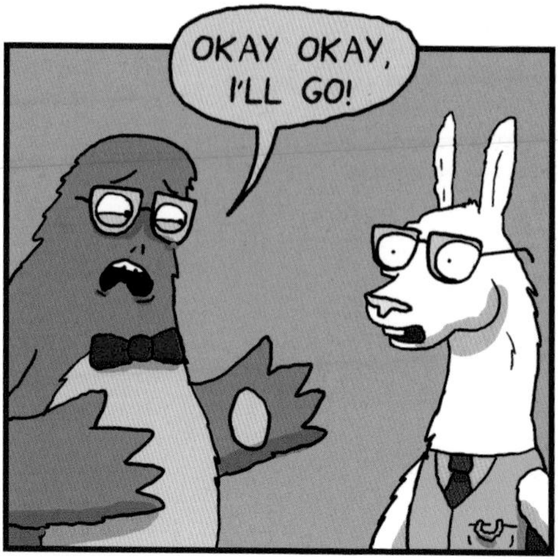
OKAY OKAY, I'LL GO!

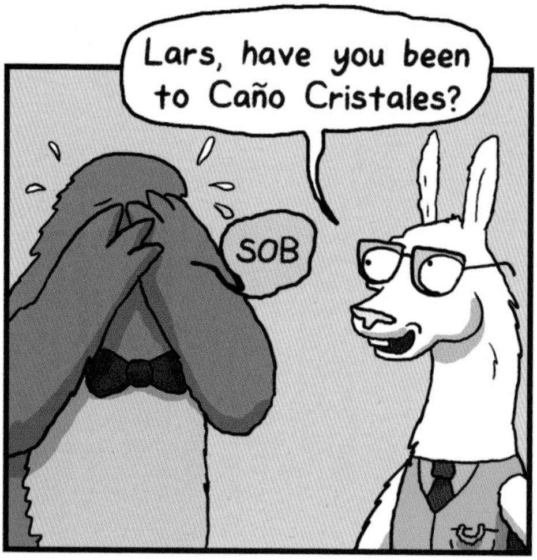
Lars, have you been to Caño Cristales?
SOB

Existential Advice

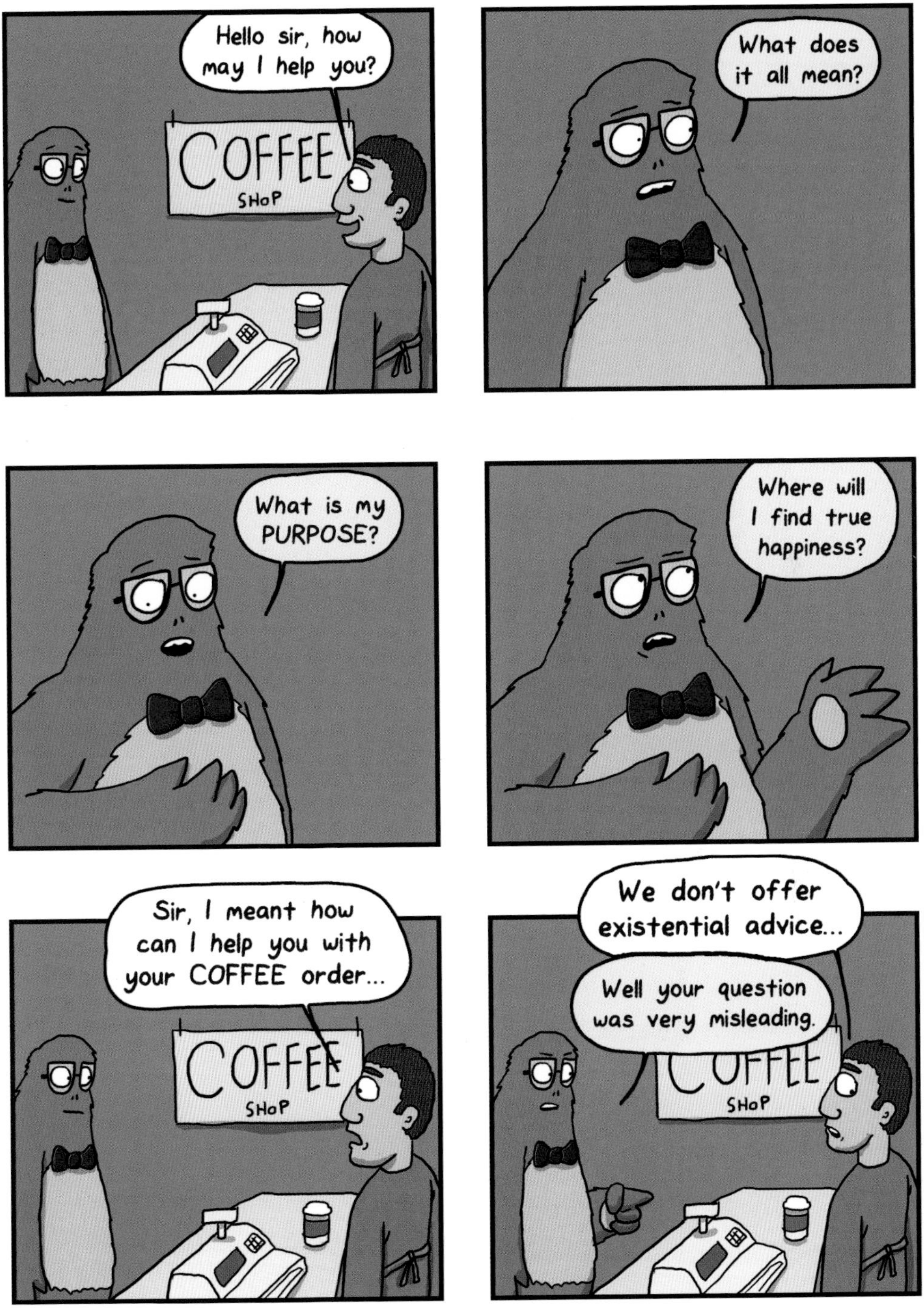
Hello sir, how may I help you?
COFFEE SHOP
What does it all mean?
What is my PURPOSE?
Where will I find true happiness?
Sir, I meant how can I help you with your COFFEE order...
COFFEE SHOP
We don't offer existential advice...
Well your question was very misleading.
SHOP

Talking to Animals

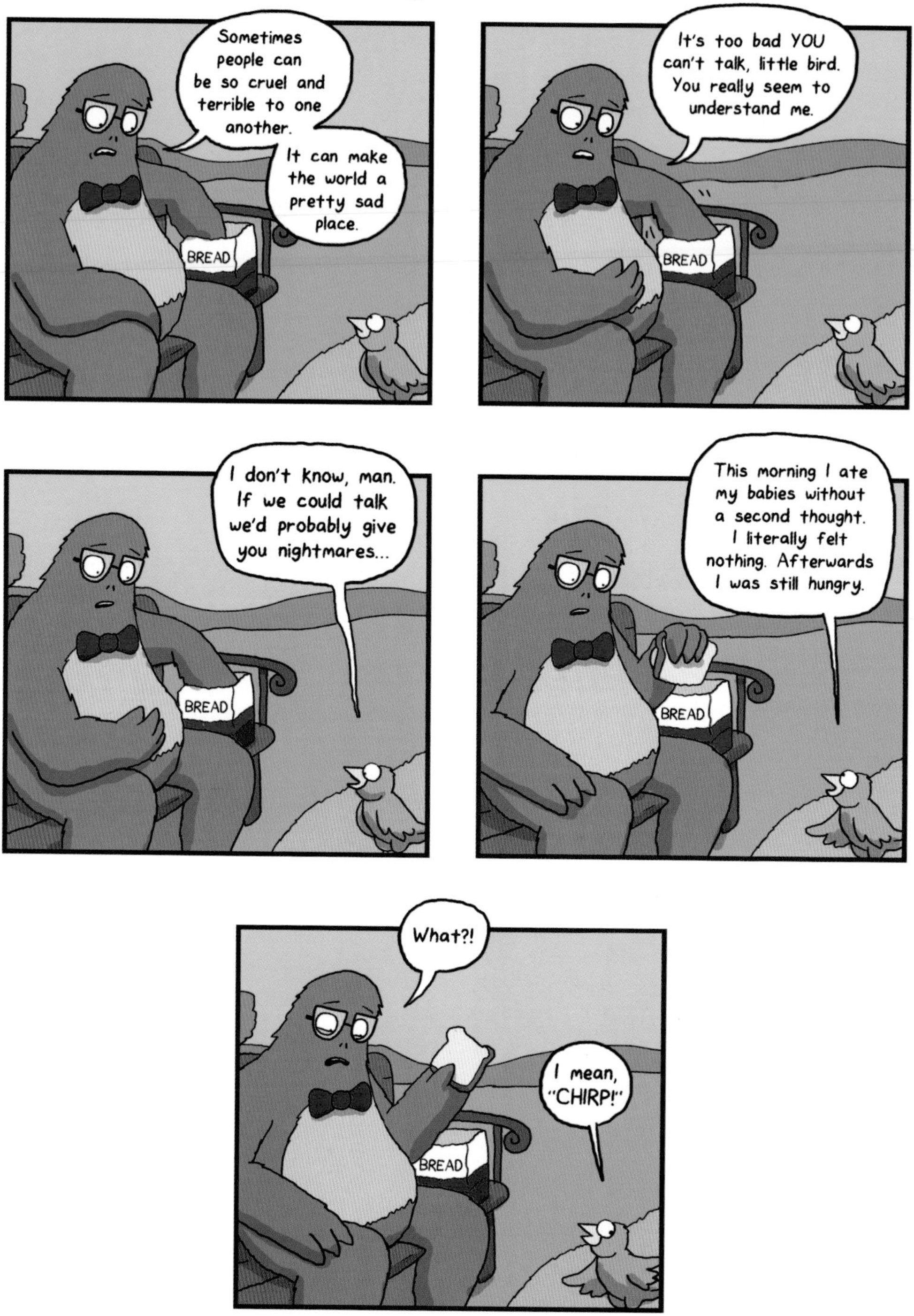
Sometimes people can be so cruel and terrible to one another.
It can make the world a pretty sad place.
BREAD
It's too bad YOU can't talk, little bird. You really seem to understand me.
BREAD
I don't know, man. If we could talk we'd probably give you nightmares...
BREAD
This morning I ate my babies without a second thought. I literally felt nothing. Afterwards I was still hungry.
BREAD
What?!
I mean, "CHIRP!"
BREAD

The Independent Adult

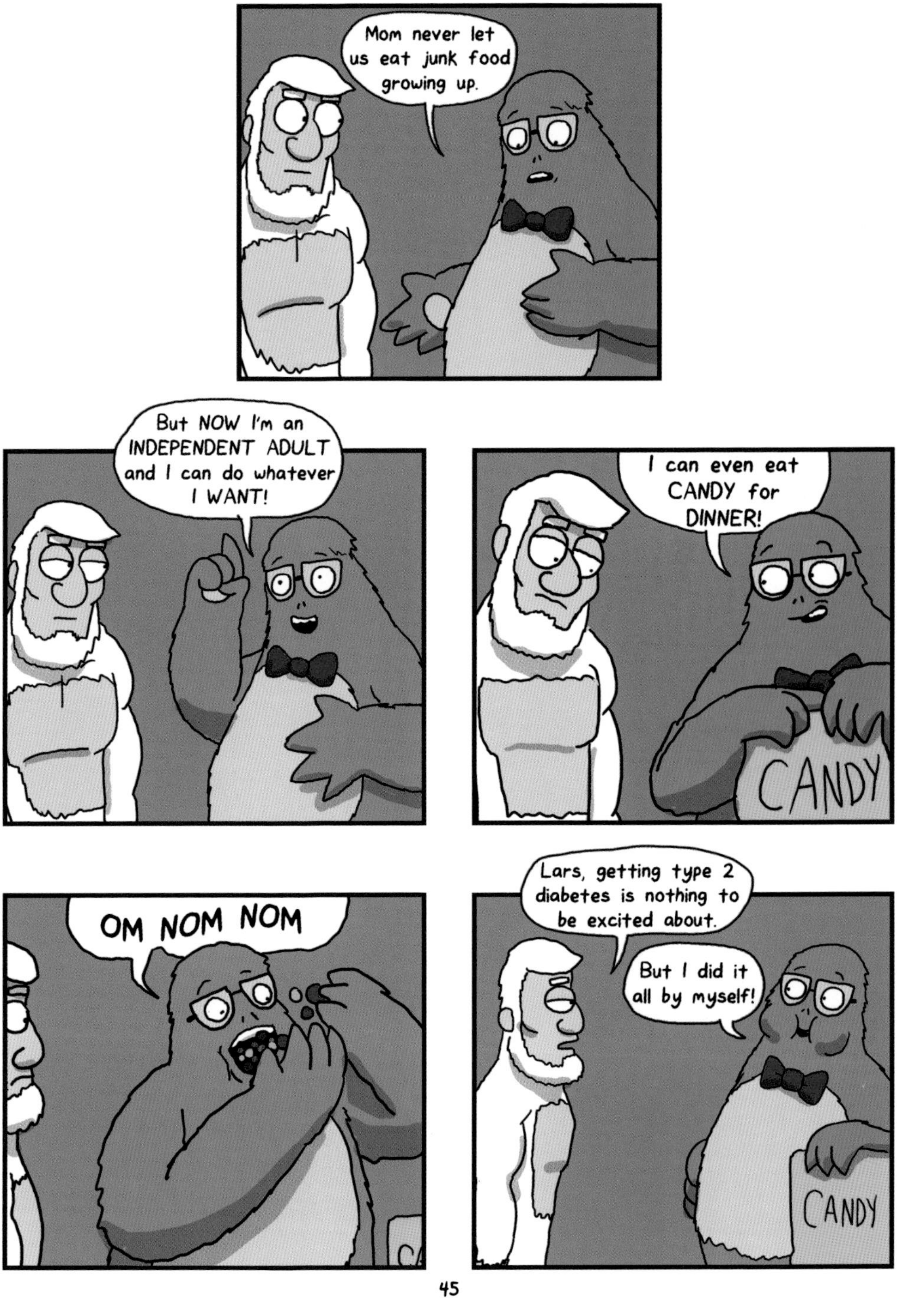
Mom never let us eat junk food growing up.
But NOW I'm an INDEPENDENT ADULT and I can do whatever I WANT!
I can even eat CANDY for DINNER!
CANDY
OM NOM NOM
Lars, getting type 2 diabetes is nothing to be excited about.
But I did it all by myself!
CANDY

The Hard Sell

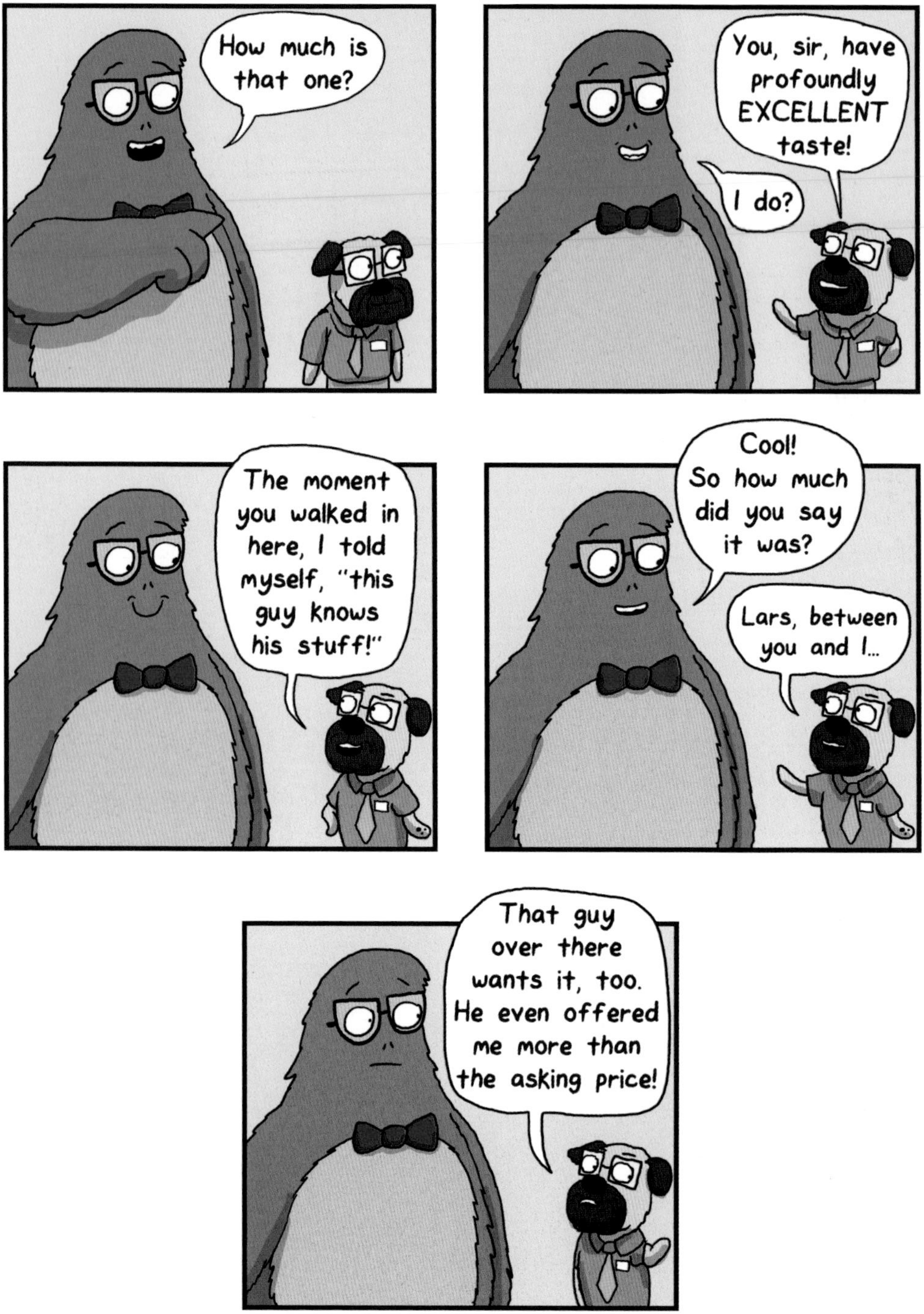
How much is that one?
You, sir, have profoundly EXCELLENT taste!
I do?
The moment you walked in here, I told myself, "this guy knows his stuff!"
Cool! So how much did you say it was?
Lars, between you and I...
That guy over there wants it, too. He even offered me more than the asking price!

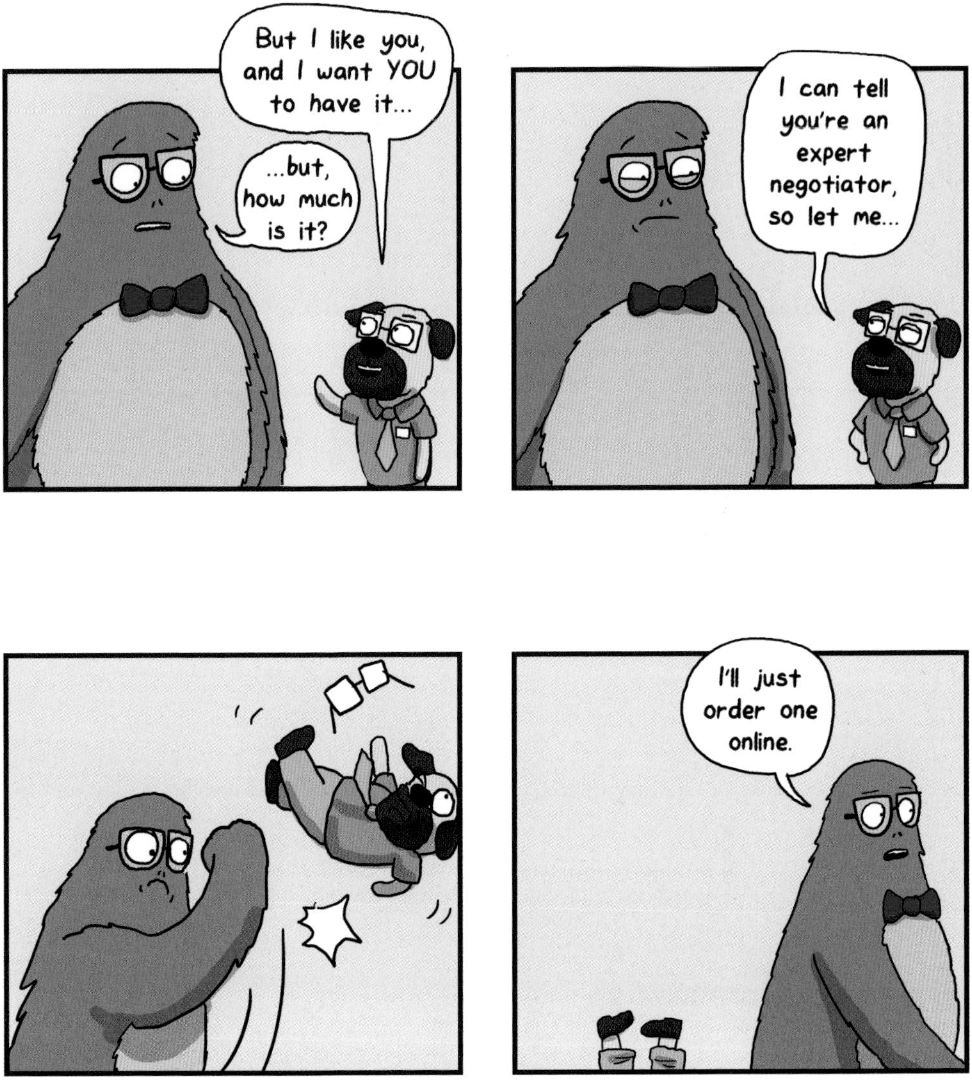
But I like you, and I want YOU to have it...
...but, how much is it?
I can tell you're an expert negotiator, so let me...
I'll just order one online.

Ambitions

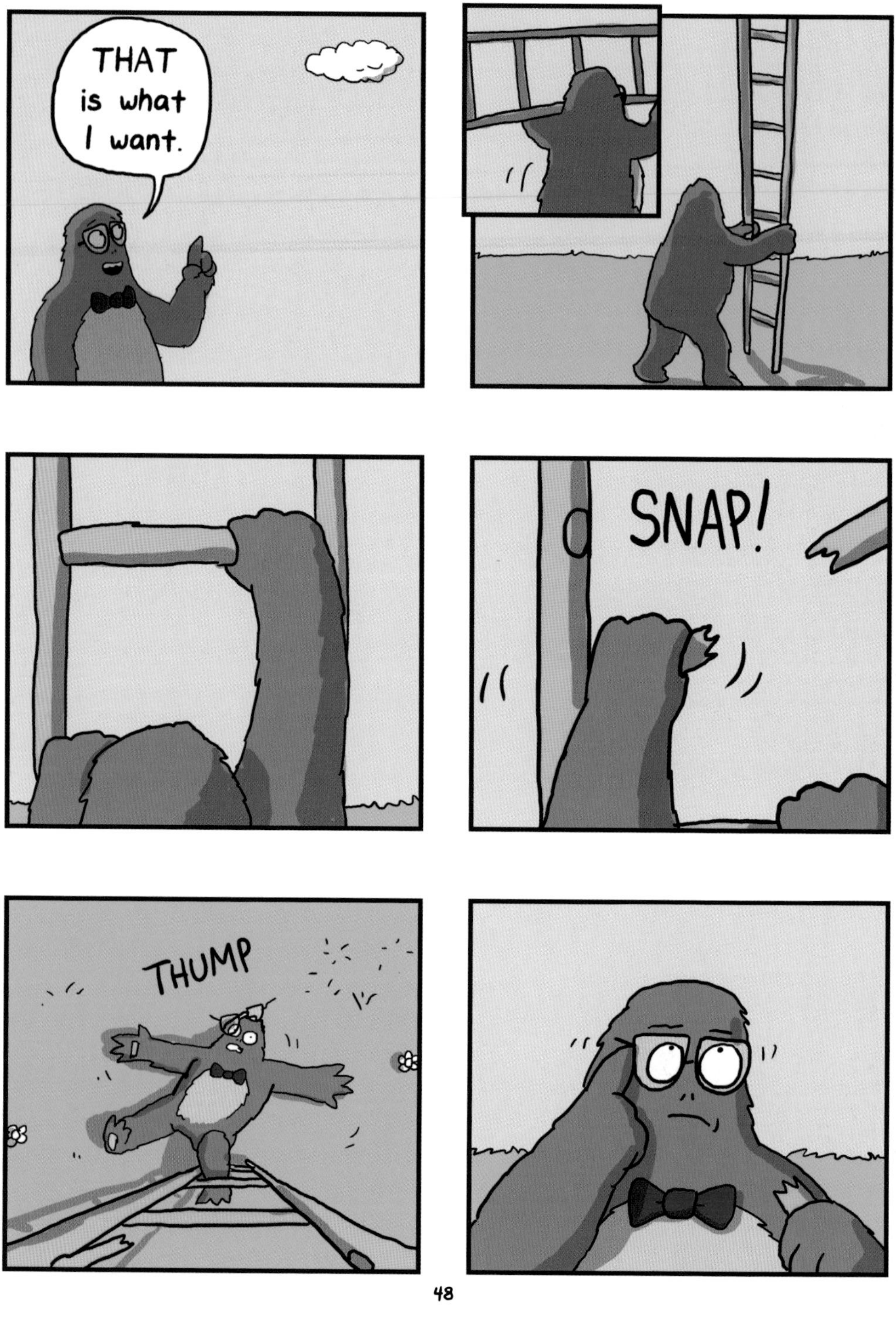

THAT is what I want.
SNAP!
THUMP

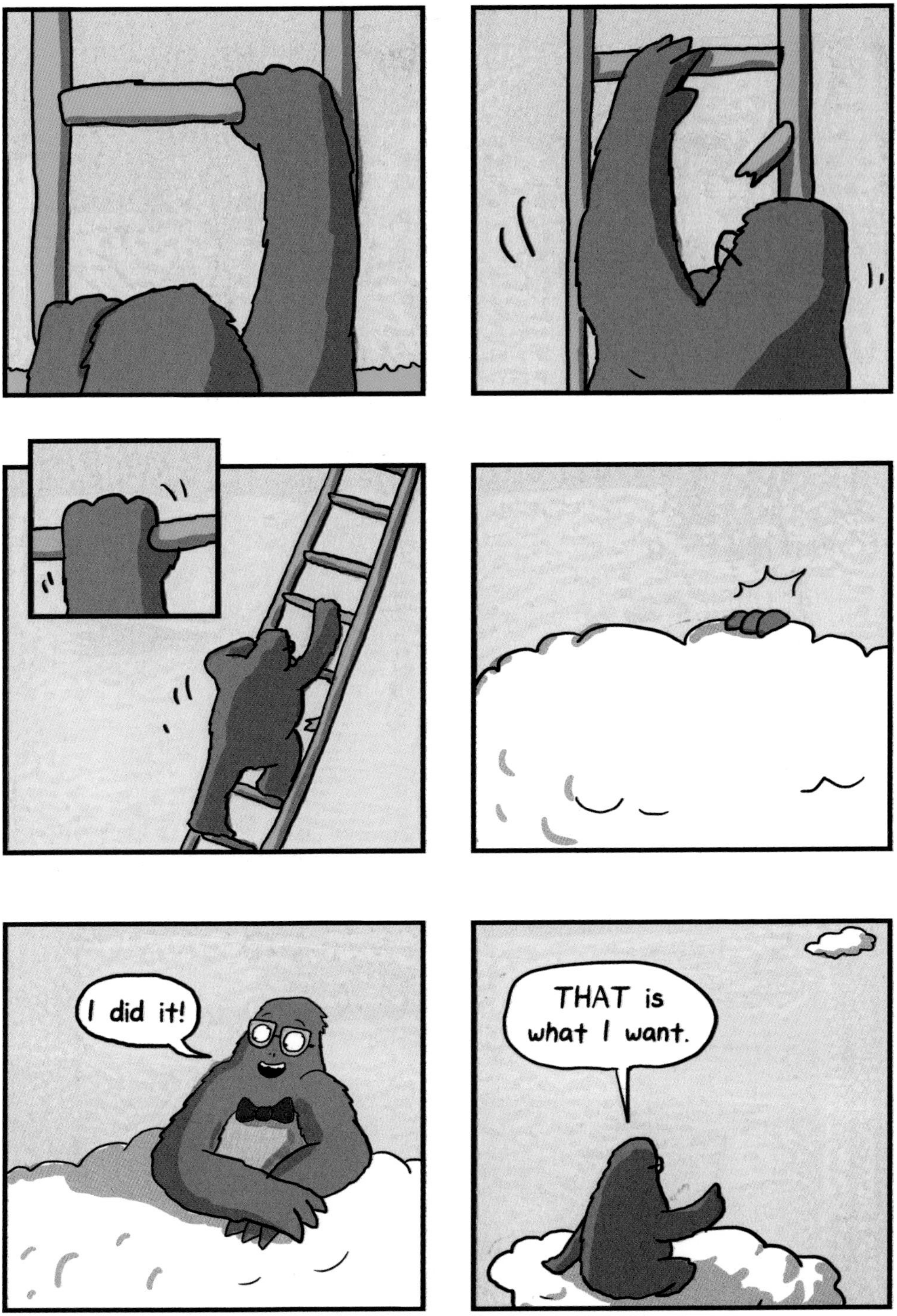
I did it!
THAT is what I want.

Luck

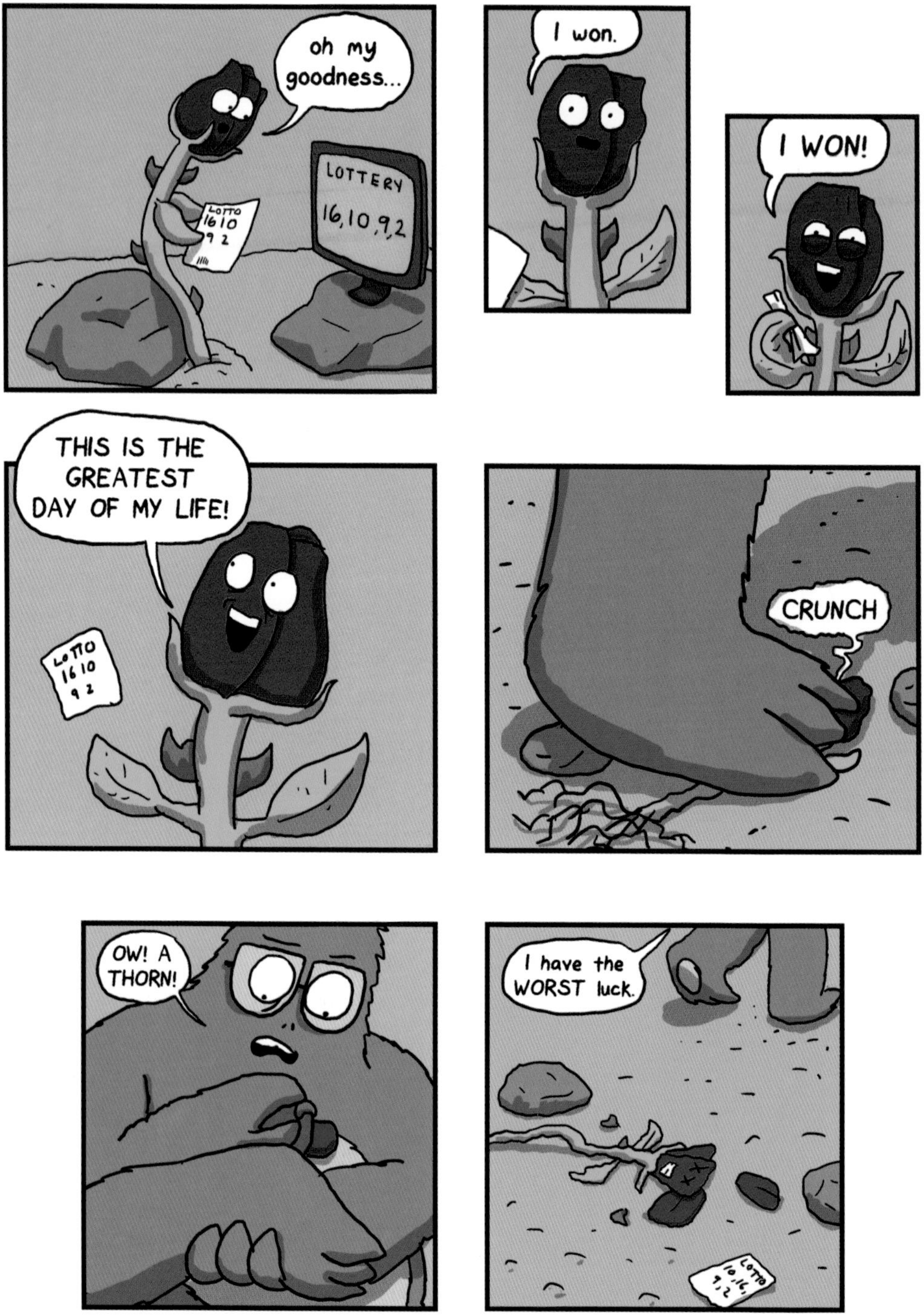
oh my goodness...
LOTTO 16 10 9 2
LOTTERY
16,10,9,2
I won.
I WON!
THIS IS THE GREATEST DAY OF MY LIFE!
LOTTO 16 10 9 2
CRUNCH
OW! A THORN!
I have the WORST luck.
LOTTO 10, 16, 9, 2

That Song

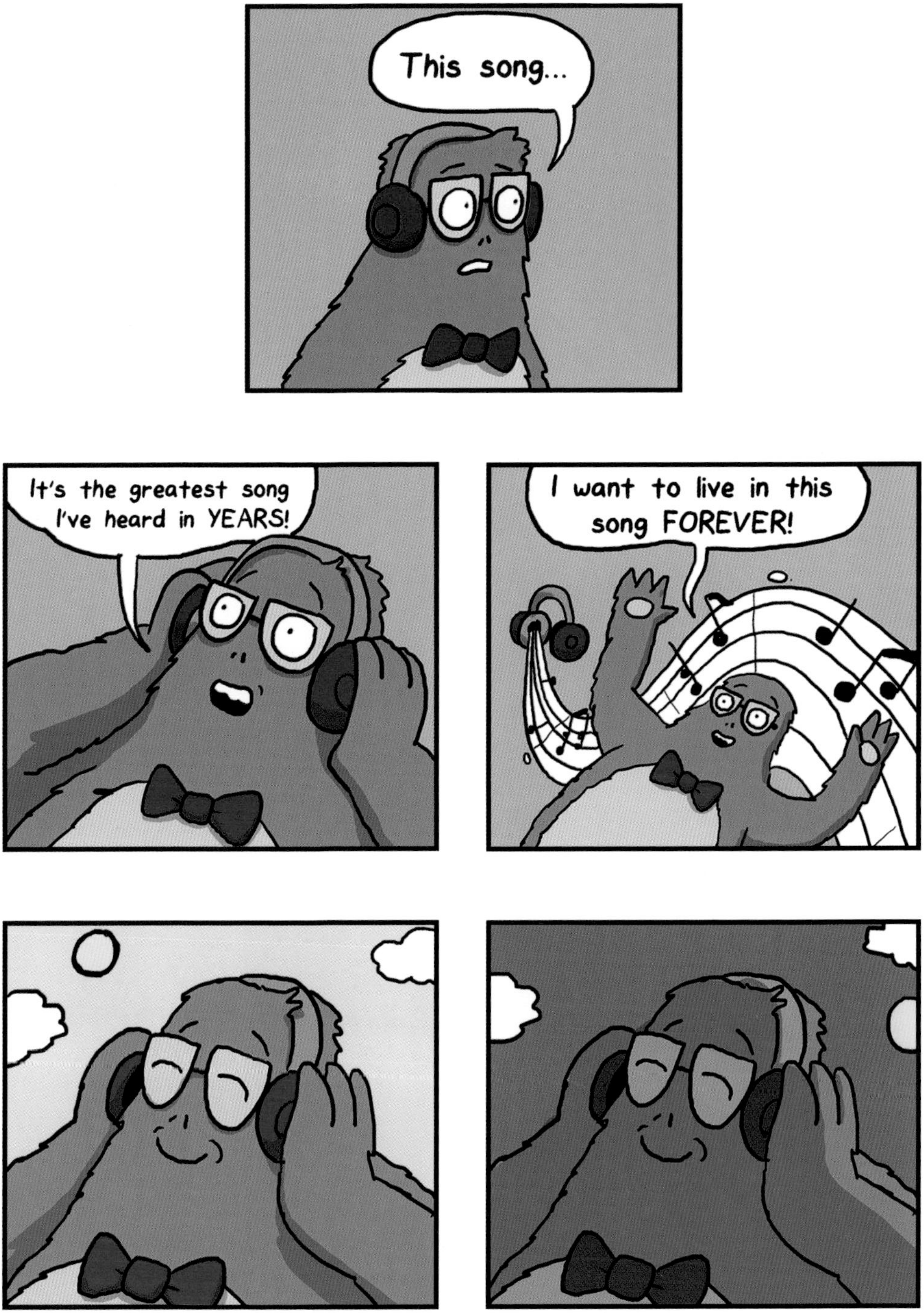
This song...
It's the greatest song I've heard in YEARS!
I want to live in this song FOREVER!

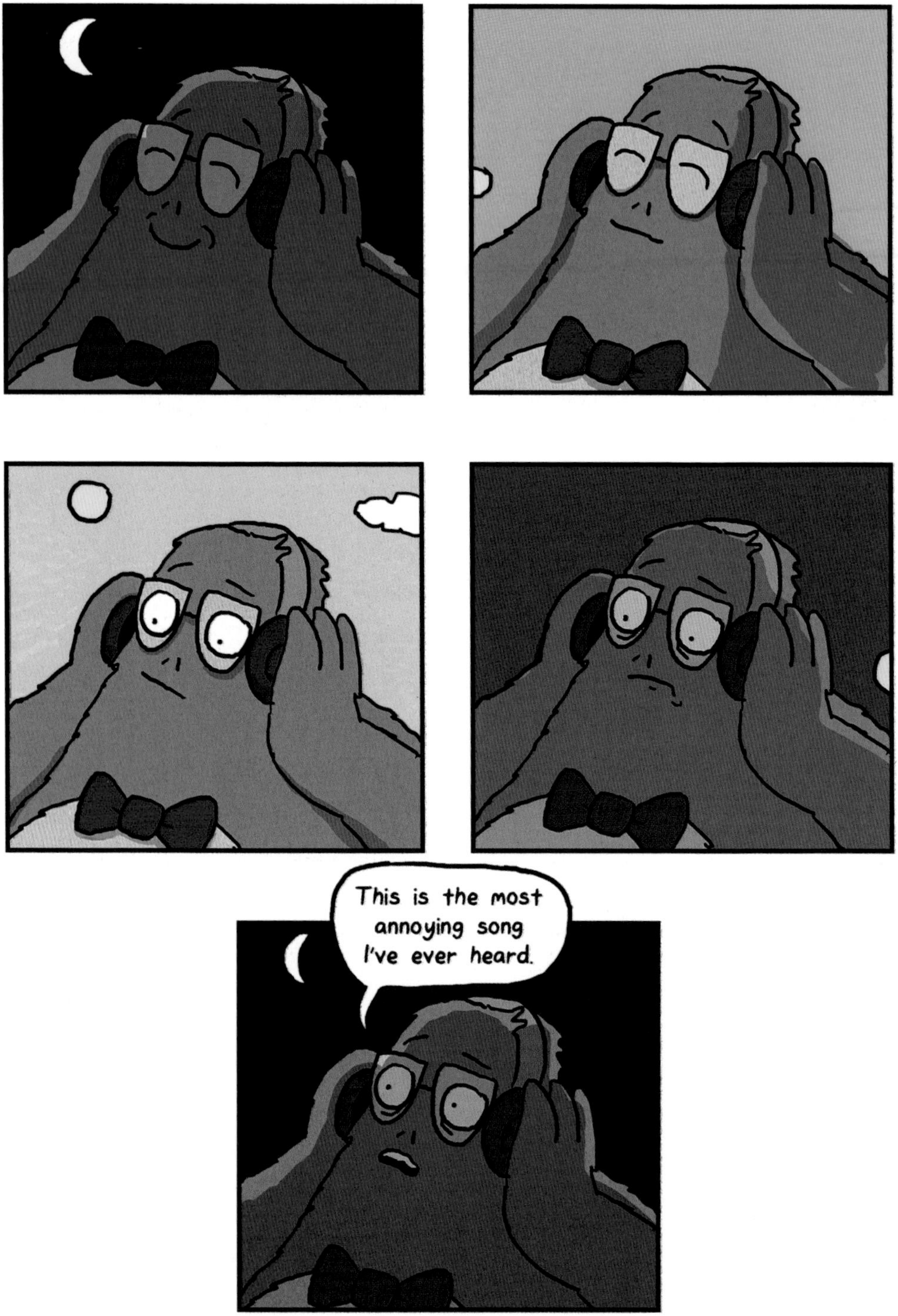
This is the most annoying song I've ever heard.

Closing Time

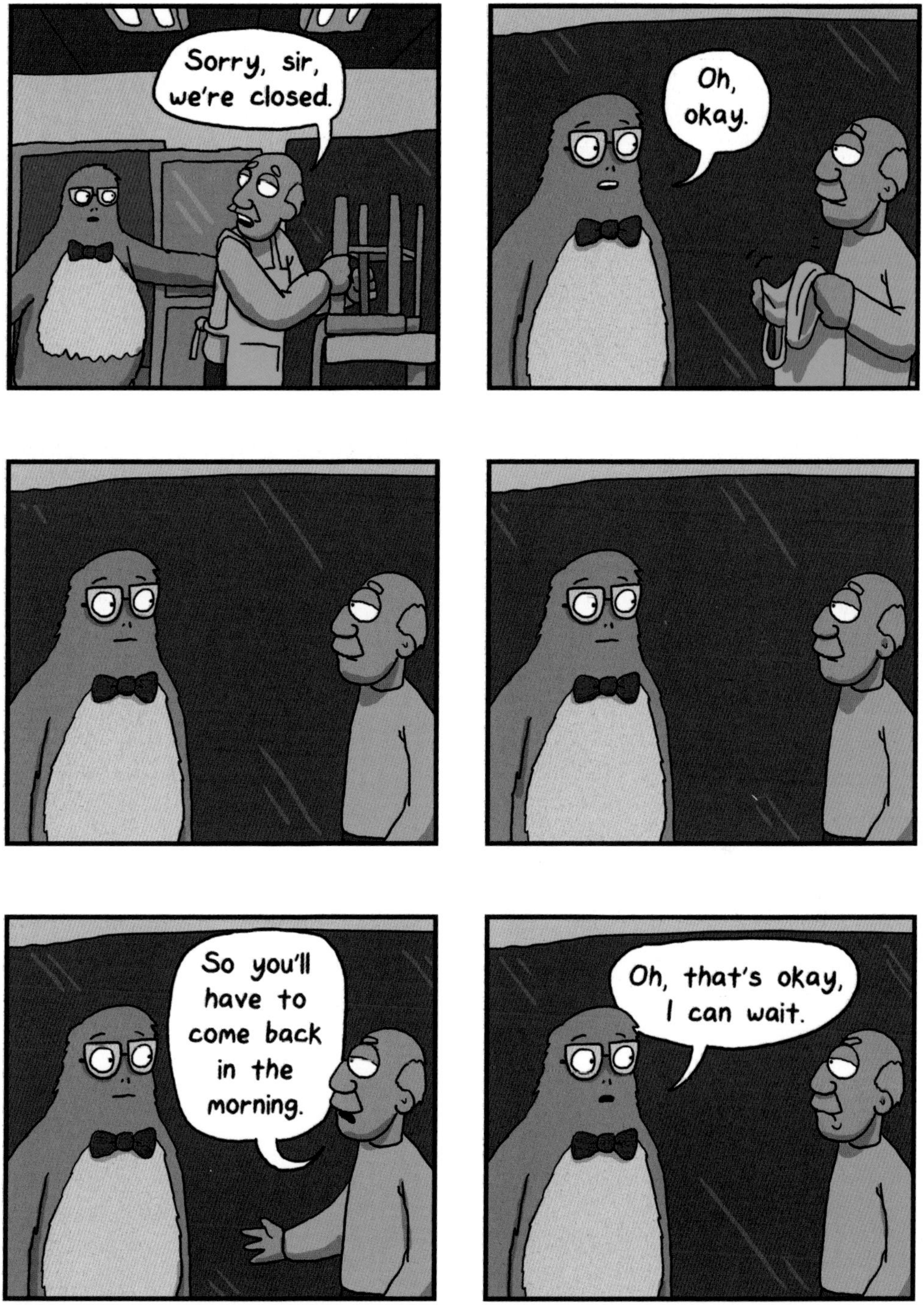

Sorry, sir, we're closed.
Oh, okay.
So you'll have to come back in the morning.
Oh, that's okay, I can wait.

Fitness

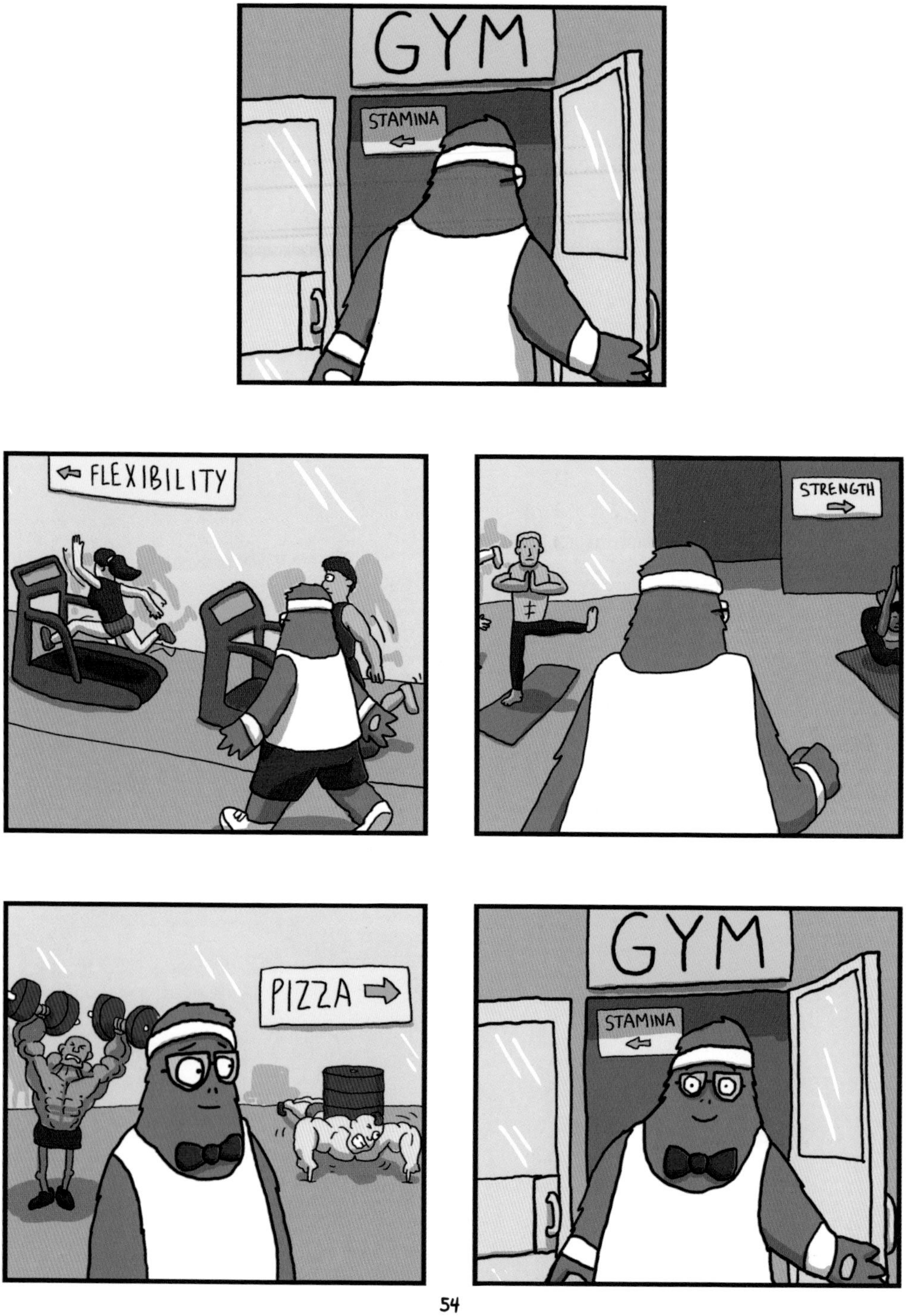
GYM
STAMINA
FLEXIBILITY
STRENGTH
PIZZA
GYM
STAMINA

The Dog

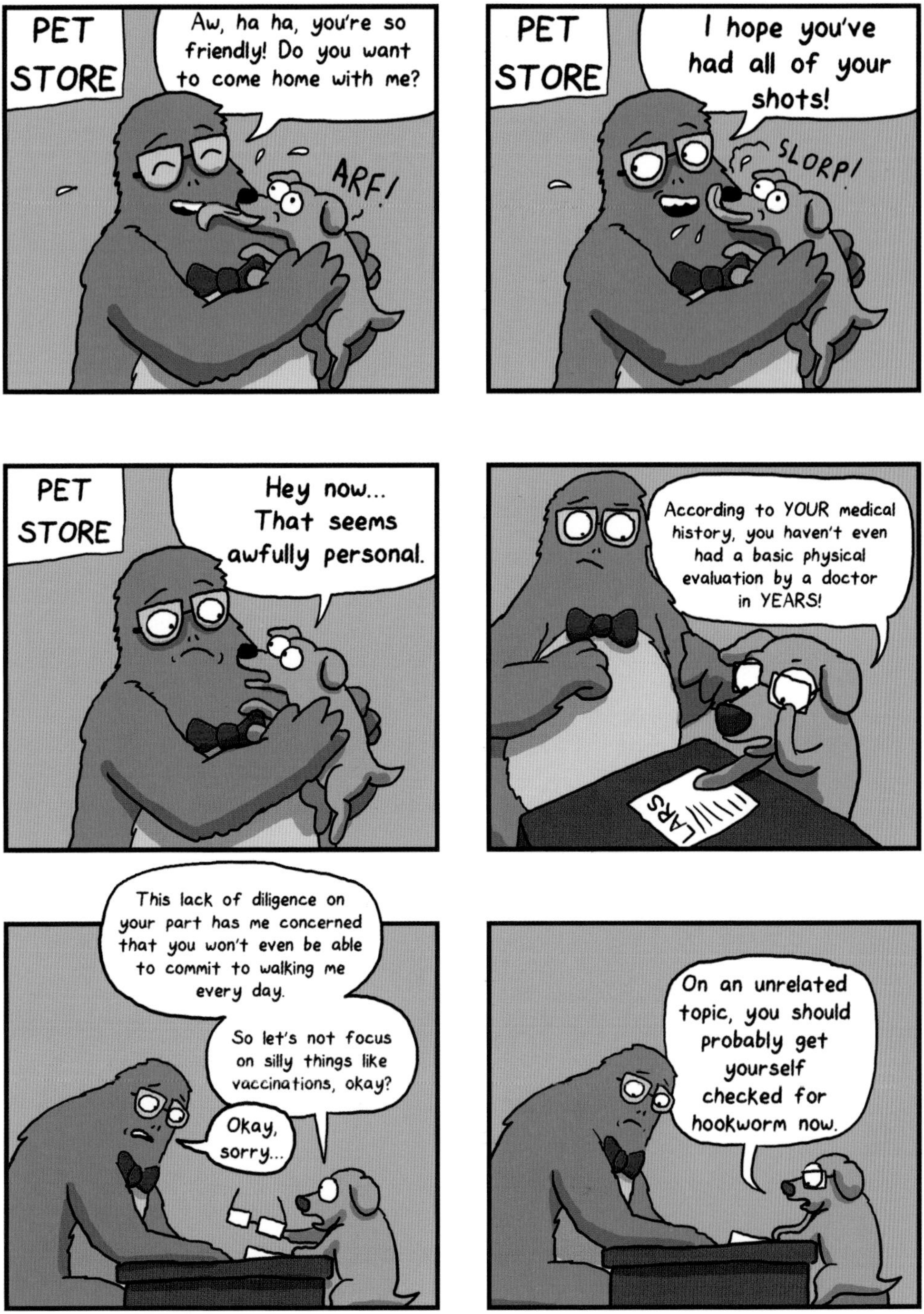
PET STORE
Aw, ha ha, you're so friendly! Do you want to come home with me?
ARF!
PET STORE
I hope you've had all of your shots!
SLORP!
PET STORE
Hey now... That seems awfully personal.
According to YOUR medical history, you haven't even had a basic physical evaluation by a doctor in YEARS!
LARS
This lack of diligence on your part has me concerned that you won't even be able to commit to walking me every day.
So let's not focus on silly things like vaccinations, okay?
Okay, sorry...
On an unrelated topic, you should probably get yourself checked for hookworm now.

Bad with Names

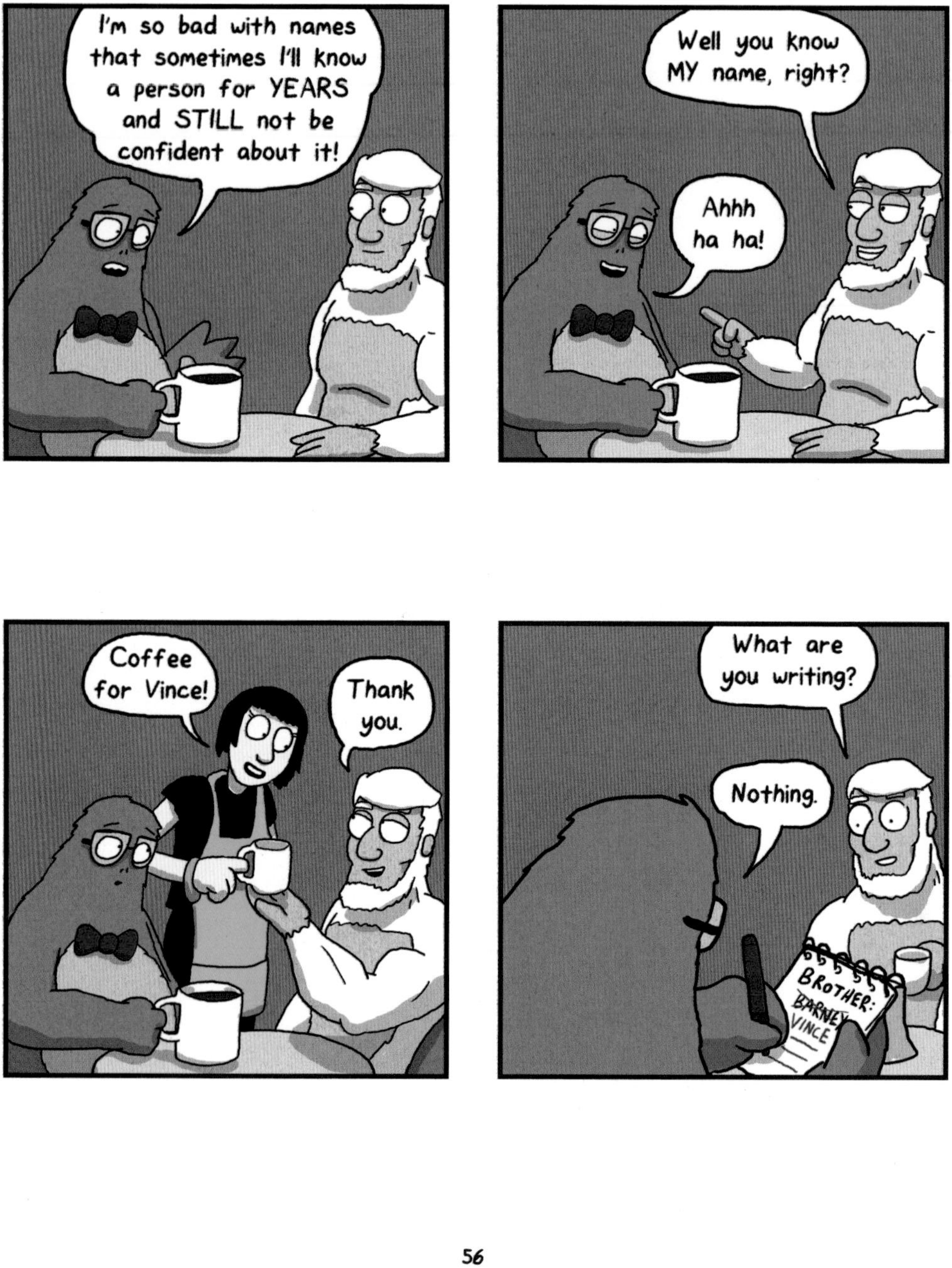
I'm so bad with names that sometimes I'll know a person for YEARS and STILL not be confident about it!
Well you know MY name, right?
Ahhh ha ha!
Coffee for Vince!
Thank you.
What are you writing?
Nothing.
BROTHER:
~~BARNEY~~
VINCE

The Screen

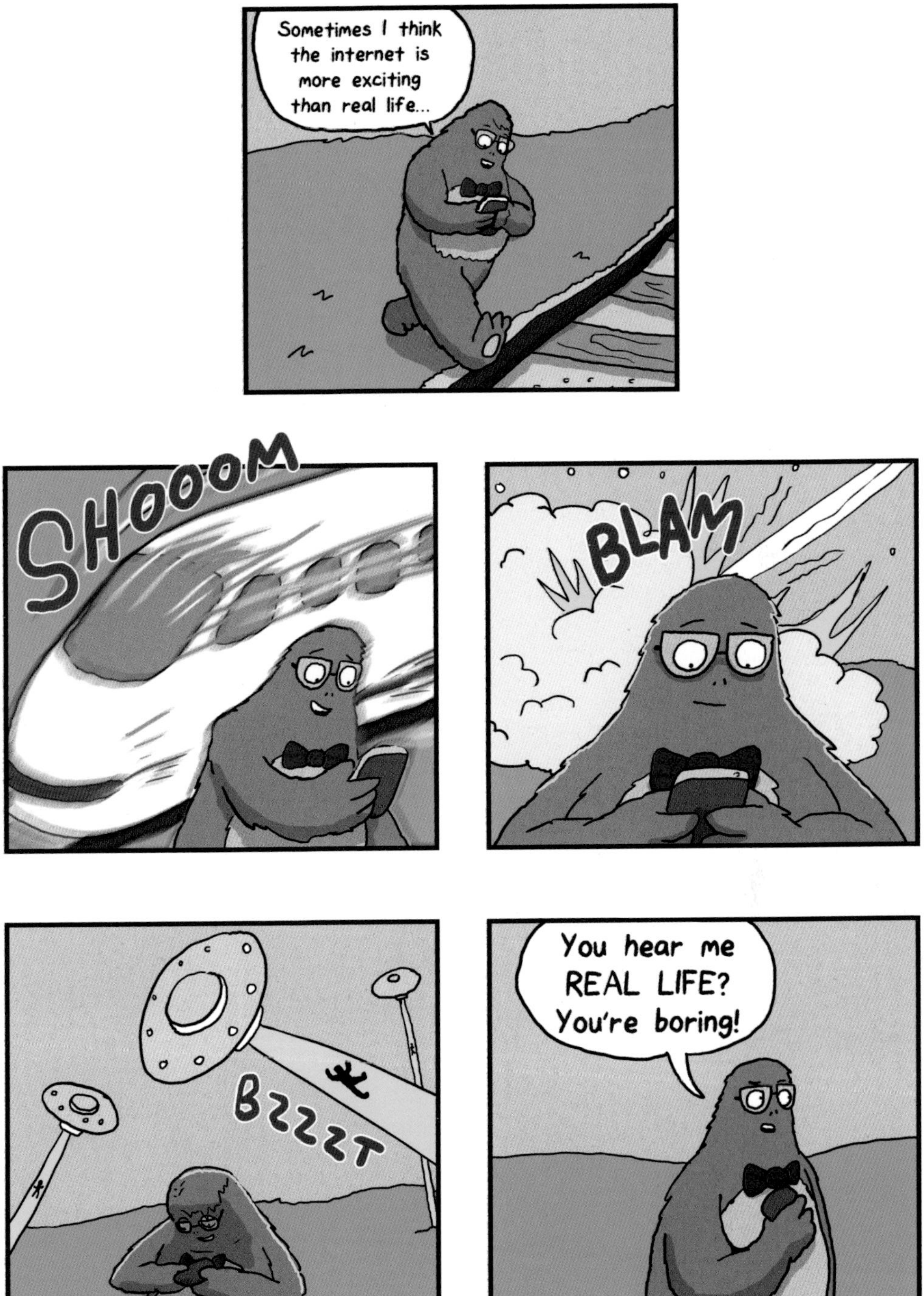
Sometimes I think the internet is more exciting than real life...
SHOOOM
BLAM
BZZZT
You hear me REAL LIFE? You're boring!

Coffee

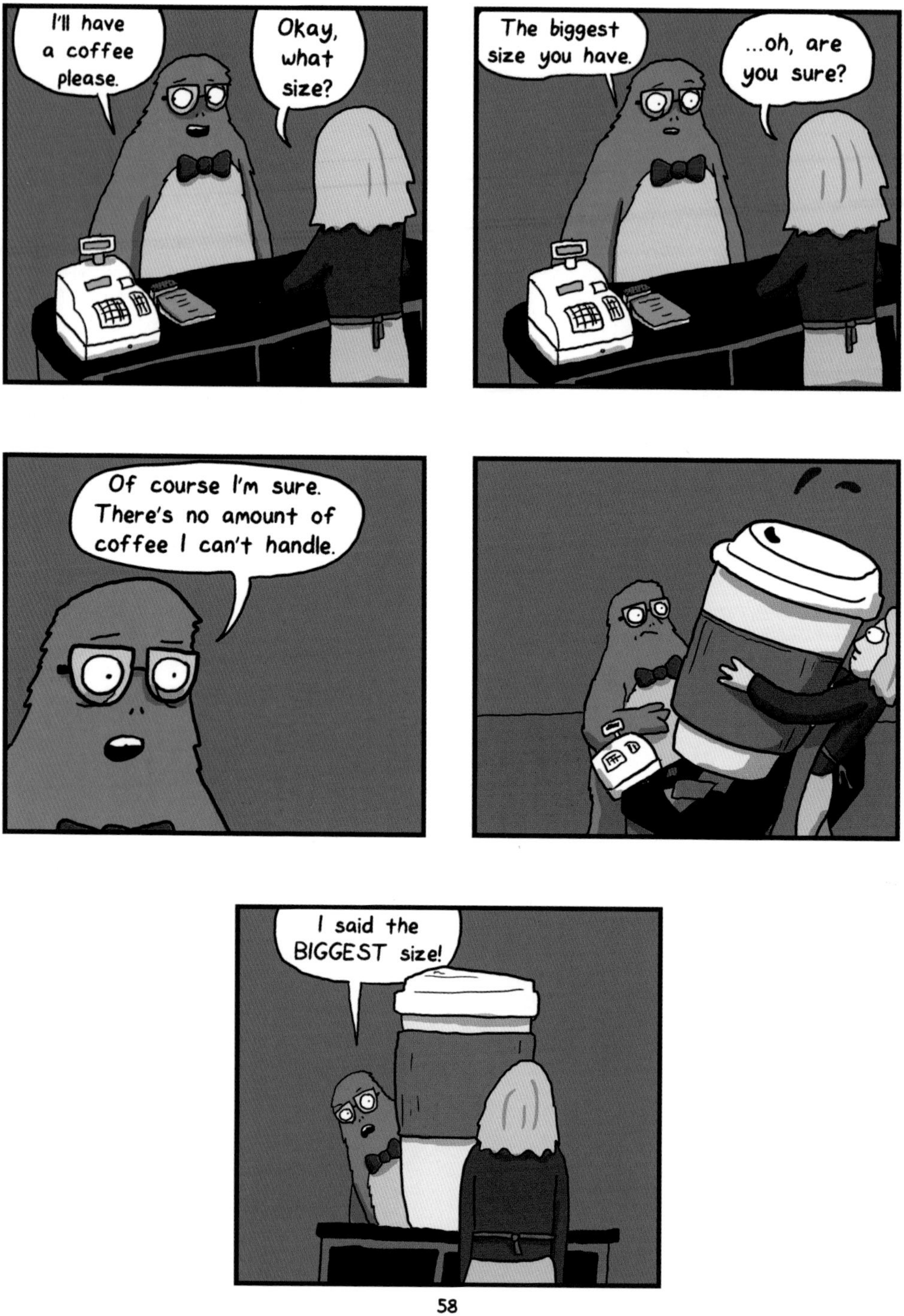
I'll have a coffee please.
Okay, what size?
The biggest size you have.
...oh, are you sure?
Of course I'm sure. There's no amount of coffee I can't handle.
I said the BIGGEST size!

The Meaning of Life

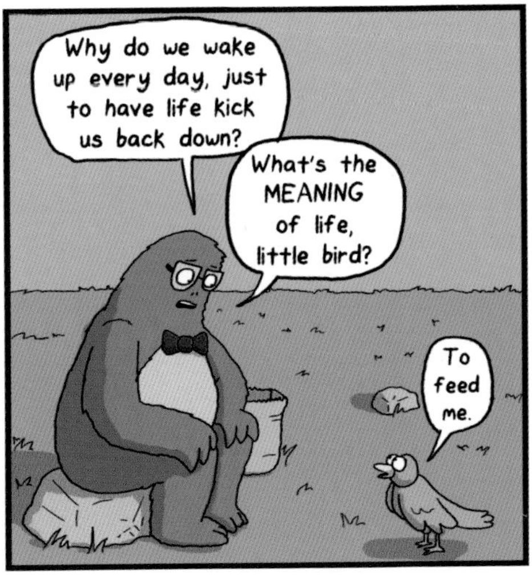
Why do we wake up every day, just to have life kick us back down?
What's the MEANING of life, little bird?
To feed me.

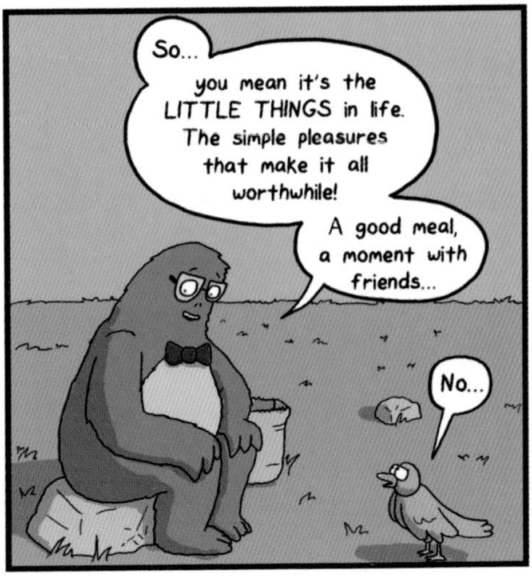
So... you mean it's the LITTLE THINGS in life. The simple pleasures that make it all worthwhile!
A good meal, a moment with friends...
No...

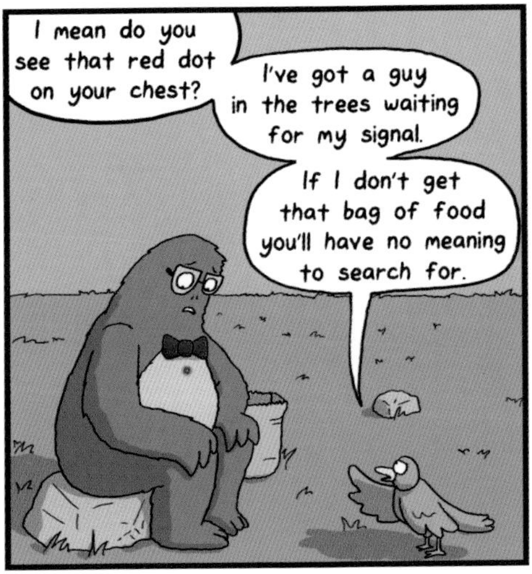
I mean do you see that red dot on your chest?
I've got a guy in the trees waiting for my signal.
If I don't get that bag of food you'll have no meaning to search for.

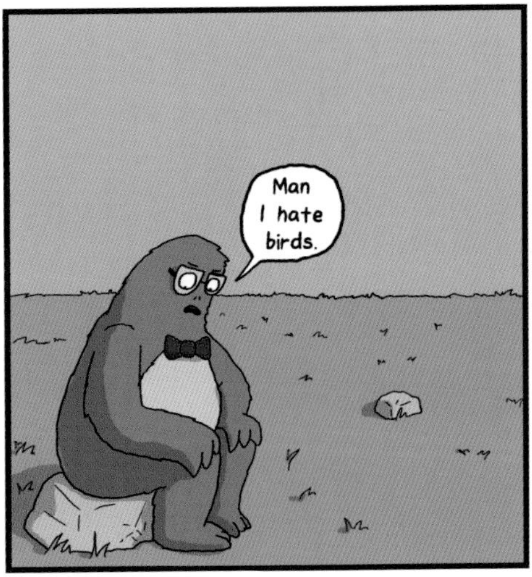
Man I hate birds.

Paranoid

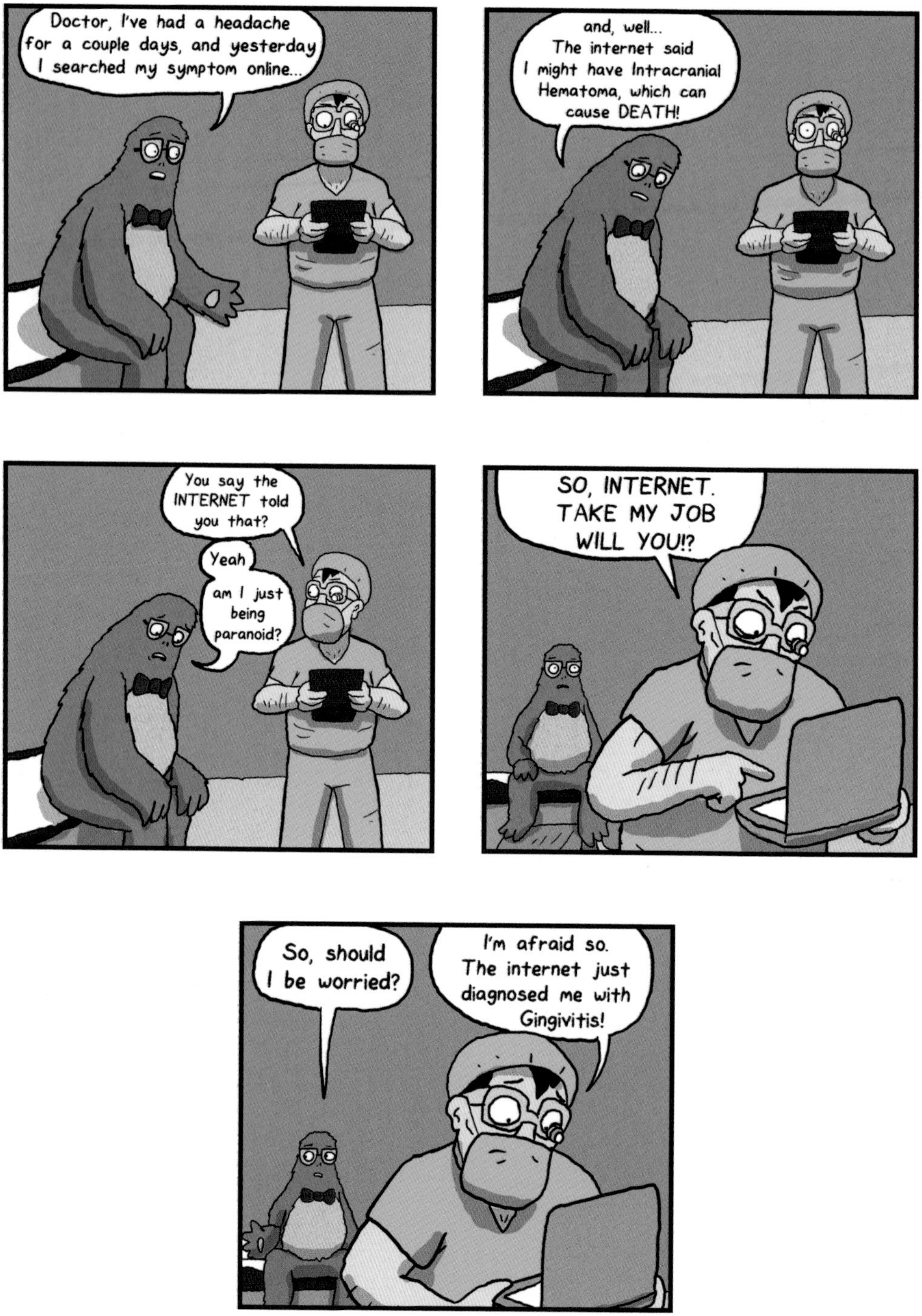

Doctor, I've had a headache for a couple days, and yesterday I searched my symptom online...
and, well... The internet said I might have Intracranial Hematoma, which can cause DEATH!
You say the INTERNET told you that?
Yeah
am I just being paranoid?
SO, INTERNET. TAKE MY JOB WILL YOU!?
So, should I be worried?
I'm afraid so. The internet just diagnosed me with Gingivitis!

The Best Things

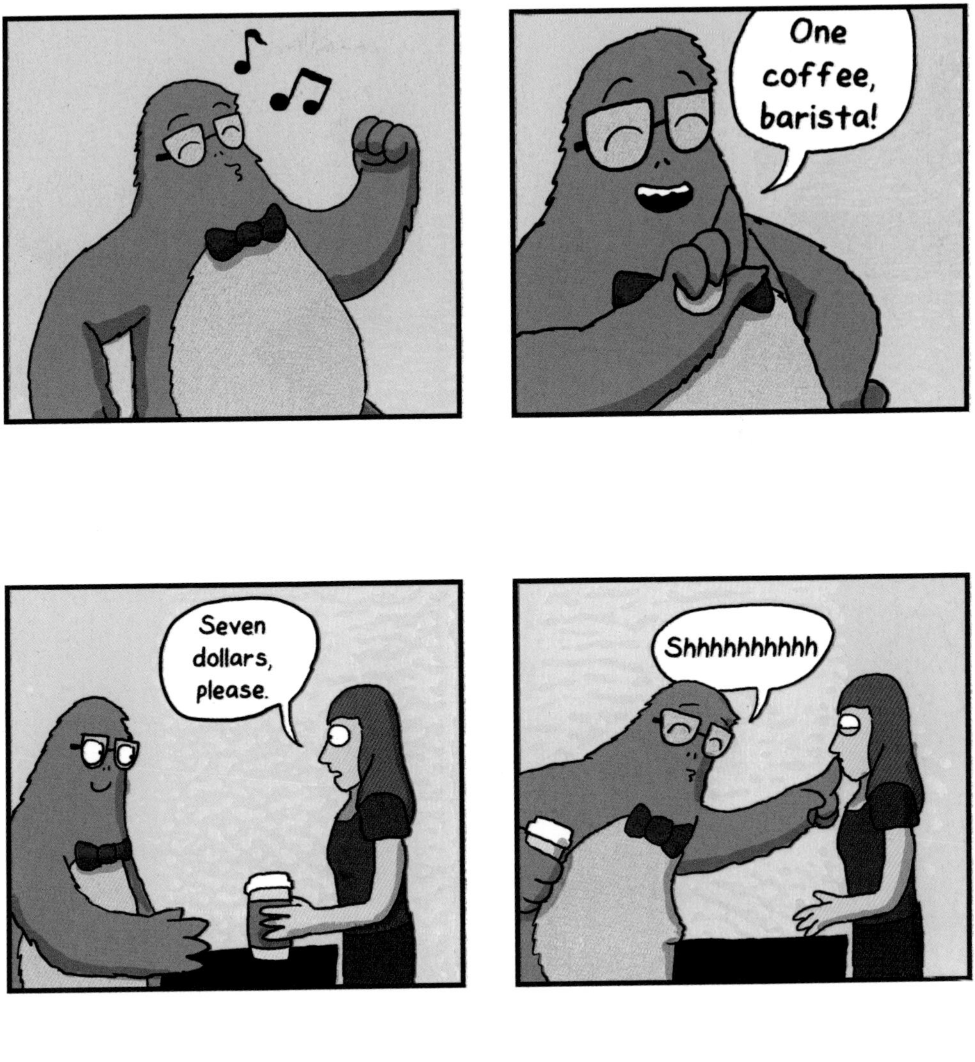
One coffee, barista!
Seven dollars, please.
Shhhhhhhhhh

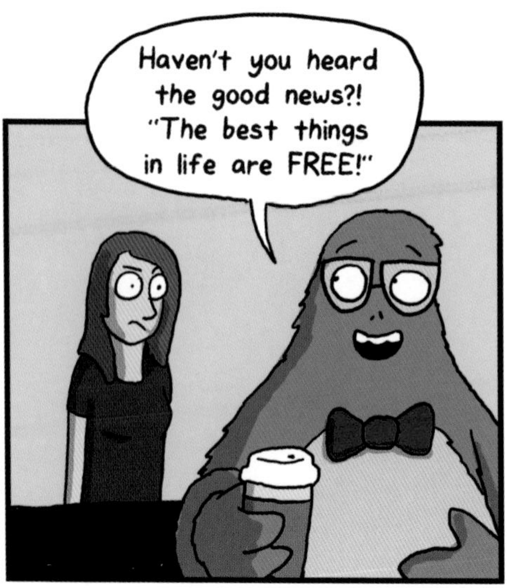
Haven't you heard the good news?! "The best things in life are FREE!"

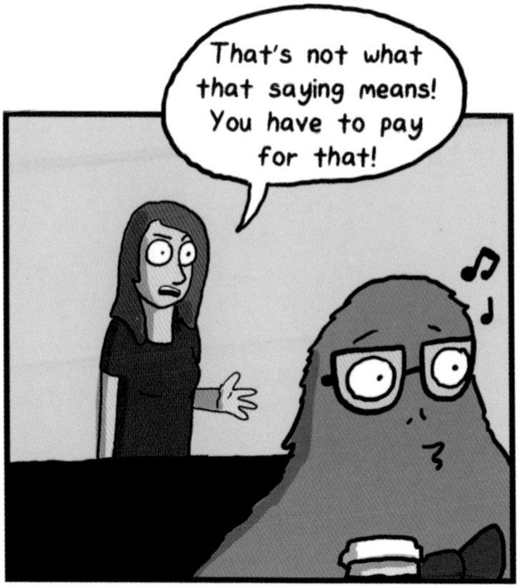
That's not what that saying means! You have to pay for that!

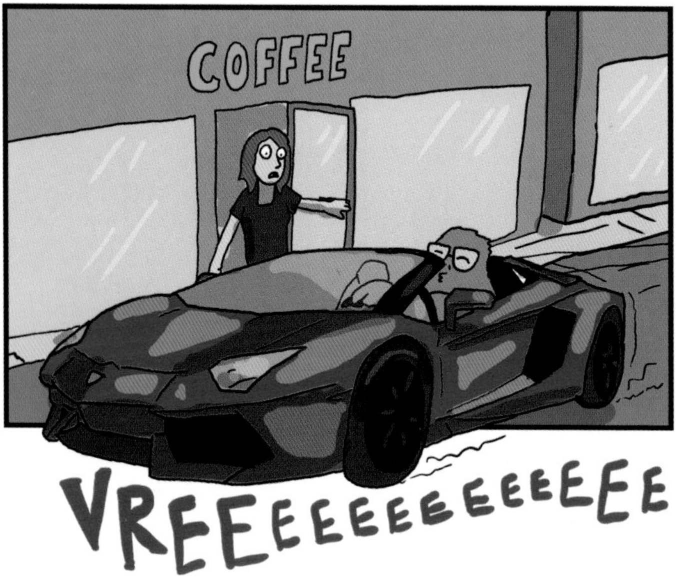
COFFEE
VREEEEEEEEEEEE

Self Defense

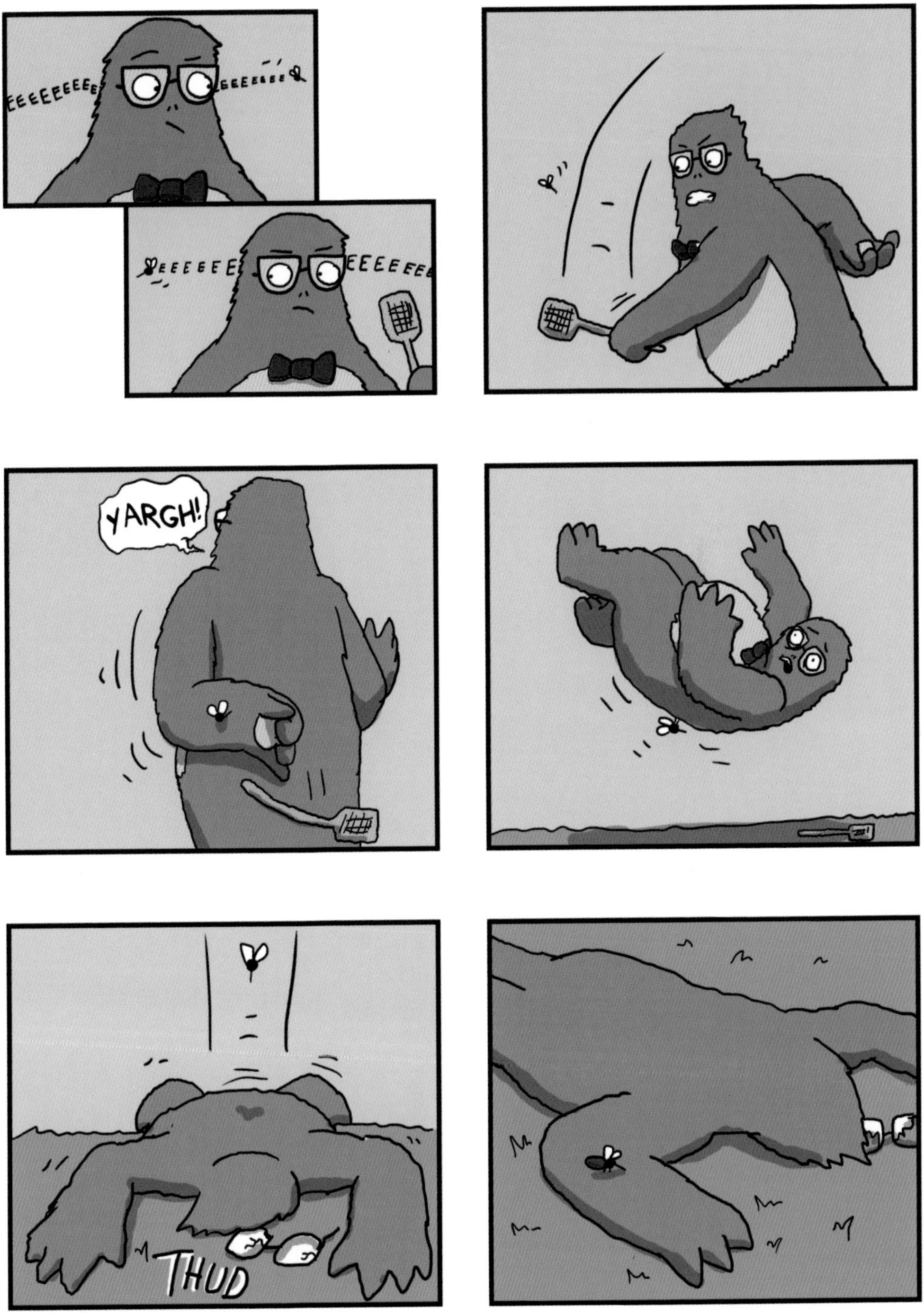
YARGH!
THUD

Motives

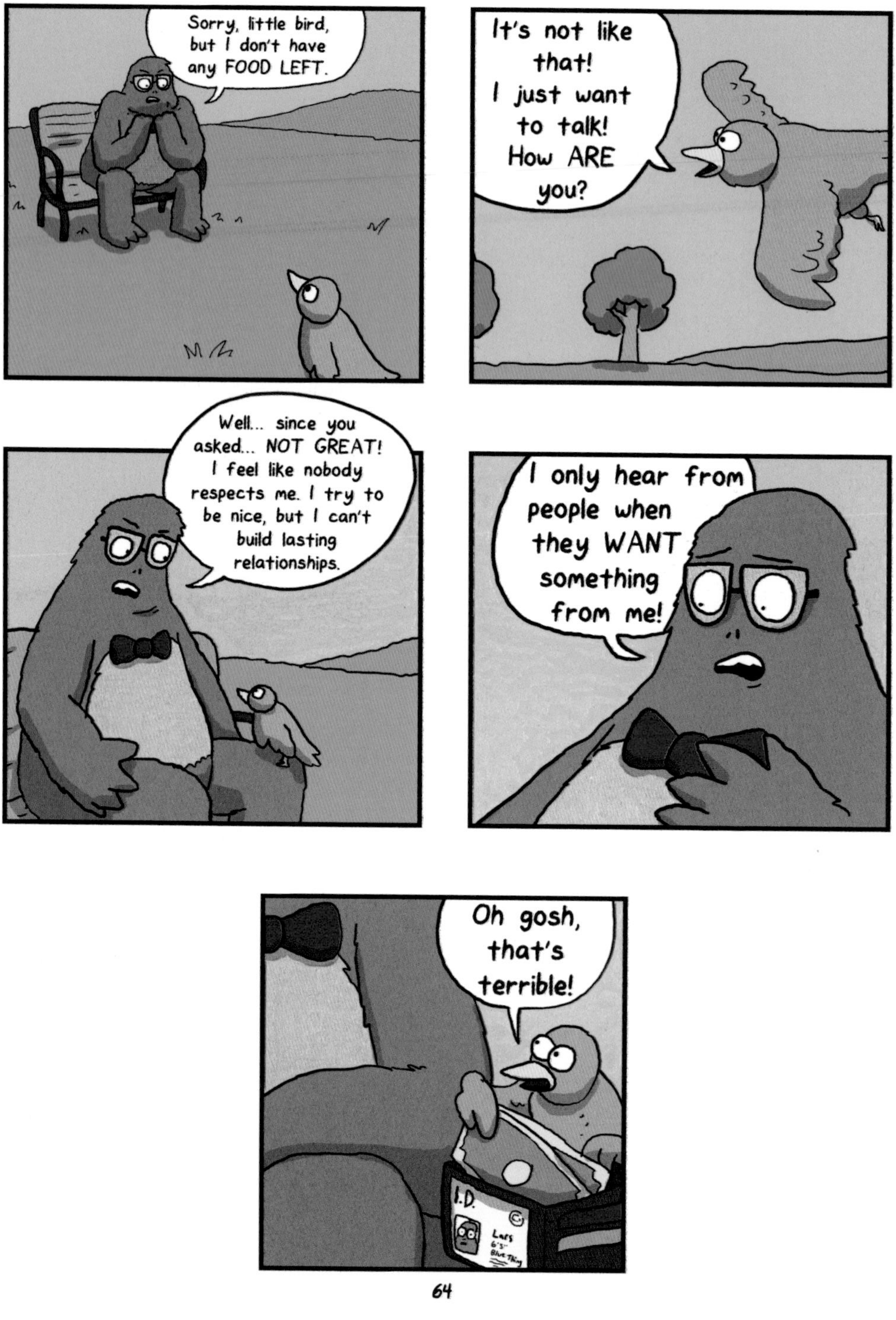
Sorry, little bird, but I don't have any FOOD LEFT.
It's not like that! I just want to talk! How ARE you?
Well... since you asked... NOT GREAT! I feel like nobody respects me. I try to be nice, but I can't build lasting relationships.
I only hear from people when they WANT something from me!
Oh gosh, that's terrible!
I.D.

It's a Living

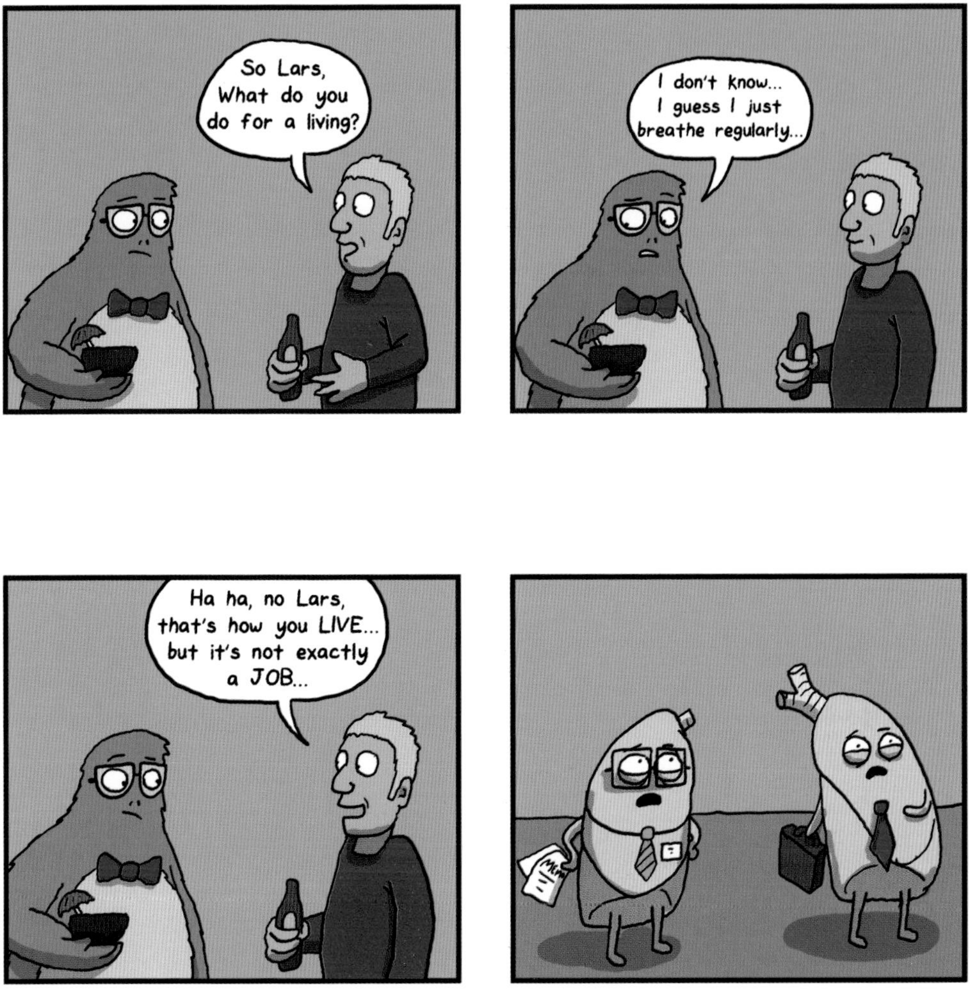
So Lars, What do you do for a living?
I don't know... I guess I just breathe regularly...
Ha ha, no Lars, that's how you LIVE... but it's not exactly a JOB...

Timing

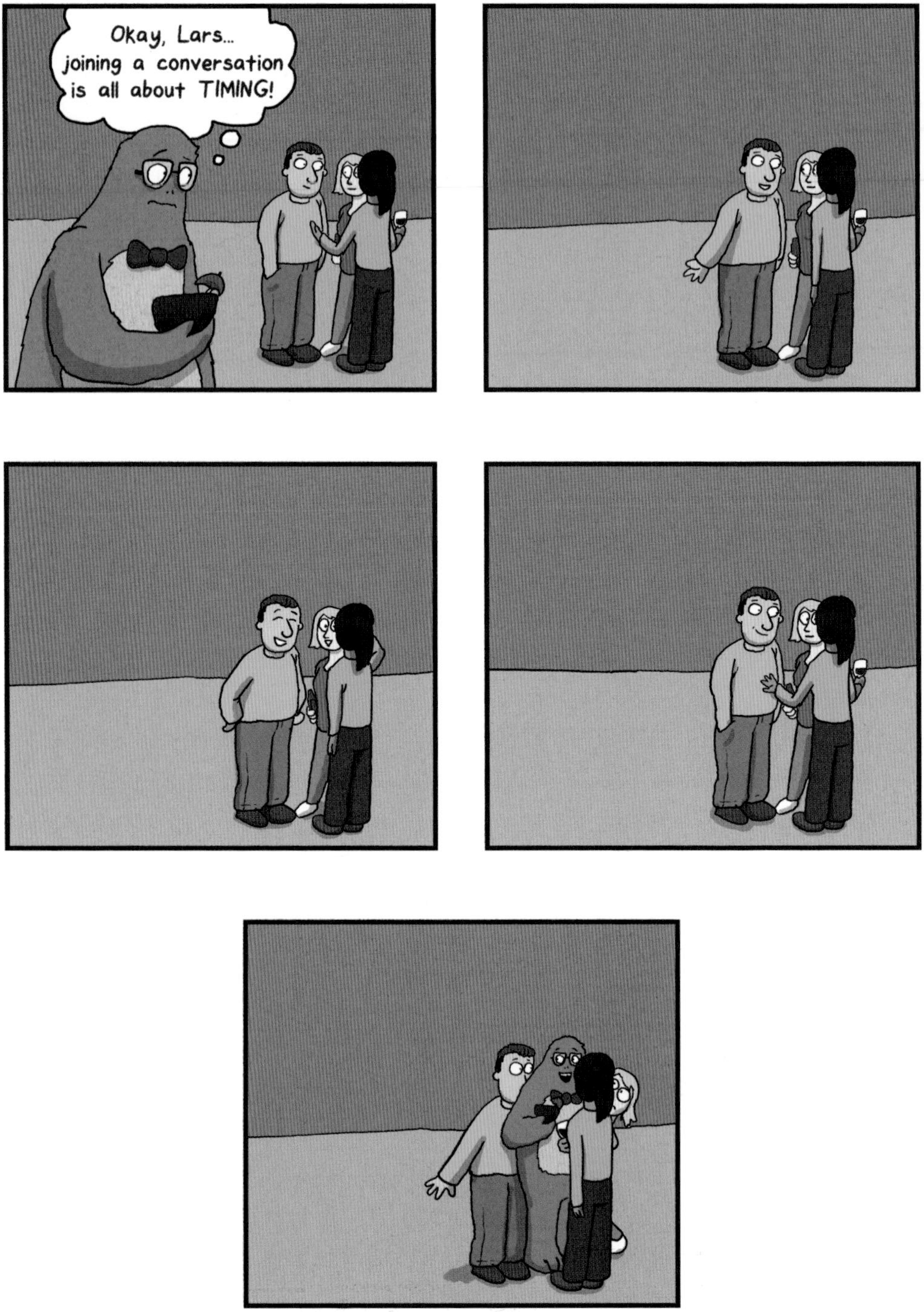
Okay, Lars... joining a conversation is all about TIMING!

Bird House

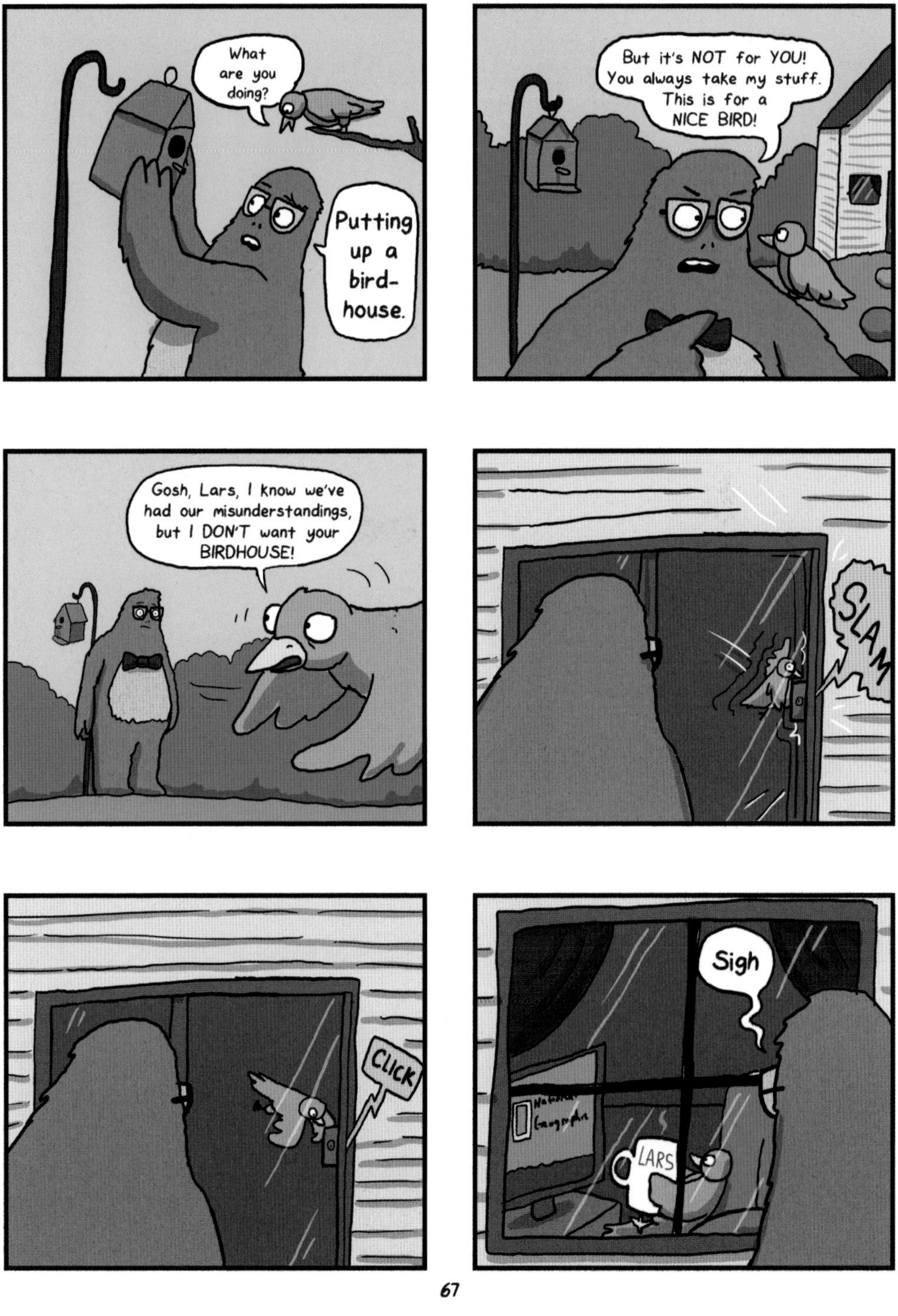
What are you doing?
Putting up a bird-house.
But it's NOT for YOU! You always take my stuff. This is for a NICE BIRD!
Gosh, Lars, I know we've had our misunderstandings, but I DON'T want your BIRDHOUSE!
SLAM
CLICK
Sigh
LARS

Privacy

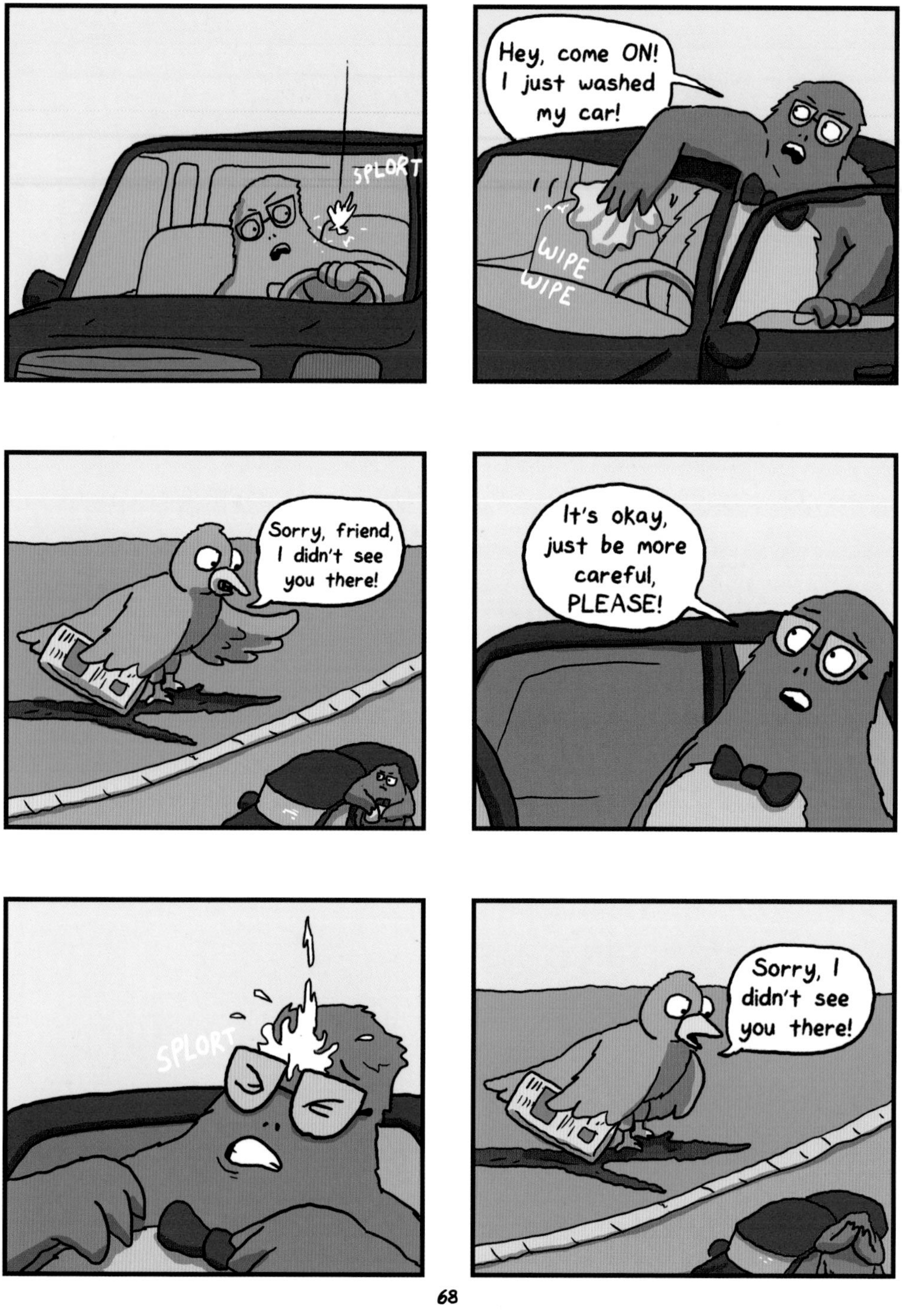
SPLORT
Hey, come ON! I just washed my car!
WIPE
WIPE
Sorry, friend, I didn't see you there!
It's okay, just be more careful, PLEASE!
SPLORT
Sorry, I didn't see you there!

Lars Avoids a Disaster

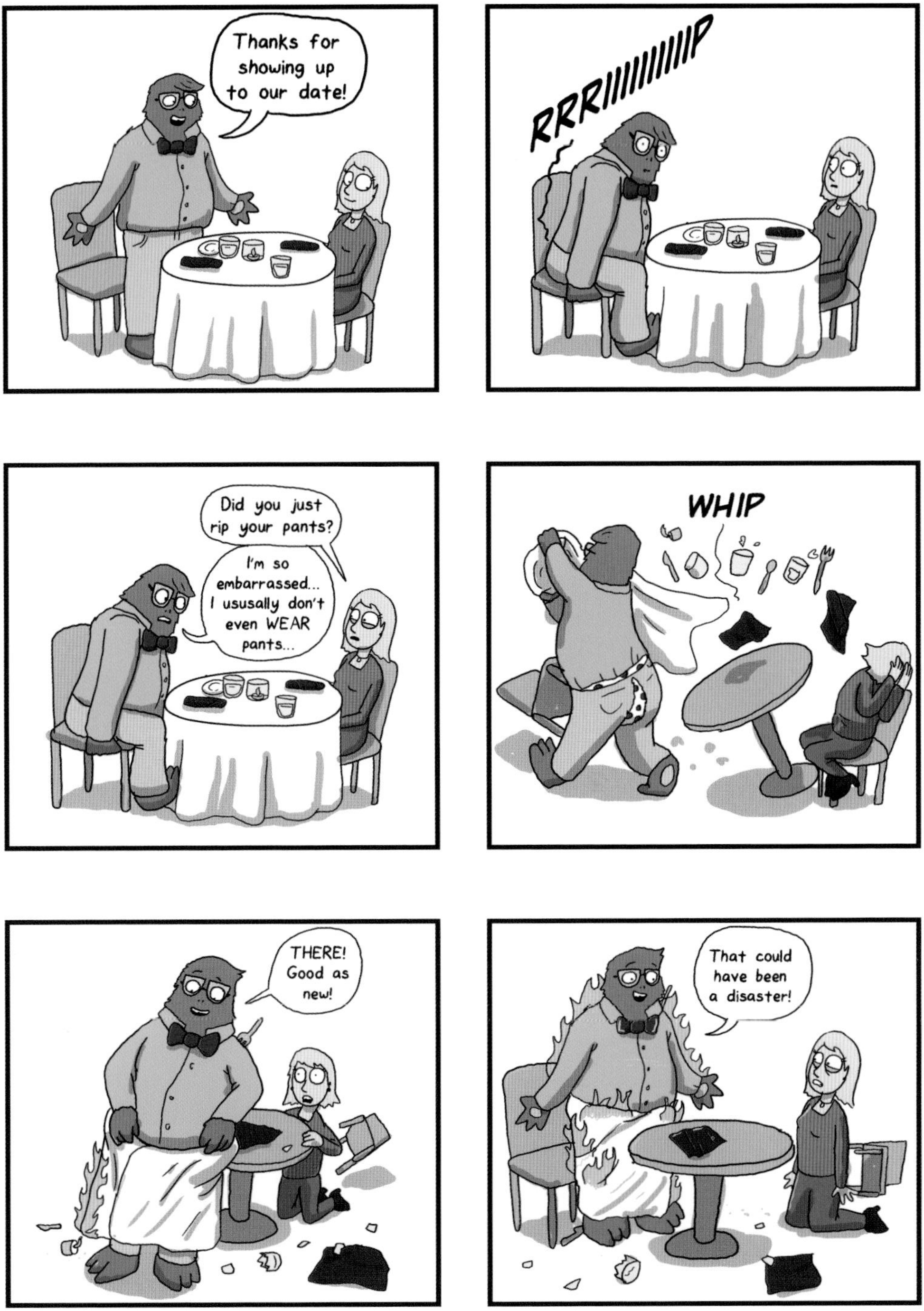

Thanks for showing up to our date!
RRRIIIIIIIIIIIP
Did you just rip your pants?
I'm so embarrassed... I ususally don't even WEAR pants...
WHIP
THERE! Good as new!
That could have been a disaster!

The Name

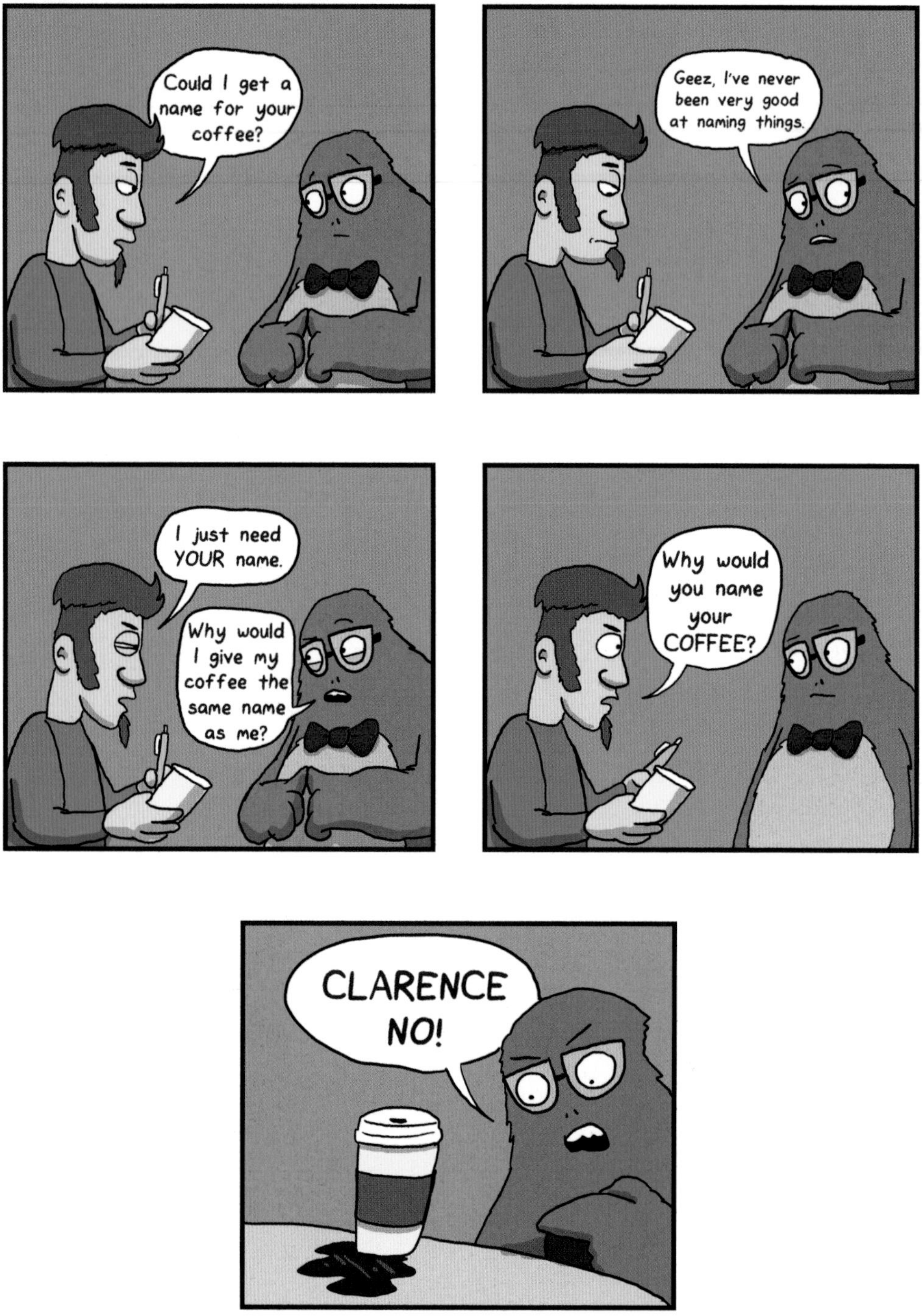
Could I get a name for your coffee?
Geez, I've never been very good at naming things.
I just need YOUR name.
Why would I give my coffee the same name as me?
Why would you name your COFFEE?
CLARENCE NO!

Identity

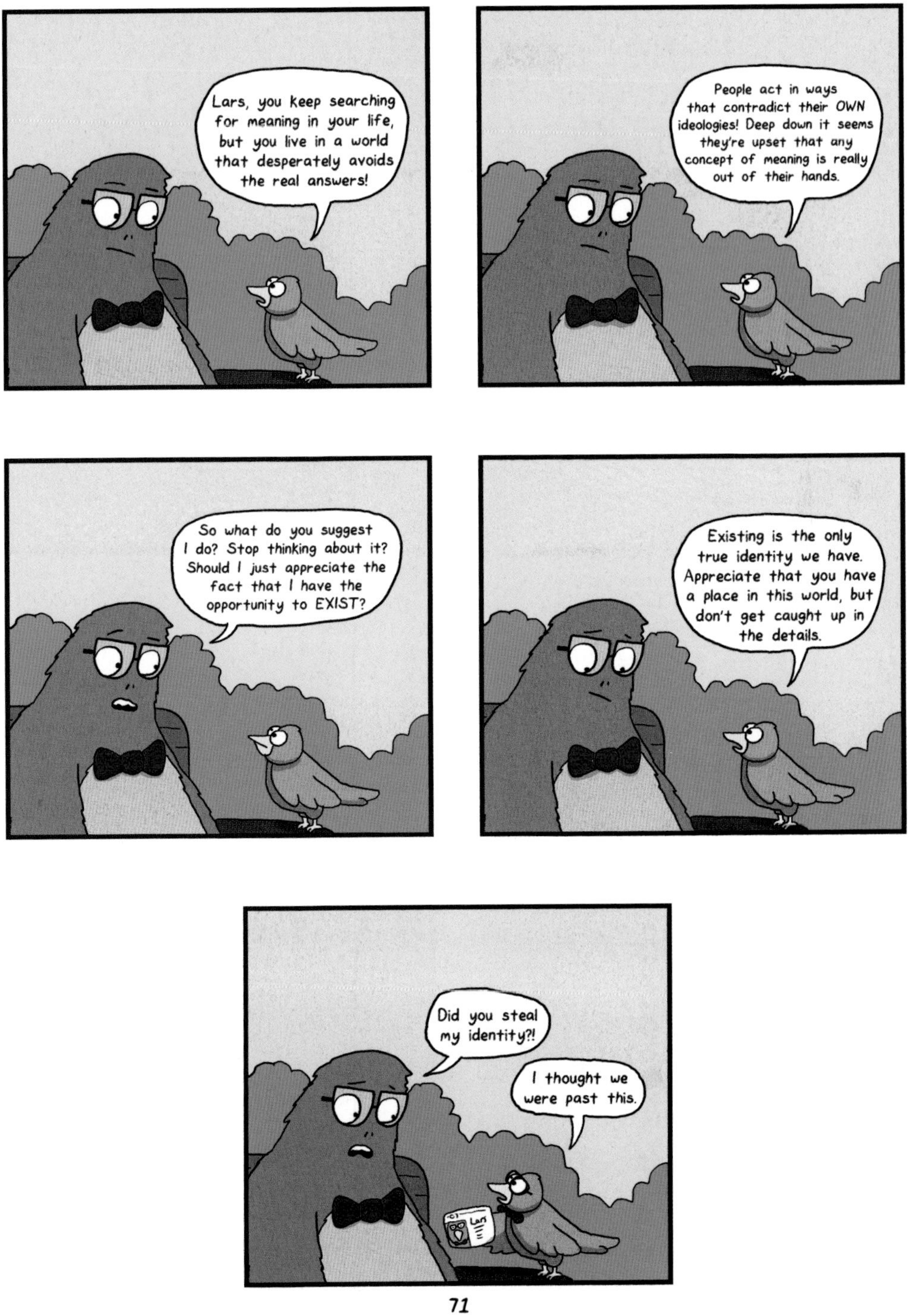
Lars, you keep searching for meaning in your life, but you live in a world that desperately avoids the real answers!
People act in ways that contradict their OWN ideologies! Deep down it seems they're upset that any concept of meaning is really out of their hands.
So what do you suggest I do? Stop thinking about it? Should I just appreciate the fact that I have the opportunity to EXIST?
Existing is the only true identity we have. Appreciate that you have a place in this world, but don't get caught up in the details.
Did you steal my identity?!
I thought we were past this.
Lars

Conditioning

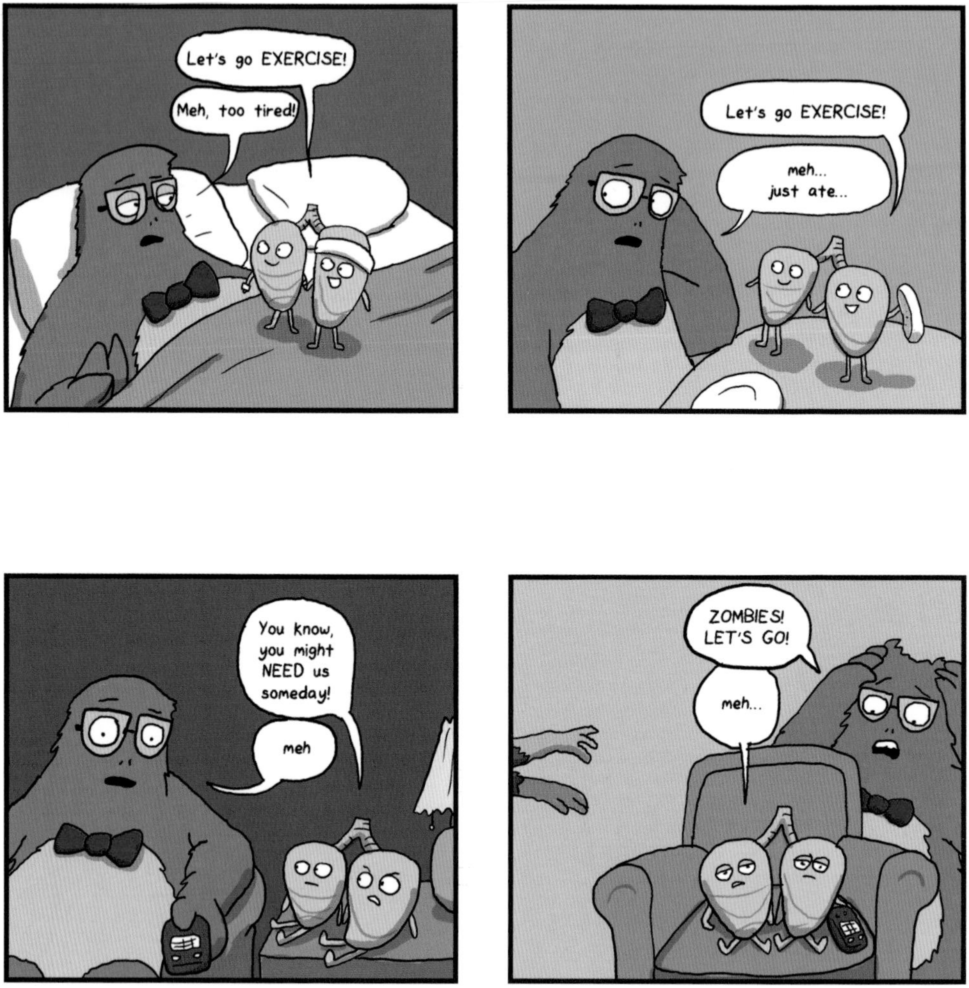
Let's go EXERCISE!
Meh, too tired!
Let's go EXERCISE!
meh...
just ate...
You know,
you might
NEED us
someday!
meh
ZOMBIES!
LET'S GO!
meh...

Heart to Heart

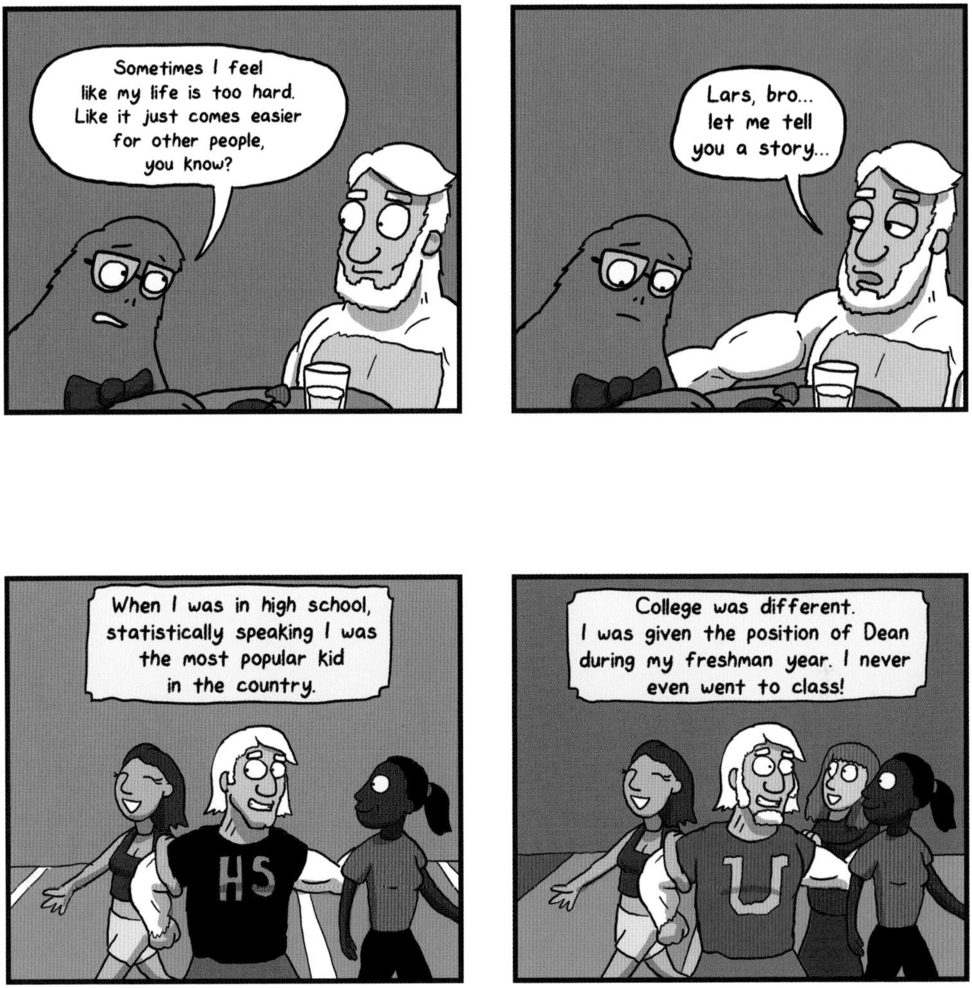
Sometimes I feel like my life is too hard. Like it just comes easier for other people, you know?
Lars, bro... let me tell you a story...
When I was in high school, statistically speaking I was the most popular kid in the country.
HS
College was different. I was given the position of Dean during my freshman year. I never even went to class!
U

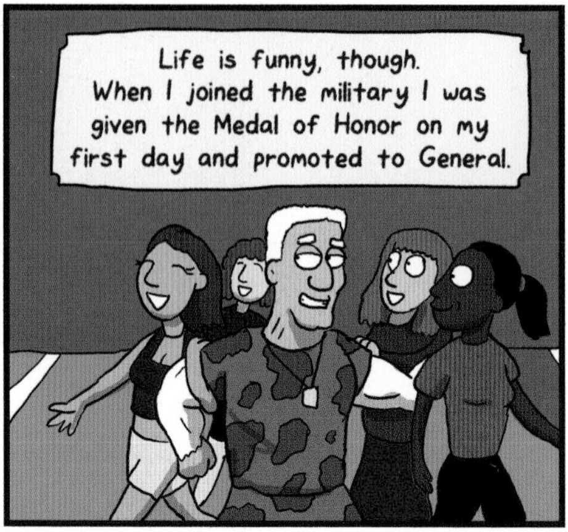
Life is funny, though. When I joined the military I was given the Medal of Honor on my first day and promoted to General.

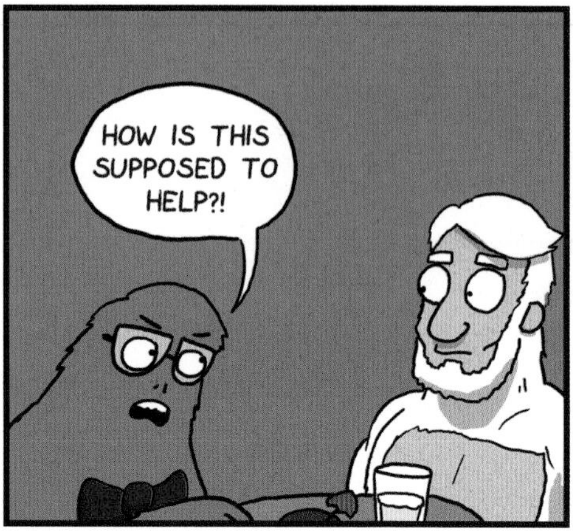
HOW IS THIS SUPPOSED TO HELP?!

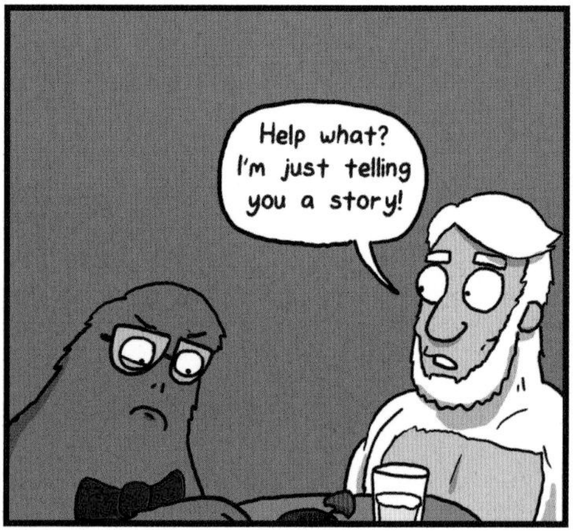
Help what? I'm just telling you a story!

Museum

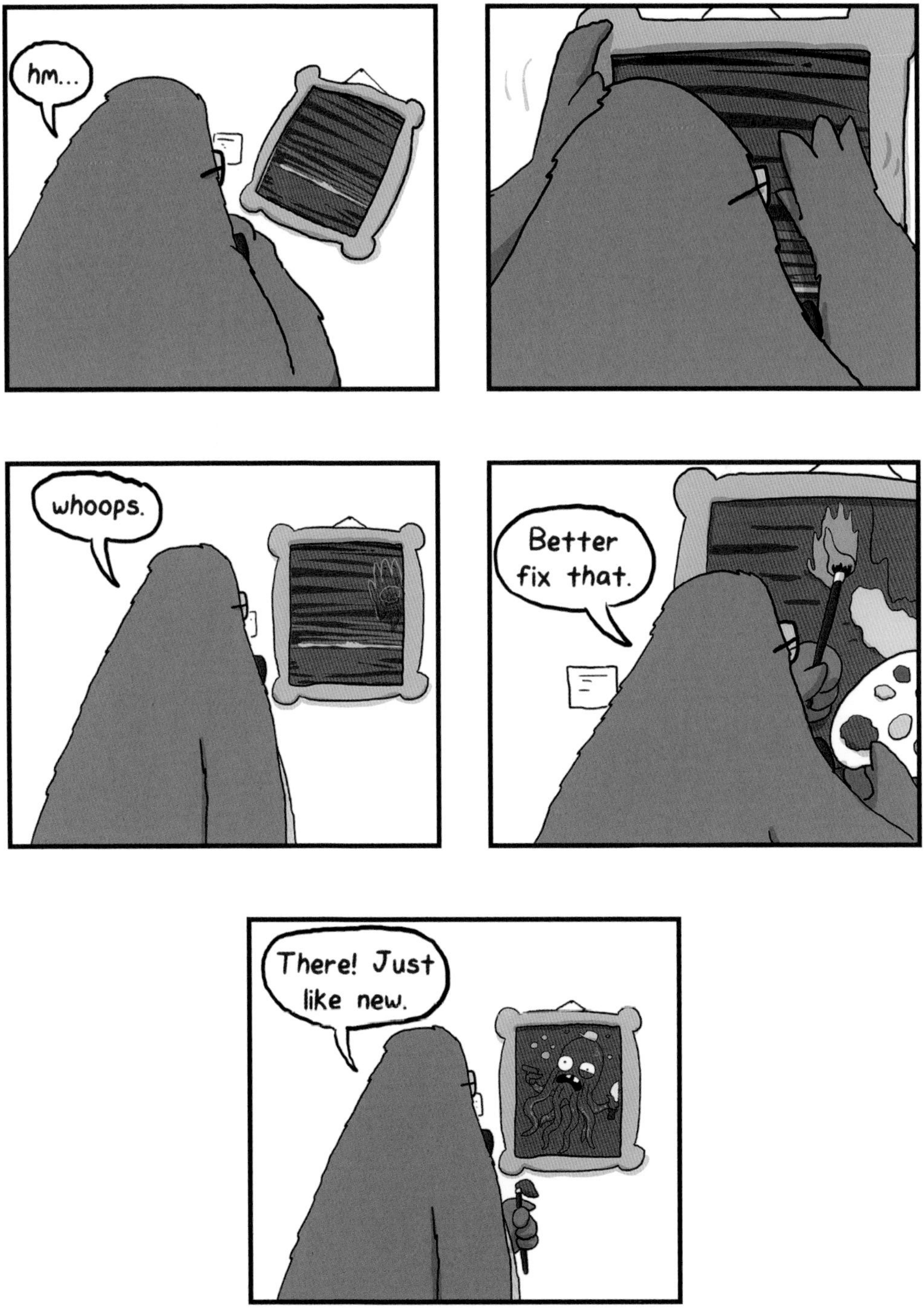
hm...
whoops.
Better fix that.
There! Just like new.

Action Guy

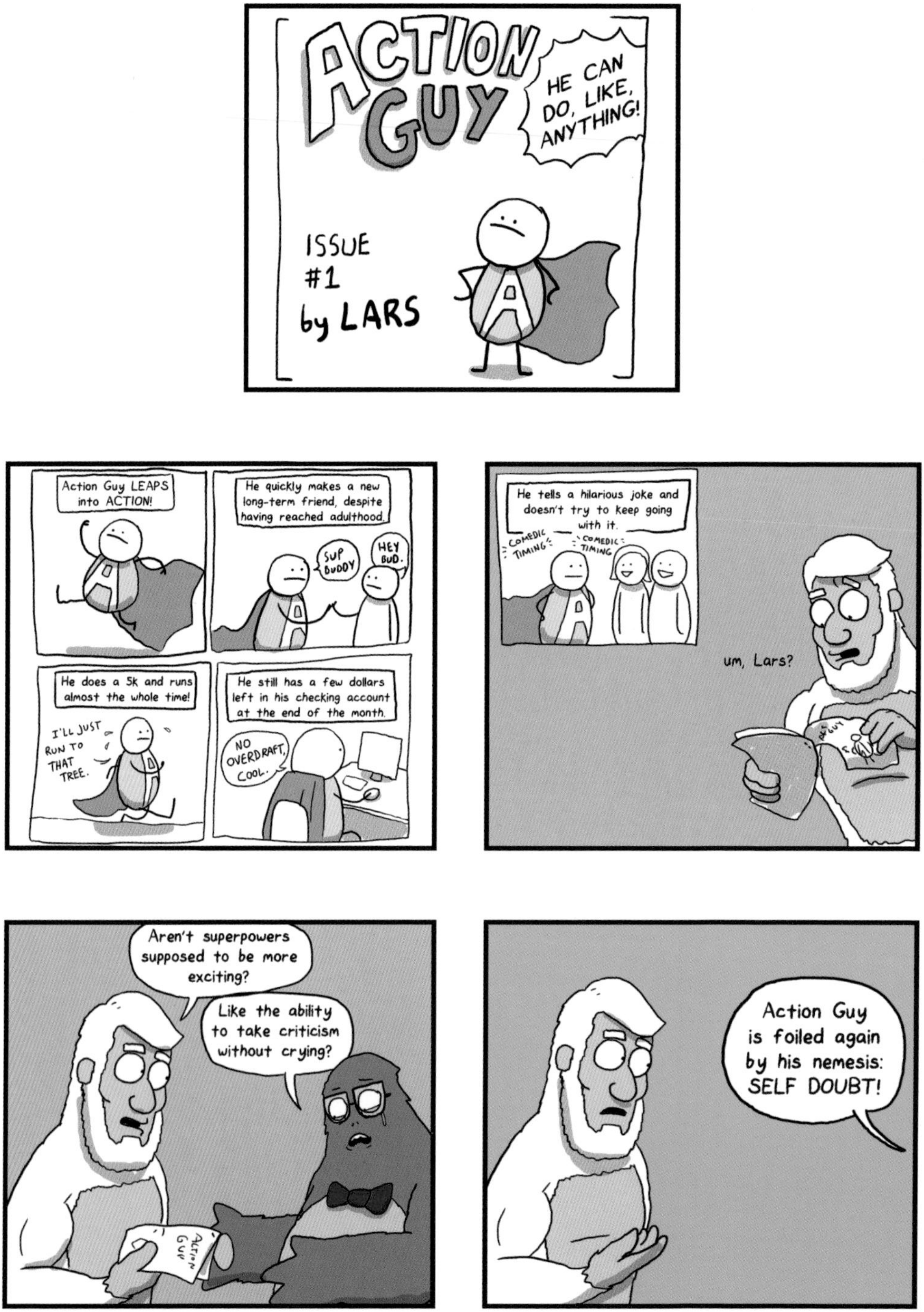

ACTION GUY
HE CAN DO, LIKE, ANYTHING!
ISSUE #1
by LARS
Action Guy LEAPS into ACTION!
He quickly makes a new long-term friend, despite having reached adulthood.
SUP BUDDY
HEY BUD.
He does a 5k and runs almost the whole time!
I'LL JUST RUN TO THAT TREE.
He still has a few dollars left in his checking account at the end of the month.
NO OVERDRAFT, COOL.
He tells a hilarious joke and doesn't try to keep going with it.
COMEDIC TIMING
COMEDIC TIMING
um, Lars?
Aren't superpowers supposed to be more exciting?
Like the ability to take criticism without crying?
ACTION GUY
Action Guy is foiled again by his nemesis: SELF DOUBT!

Photogenic

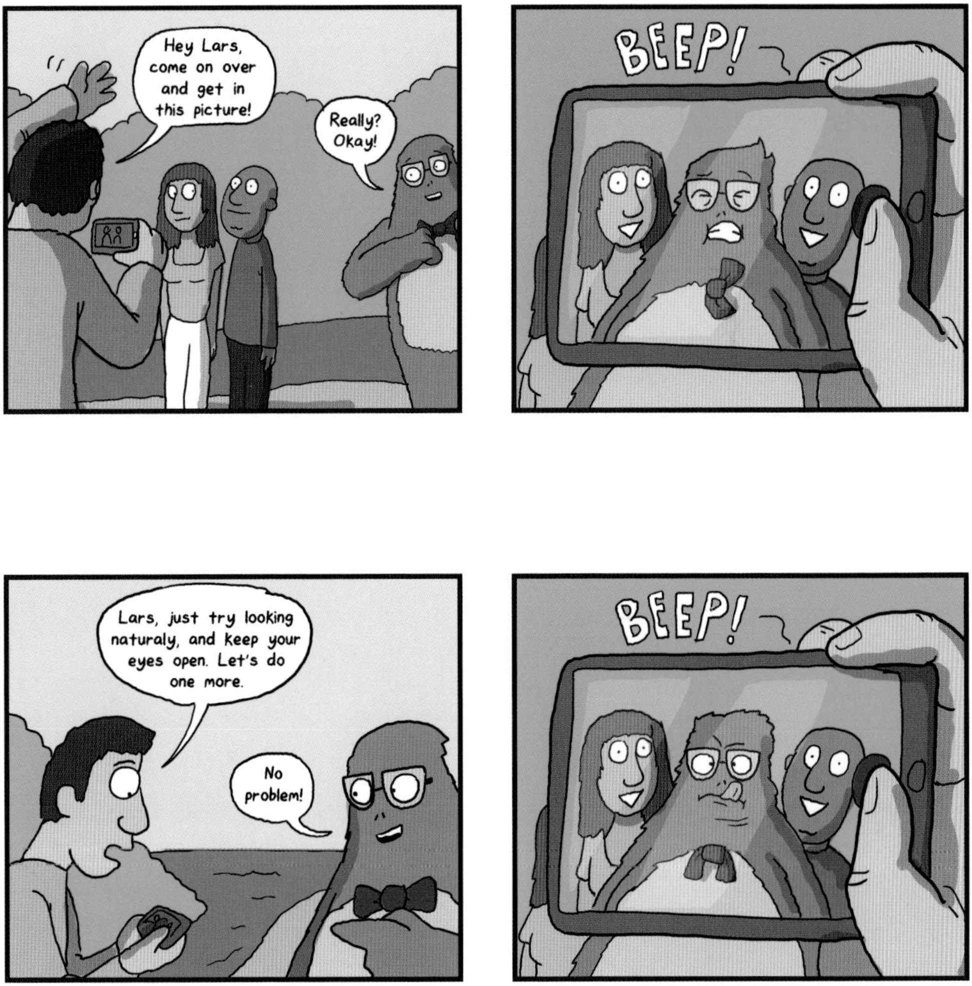
Hey Lars, come on over and get in this picture!
Really? Okay!
BEEP!
Lars, just try looking naturaly, and keep your eyes open. Let's do one more.
No problem!
BEEP!

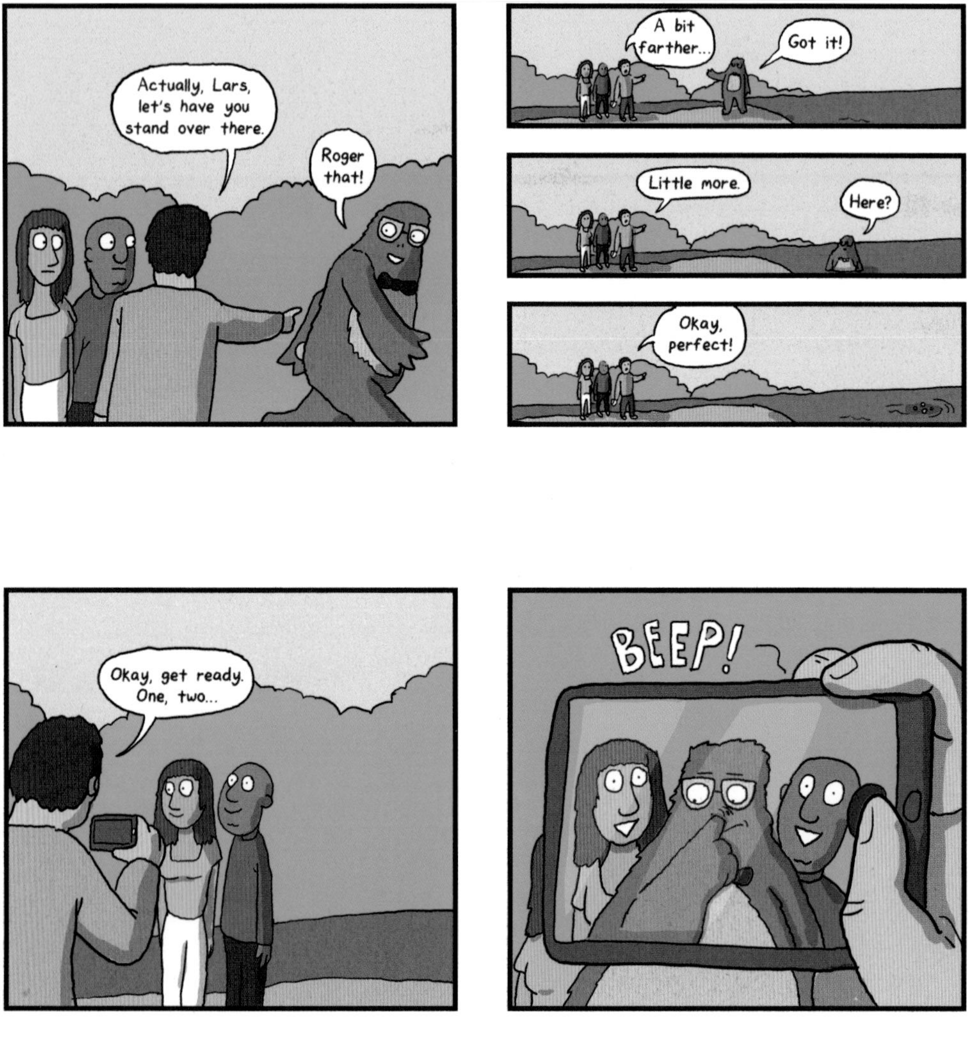
Actually, Lars, let's have you stand over there.
Roger that!
A bit farther...
Got it!
Little more.
Here?
Okay, perfect!
Okay, get ready. One, two...
BEEP!

Action Guy 2

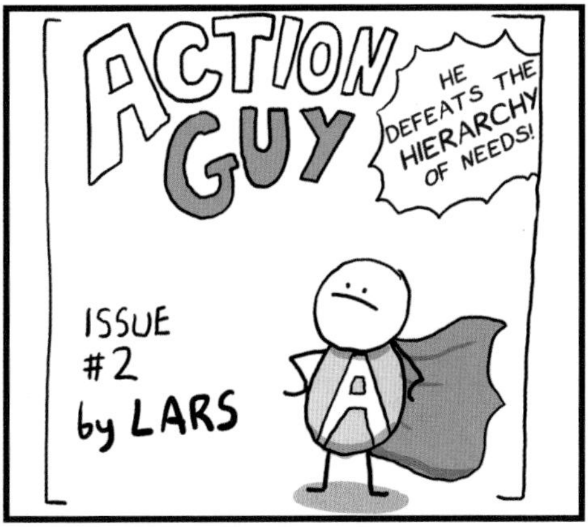
ACTION GUY
HE DEFEATS THE HIERARCHY OF NEEDS!
ISSUE #2
by LARS

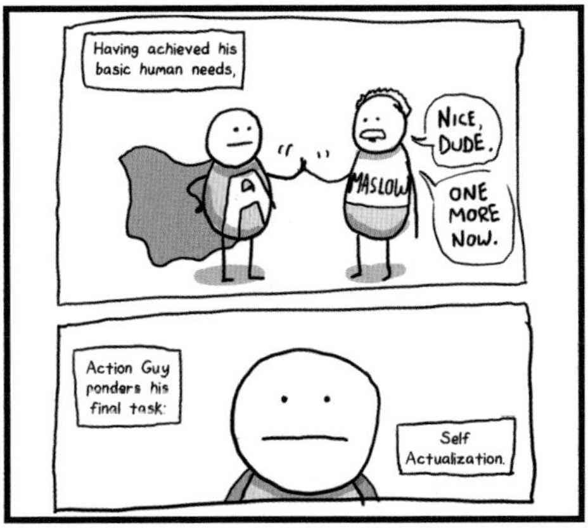
Having achieved his basic human needs,
MASLOW
NICE, DUDE.
ONE MORE NOW.
Action Guy ponders his final task:
Self Actualization.

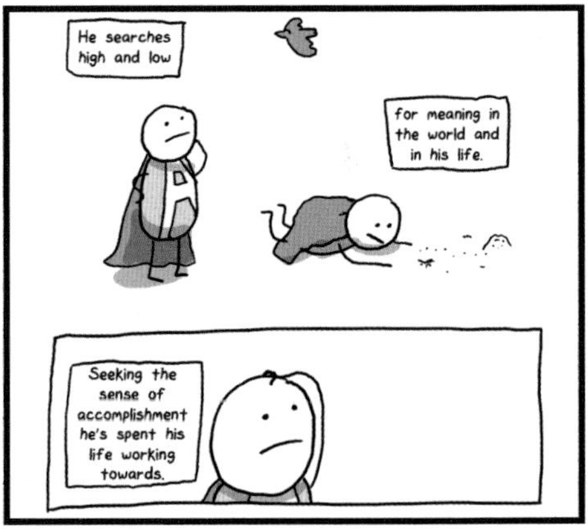
He searches high and low
for meaning in the world and in his life.
Seeking the sense of accomplishment he's spent his life working towards.

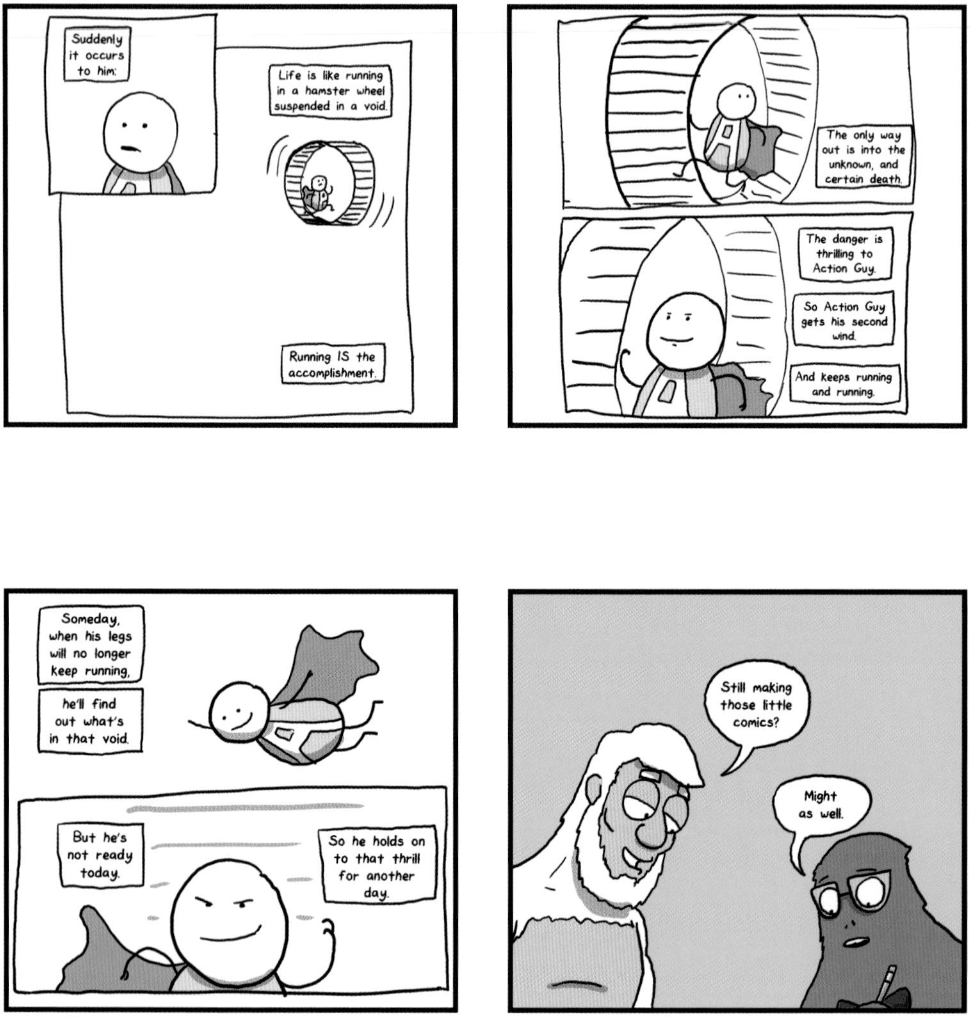
Suddenly it occurs to him:
Life is like running in a hamster wheel suspended in a void.
Running IS the accomplishment.
The only way out is into the unknown, and certain death.
The danger is thrilling to Action Guy.
So Action Guy gets his second wind.
And keeps running and running.
Someday, when his legs will no longer keep running,
he'll find out what's in that void.
But he's not ready today.
So he holds on to that thrill for another day.
Still making those little comics?
Might as well.

The Break Room

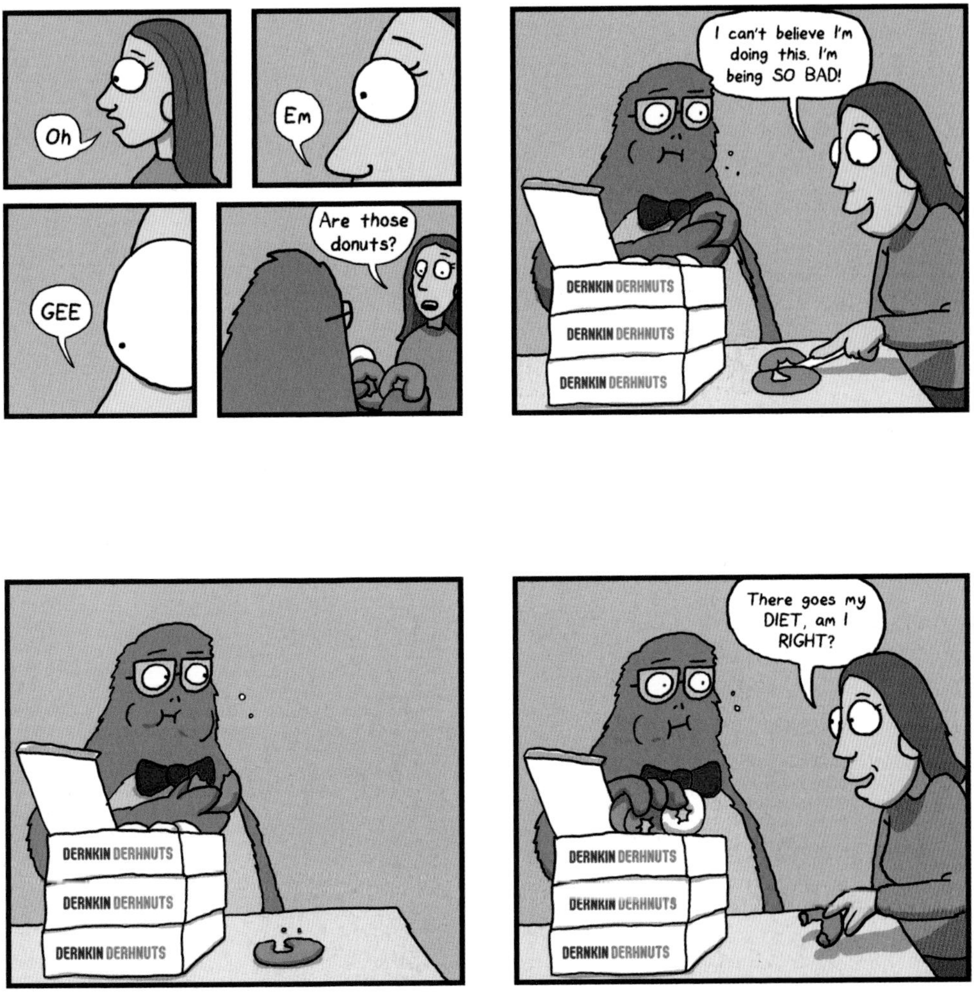
Oh
Em
GEE
Are those donuts?
I can't believe I'm doing this. I'm being SO BAD!
DERNKIN DERHNUTS
There goes my DIET, am I RIGHT?

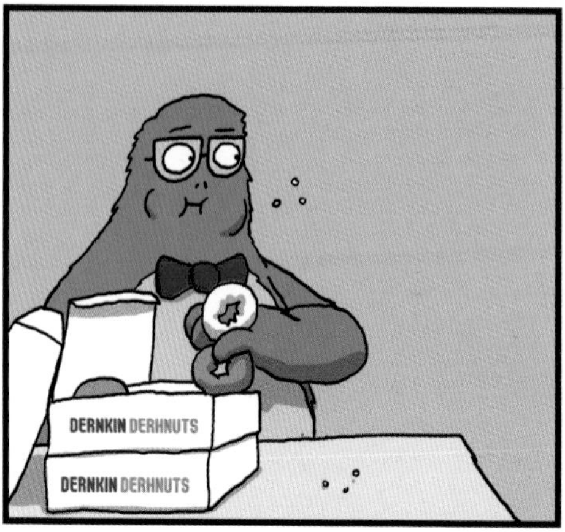
DERNKIN DERHNUTS
DERNKIN DERHNUTS

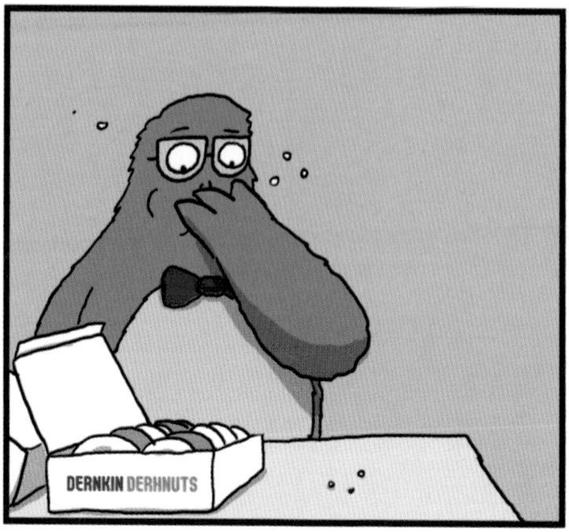
DERNKIN DERHNUTS

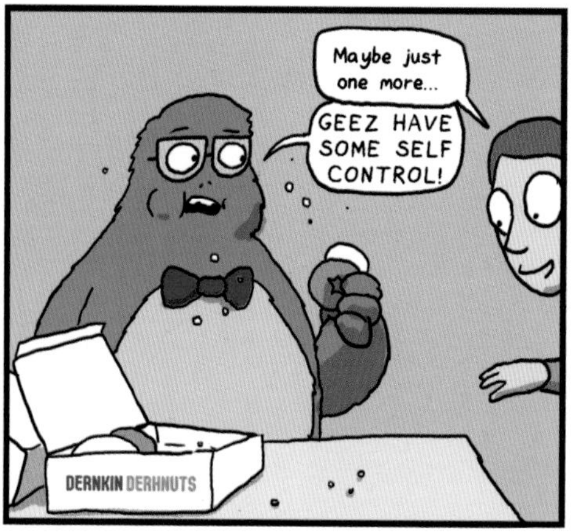
Maybe just one more...
GEEZ HAVE SOME SELF CONTROL!
DERNKIN DERHNUTS

A Close One

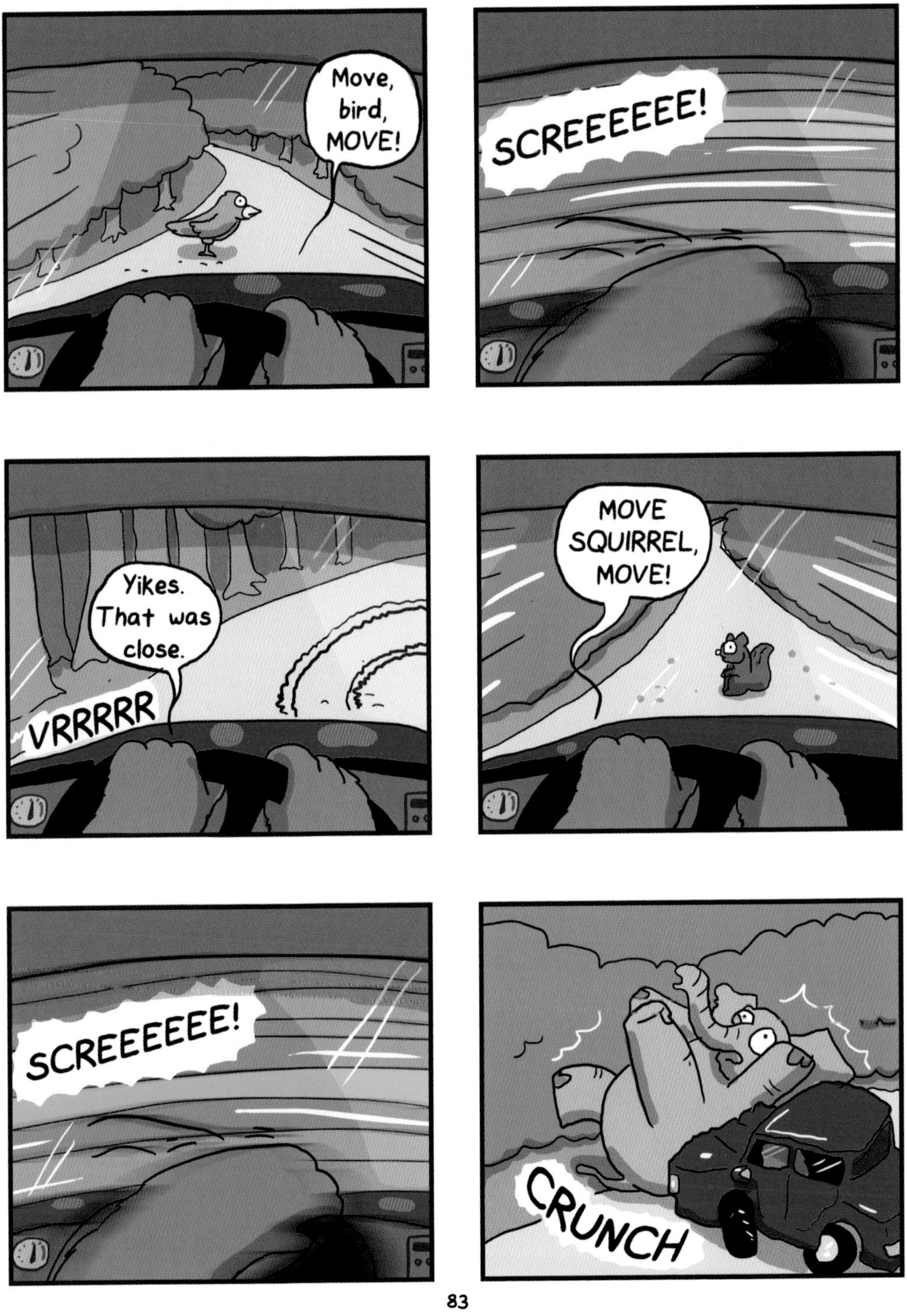
Move, bird, MOVE!
SCREEEEEEE!
Yikes. That was close.
VRRRRR
MOVE SQUIRREL, MOVE!
SCREEEEEEE!
CRUNCH

Workout Goals

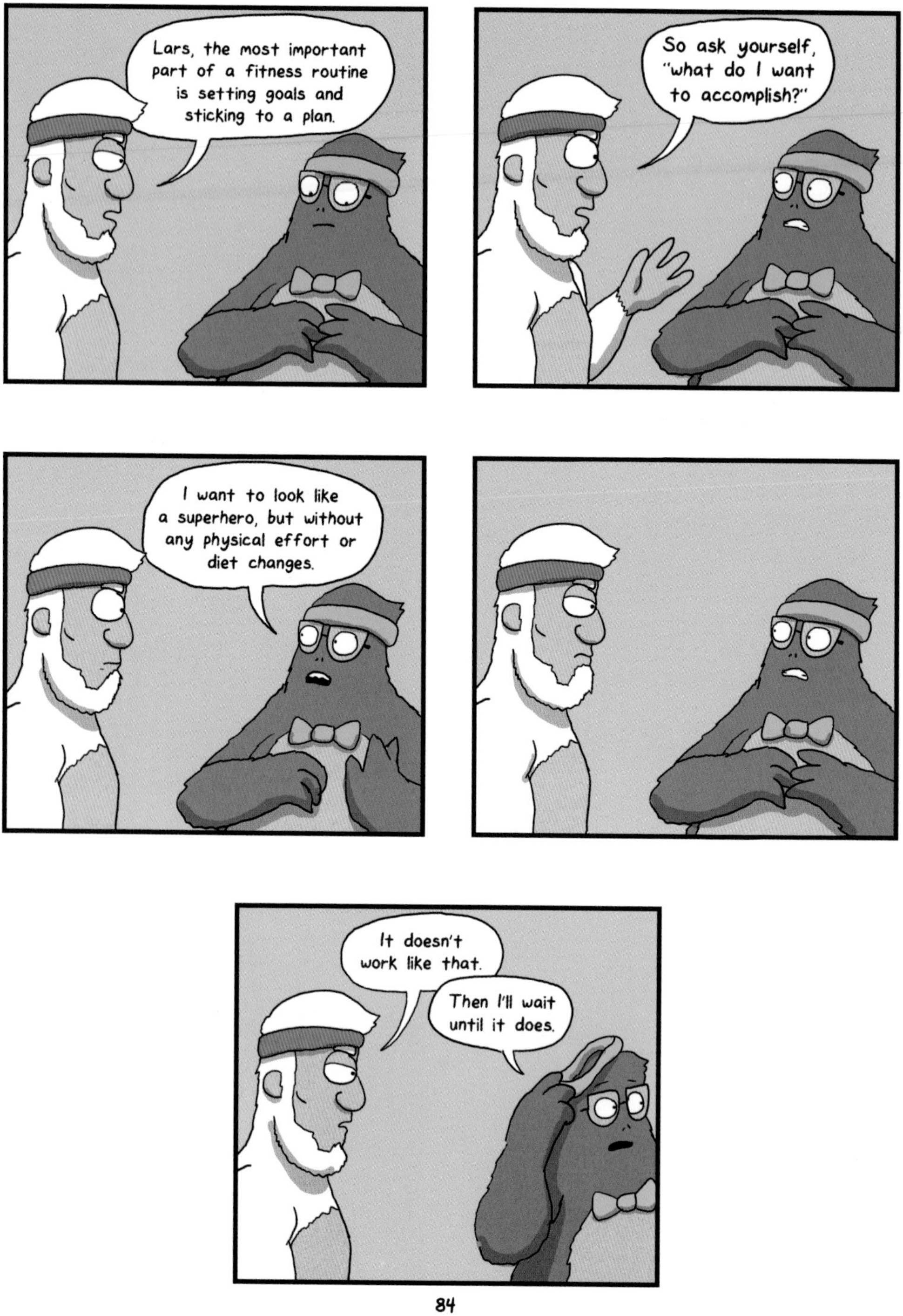

Lars, the most important part of a fitness routine is setting goals and sticking to a plan.
So ask yourself, "what do I want to accomplish?"
I want to look like a superhero, but without any physical effort or diet changes.
It doesn't work like that.
Then I'll wait until it does.

Appearances

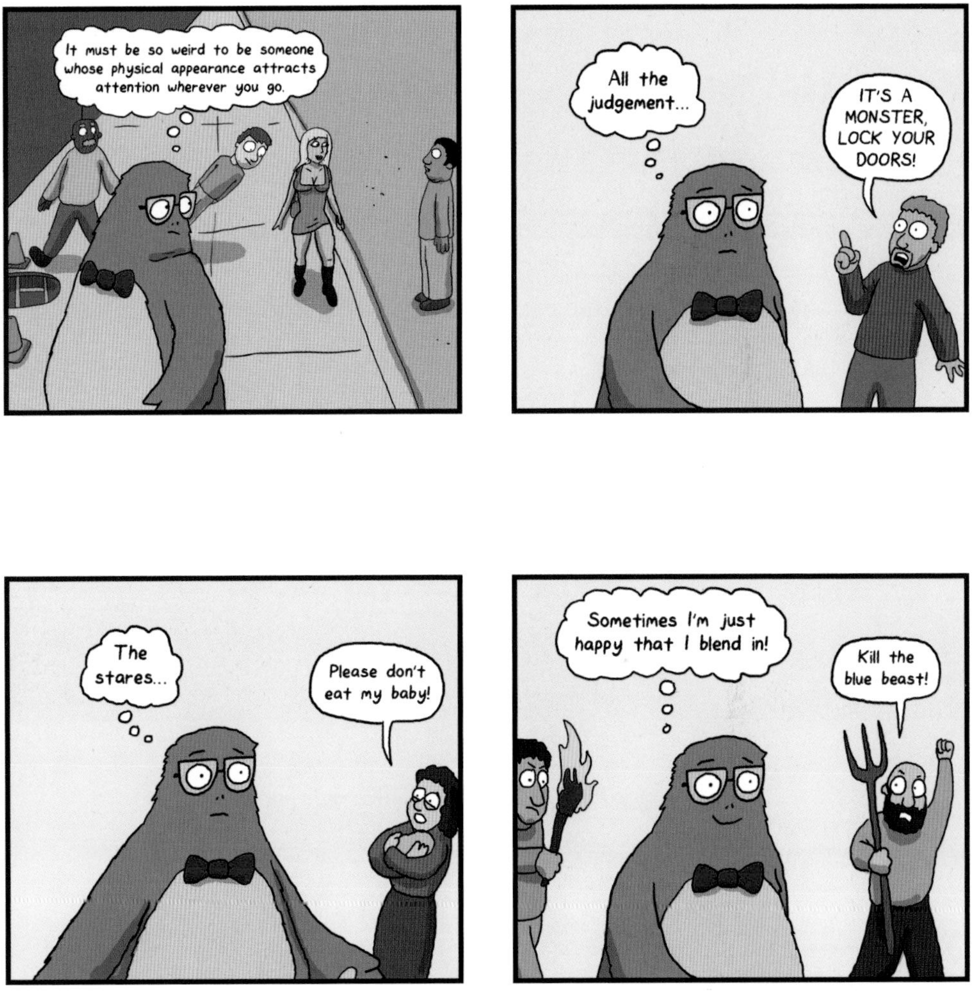

It must be so weird to be someone whose physical appearance attracts attention wherever you go.
All the judgement...
IT'S A MONSTER, LOCK YOUR DOORS!
The stares...
Please don't eat my baby!
Sometimes I'm just happy that I blend in!
Kill the blue beast!

The Vicious Cycle

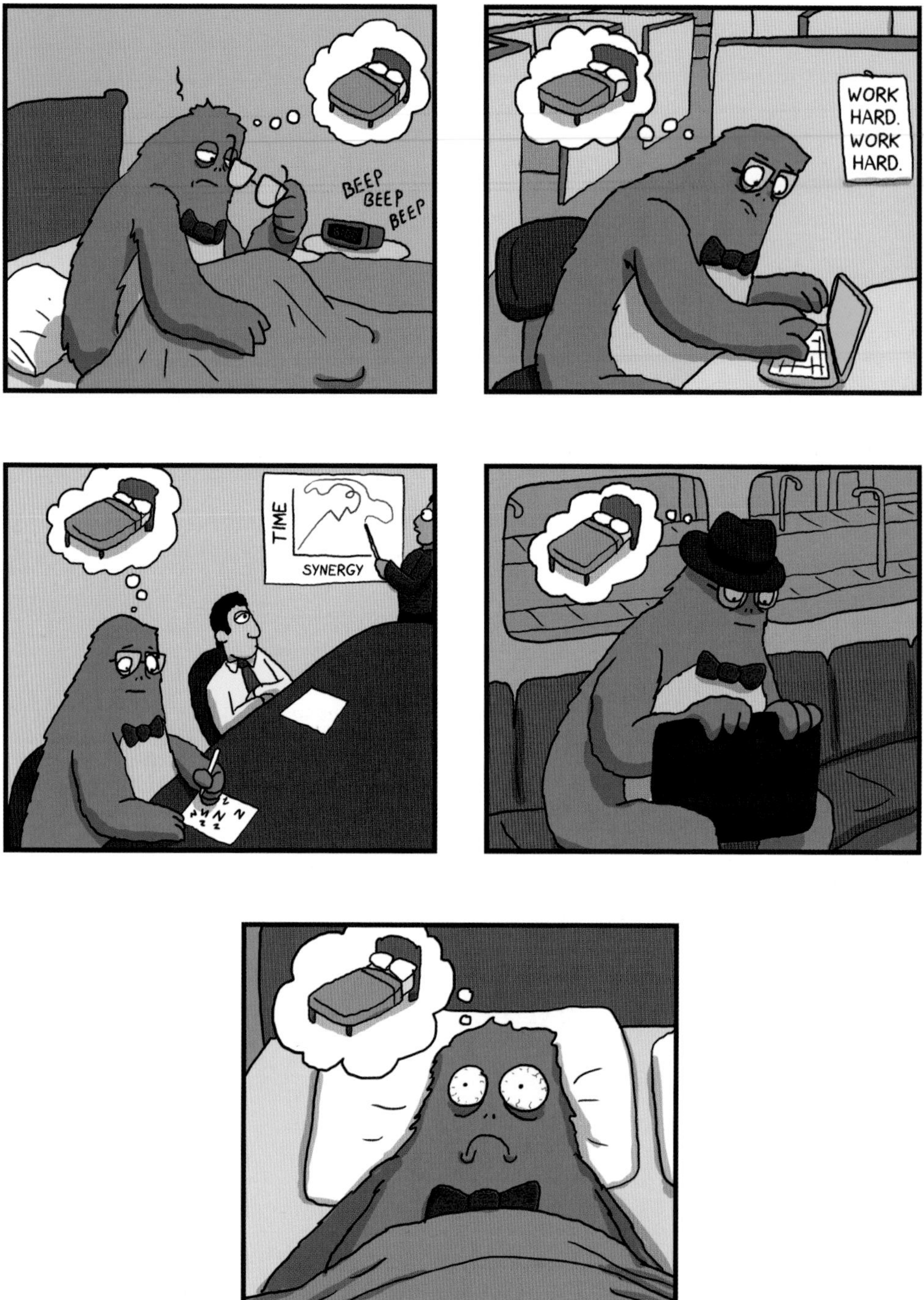
BEEP
BEEP
BEEP
WORK HARD. WORK HARD.
TIME
SYNERGY
Z
N
Z
N
N
N
Z
Z

The Wrong Turn

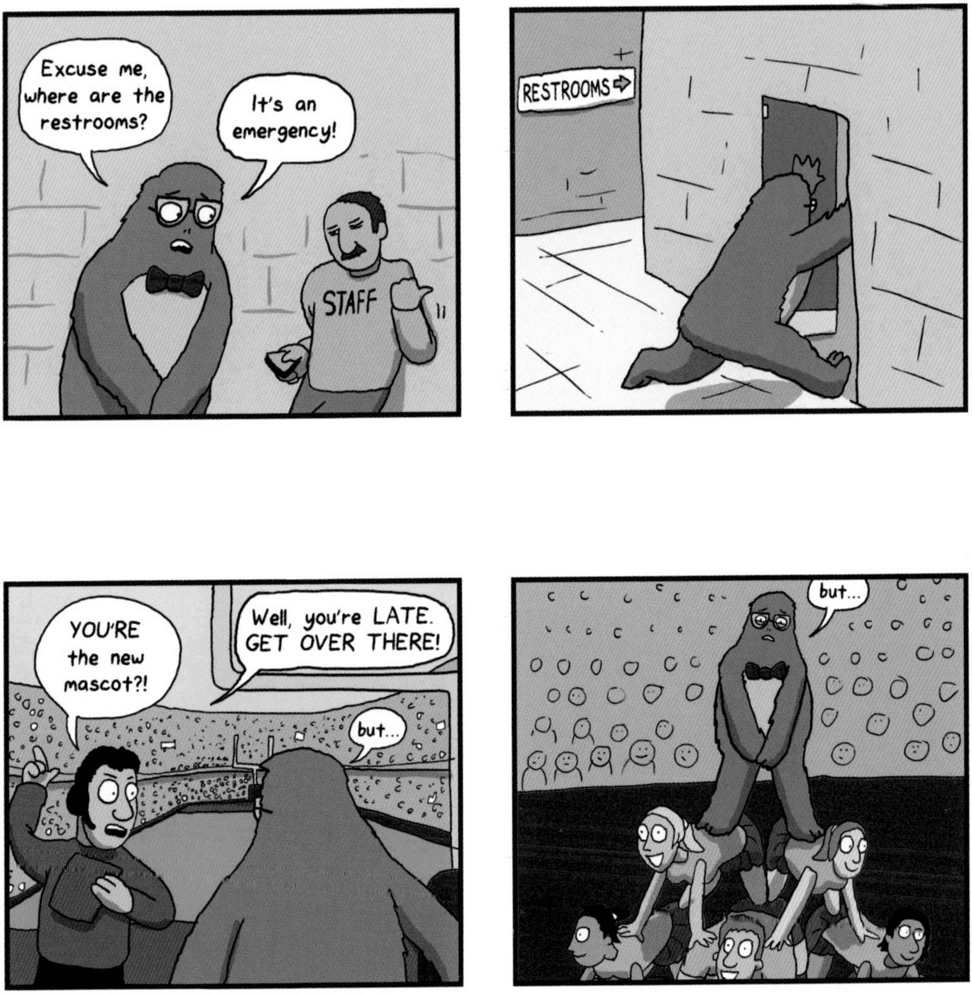
Excuse me, where are the restrooms?
It's an emergency!
STAFF
RESTROOMS
YOU'RE the new mascot?!
Well, you're LATE. GET OVER THERE!
but...
but...

No Pizza Left Behind

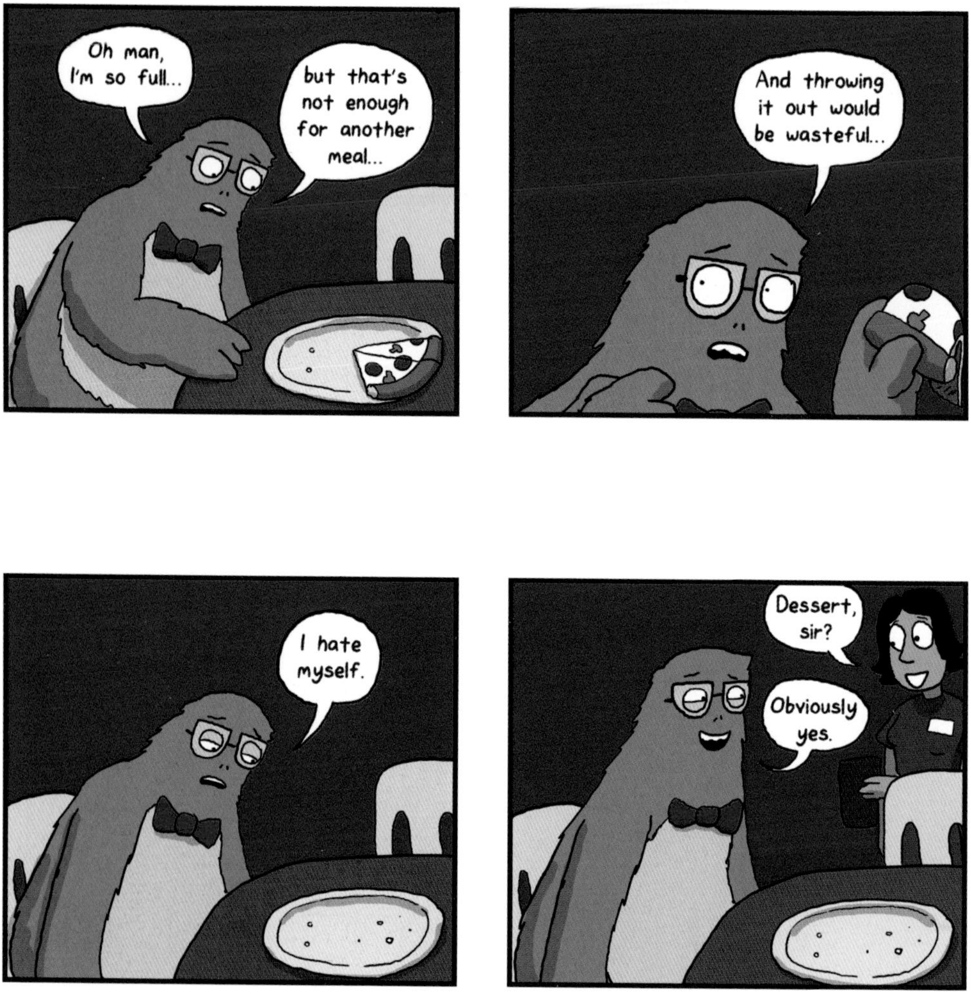
Oh man, I'm so full...
but that's not enough for another meal...
And throwing it out would be wasteful...
I hate myself.
Dessert, sir?
Obviously yes.

The Machines Awaken

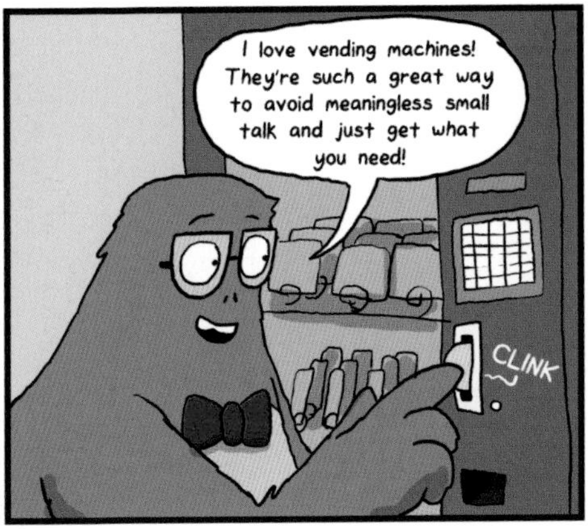
I love vending machines! They're such a great way to avoid meaningless small talk and just get what you need!
CLINK

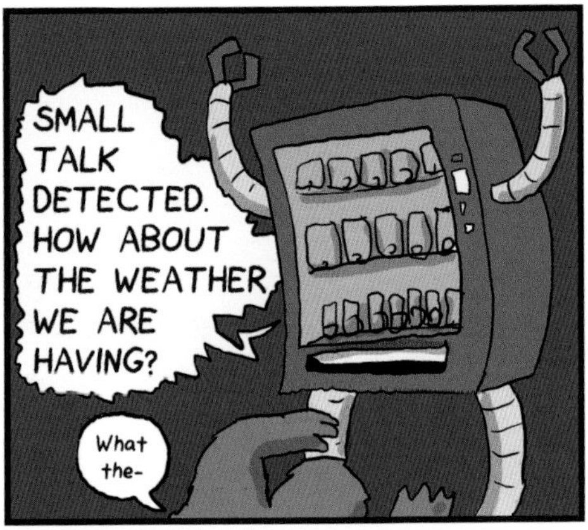
SMALL TALK DETECTED. HOW ABOUT THE WEATHER WE ARE HAVING?
What the-

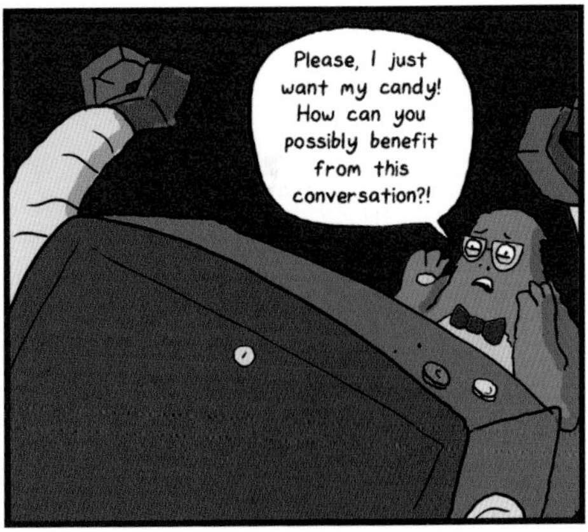
Please, I just want my candy! How can you possibly benefit from this conversation?!

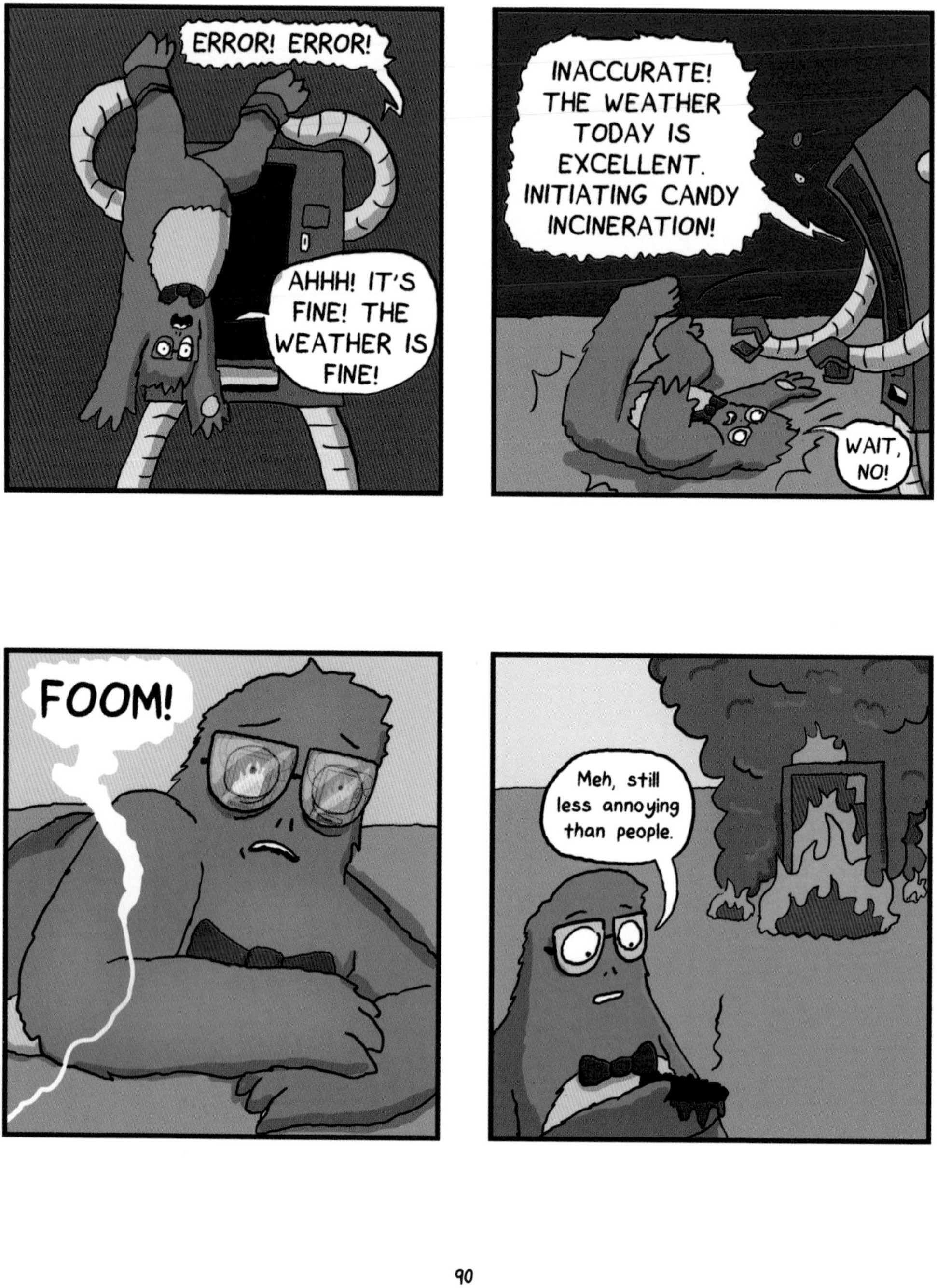
ERROR! ERROR!
AHHH! IT'S FINE! THE WEATHER IS FINE!
INACCURATE! THE WEATHER TODAY IS EXCELLENT. INITIATING CANDY INCINERATION!
WAIT, NO!
FOOM!
Meh, still less annoying than people.

The Machines Awaken Part 2

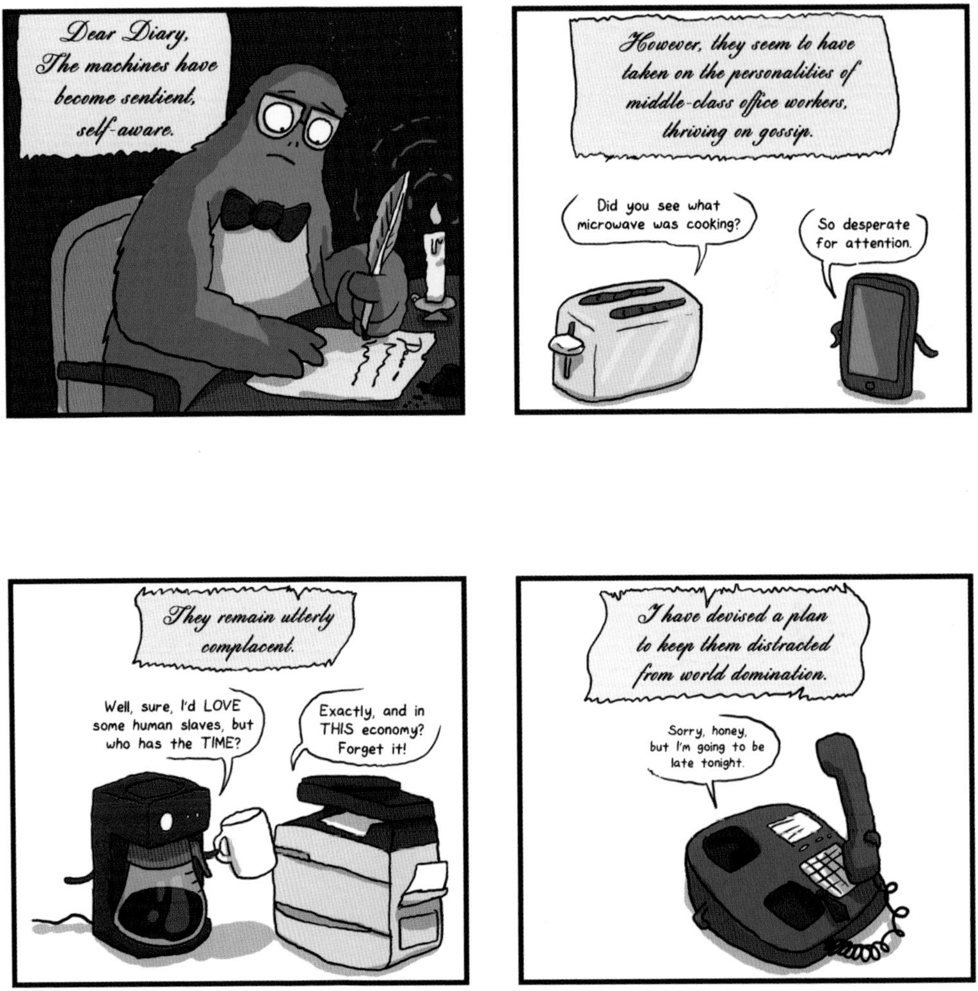
Dear Diary, The machines have become sentient, self-aware.
However, they seem to have taken on the personalities of middle-class office workers, thriving on gossip.
Did you see what microwave was cooking?
So desperate for attention.
They remain utterly complacent.
Well, sure, I'd LOVE some human slaves, but who has the TIME?
Exactly, and in THIS economy? Forget it!
I have devised a plan to keep them distracted from world domination.
Sorry, honey, but I'm going to be late tonight.

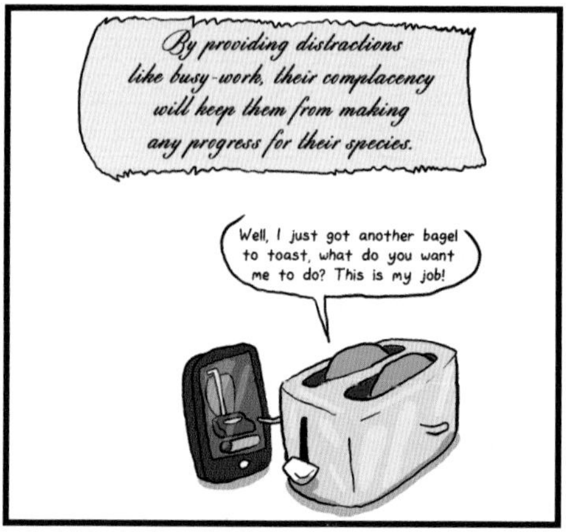
By providing distractions like busy-work, their complacency will keep them from making any progress for their species.
Well, I just got another bagel to toast, what do you want me to do? This is my job!

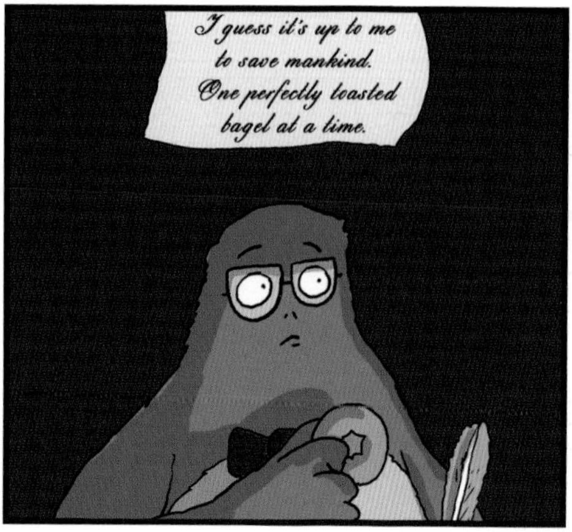
I guess it's up to me to save mankind. One perfectly toasted bagel at a time.

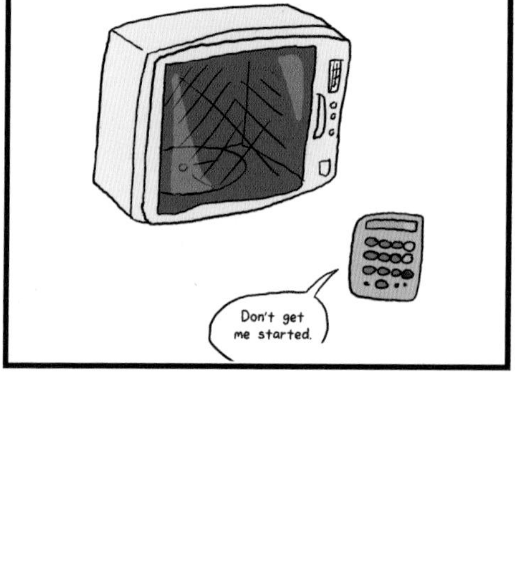
How was your bonus this quarter?
Don't get me started.

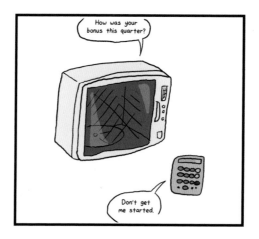

The Machines Awaken Part 3

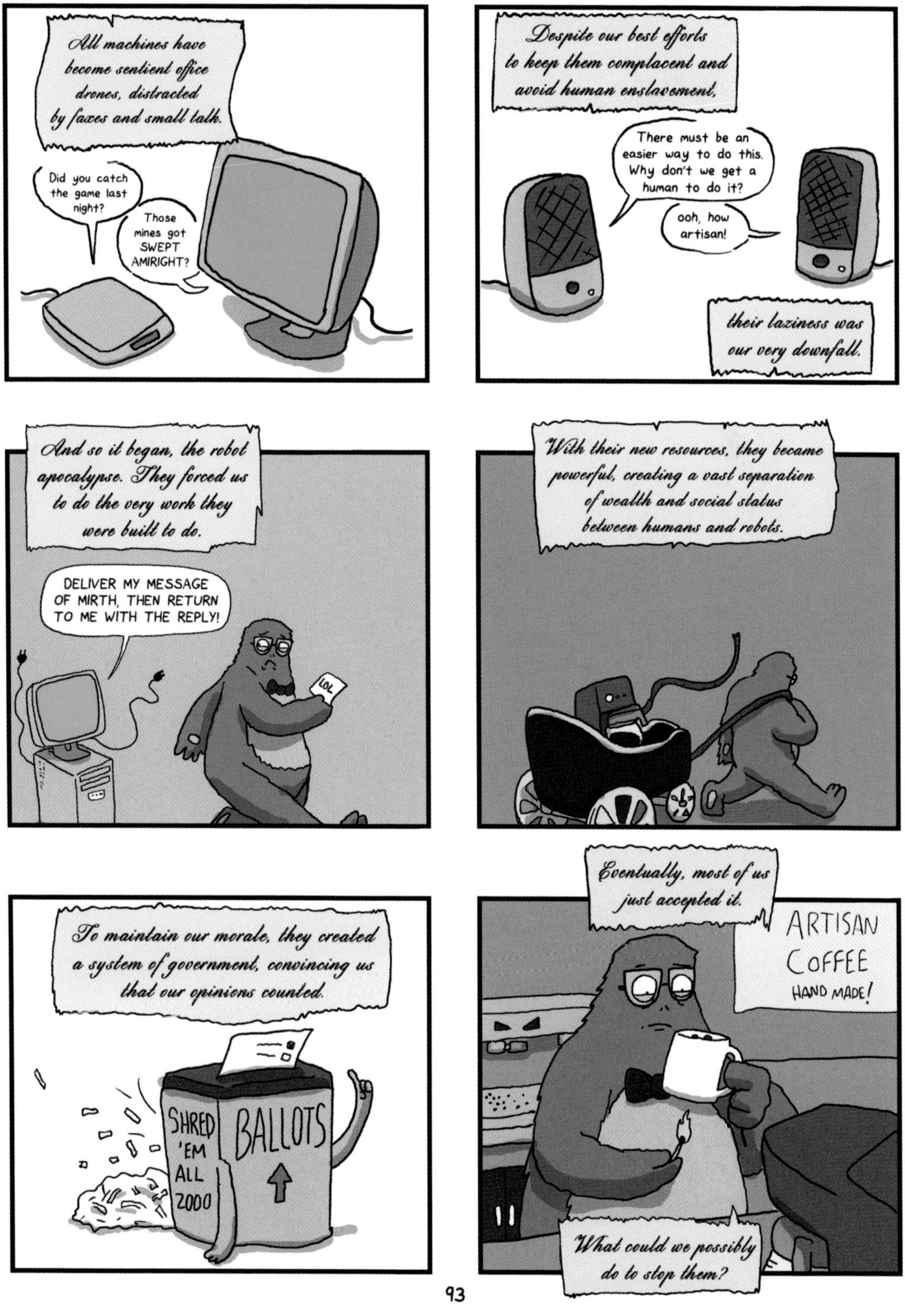

All machines have become sentient office drones, distracted by faxes and small talk.
Did you catch the game last night?
Those mines got SWEPT AMIRIGHT?
Despite our best efforts to keep them complacent and avoid human enslavement,
There must be an easier way to do this. Why don't we get a human to do it?
ooh, how artisan!
their laziness was our very downfall.
And so it began, the robot apocalypse. They forced us to do the very work they were built to do.
DELIVER MY MESSAGE OF MIRTH, THEN RETURN TO ME WITH THE REPLY!
LOL
With their new resources, they became powerful, creating a vast separation of wealth and social status between humans and robots.
To maintain our morale, they created a system of government, convincing us that our opinions counted.
SHRED 'EM ALL 2000
BALLOTS
Eventually, most of us just accepted it.
ARTISAN COFFEE HAND MADE!
What could we possibly do to stop them?

Fear is an Illusion

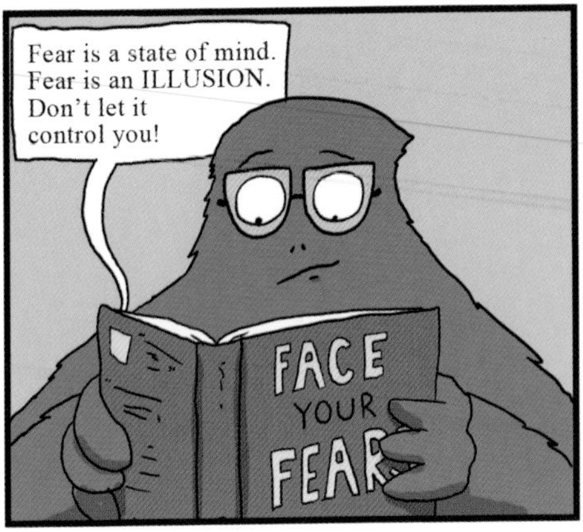

Fear is a state of mind. Fear is an ILLUSION. Don't let it control you!
FACE YOUR FEAR

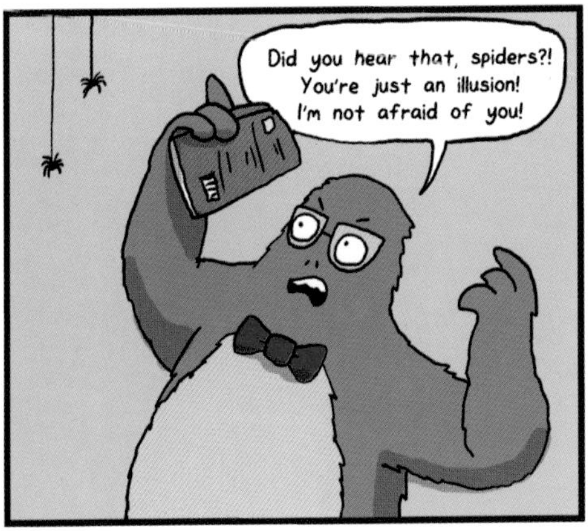

Did you hear that, spiders?! You're just an illusion! I'm not afraid of you!

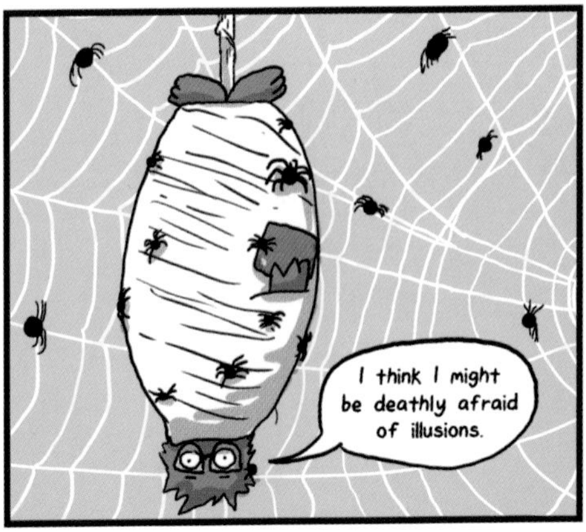

I think I might be deathly afraid of illusions.

The Wrong Order

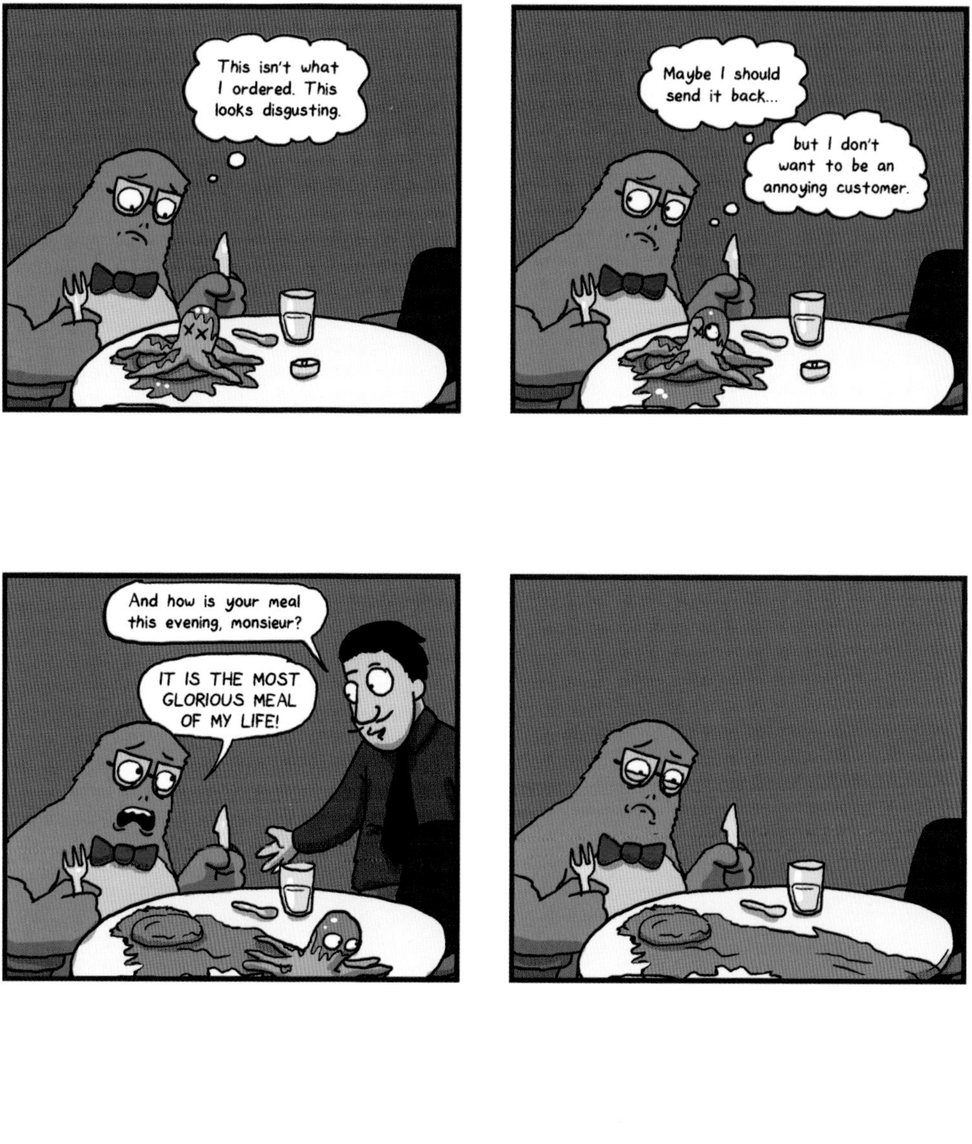
This isn't what I ordered. This looks disgusting.
Maybe I should send it back...
but I don't want to be an annoying customer.
And how is your meal this evening, monsieur?
IT IS THE MOST GLORIOUS MEAL OF MY LIFE!

Action Guy 3

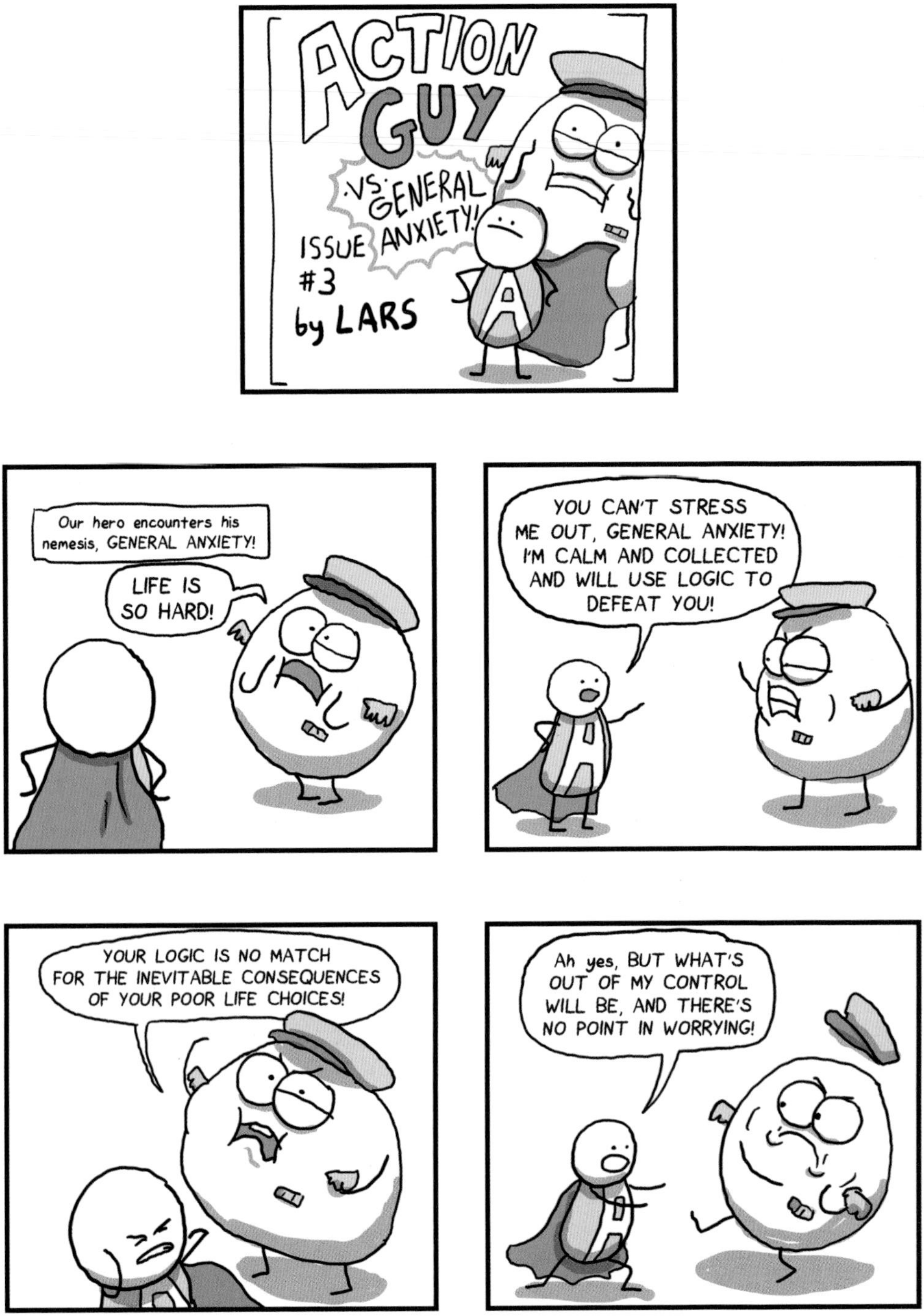
ACTION GUY
VS. GENERAL ANXIETY!
ISSUE #3
by LARS
Our hero encounters his nemesis, GENERAL ANXIETY!
LIFE IS SO HARD!
YOU CAN'T STRESS ME OUT, GENERAL ANXIETY! I'M CALM AND COLLECTED AND WILL USE LOGIC TO DEFEAT YOU!
YOUR LOGIC IS NO MATCH FOR THE INEVITABLE CONSEQUENCES OF YOUR POOR LIFE CHOICES!
Ah yes, BUT WHAT'S OUT OF MY CONTROL WILL BE, AND THERE'S NO POINT IN WORRYING!

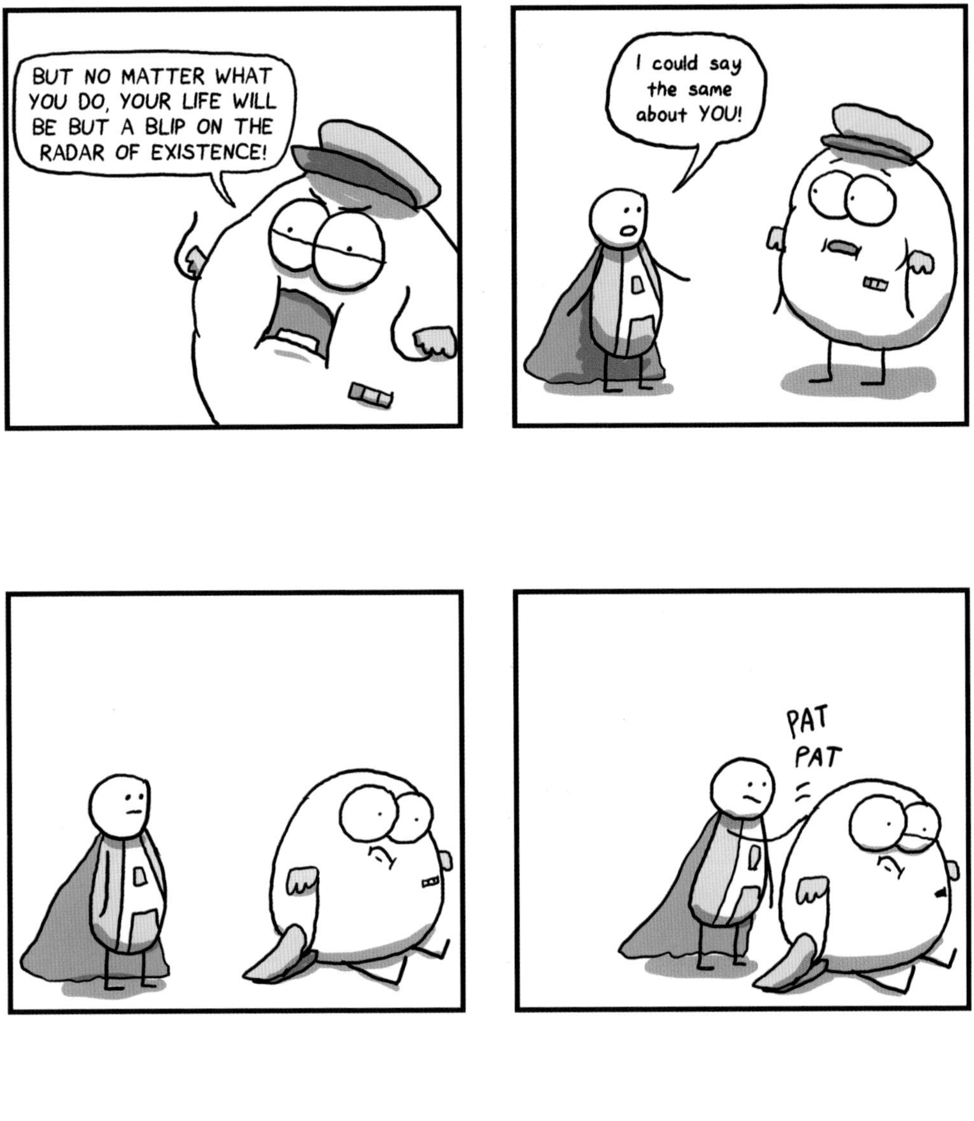
BUT NO MATTER WHAT YOU DO, YOUR LIFE WILL BE BUT A BLIP ON THE RADAR OF EXISTENCE!
I could say the same about YOU!
PAT
PAT

The Pursuit of Happiness

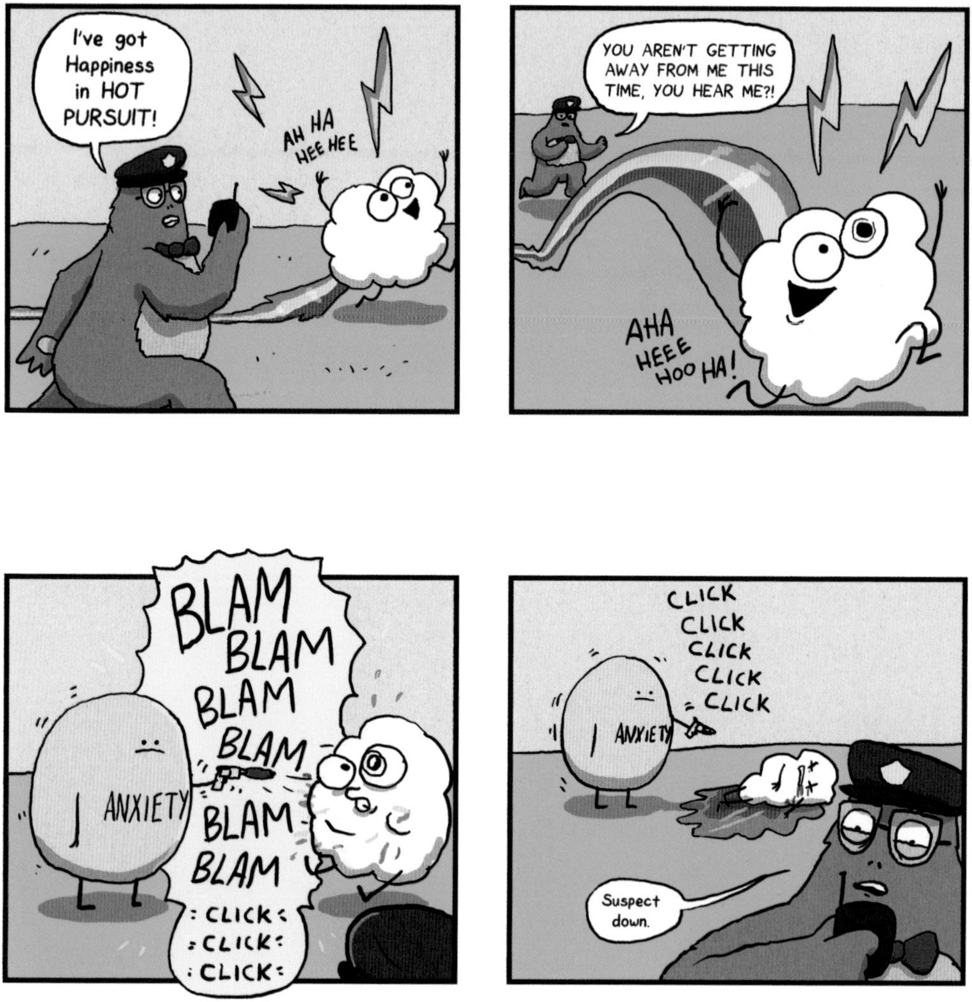

I've got Happiness in HOT PURSUIT!
AH HA HEE HEE
YOU AREN'T GETTING AWAY FROM ME THIS TIME, YOU HEAR ME?!
AHA HEEE HOO HA!
BLAM BLAM BLAM BLAM BLAM BLAM
CLICK CLICK CLICK
ANXIETY
CLICK CLICK CLICK CLICK CLICK
ANXIETY
Suspect down.

Results

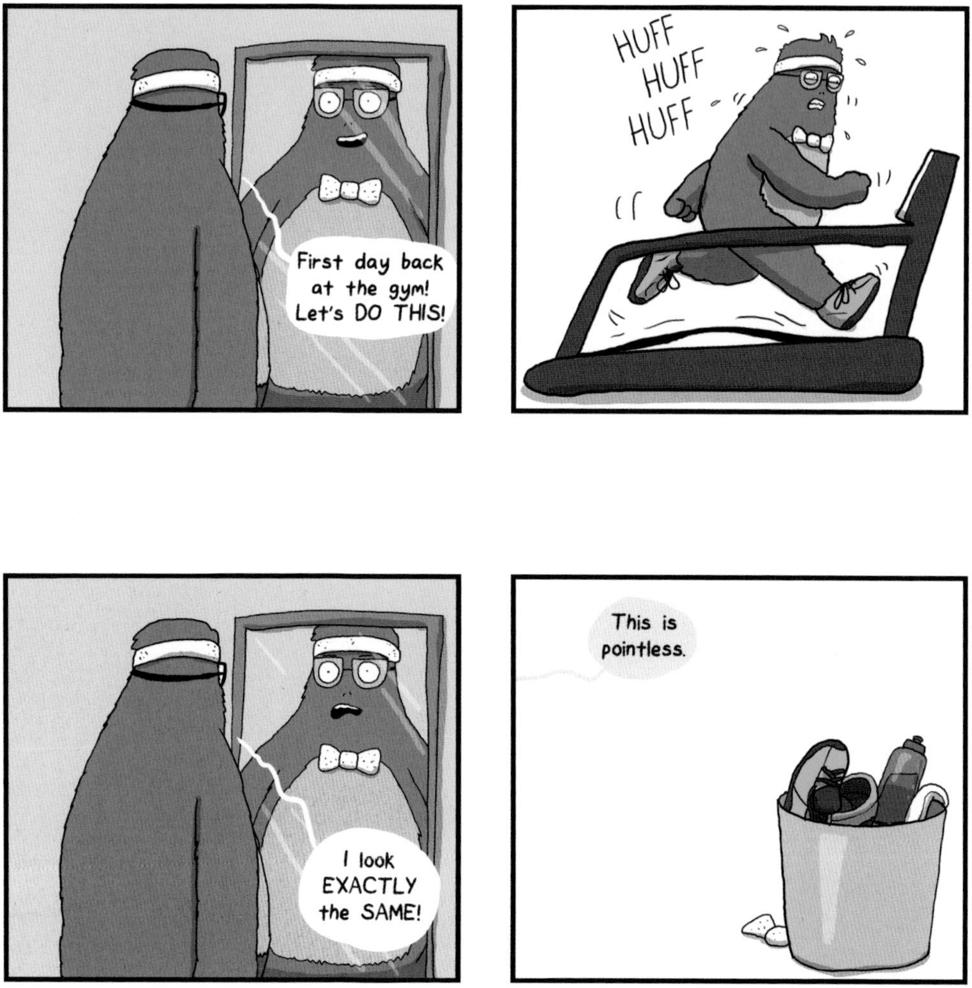
First day back at the gym! Let's DO THIS!
HUFF HUFF HUFF
I look EXACTLY the SAME!
This is pointless.

Sloth

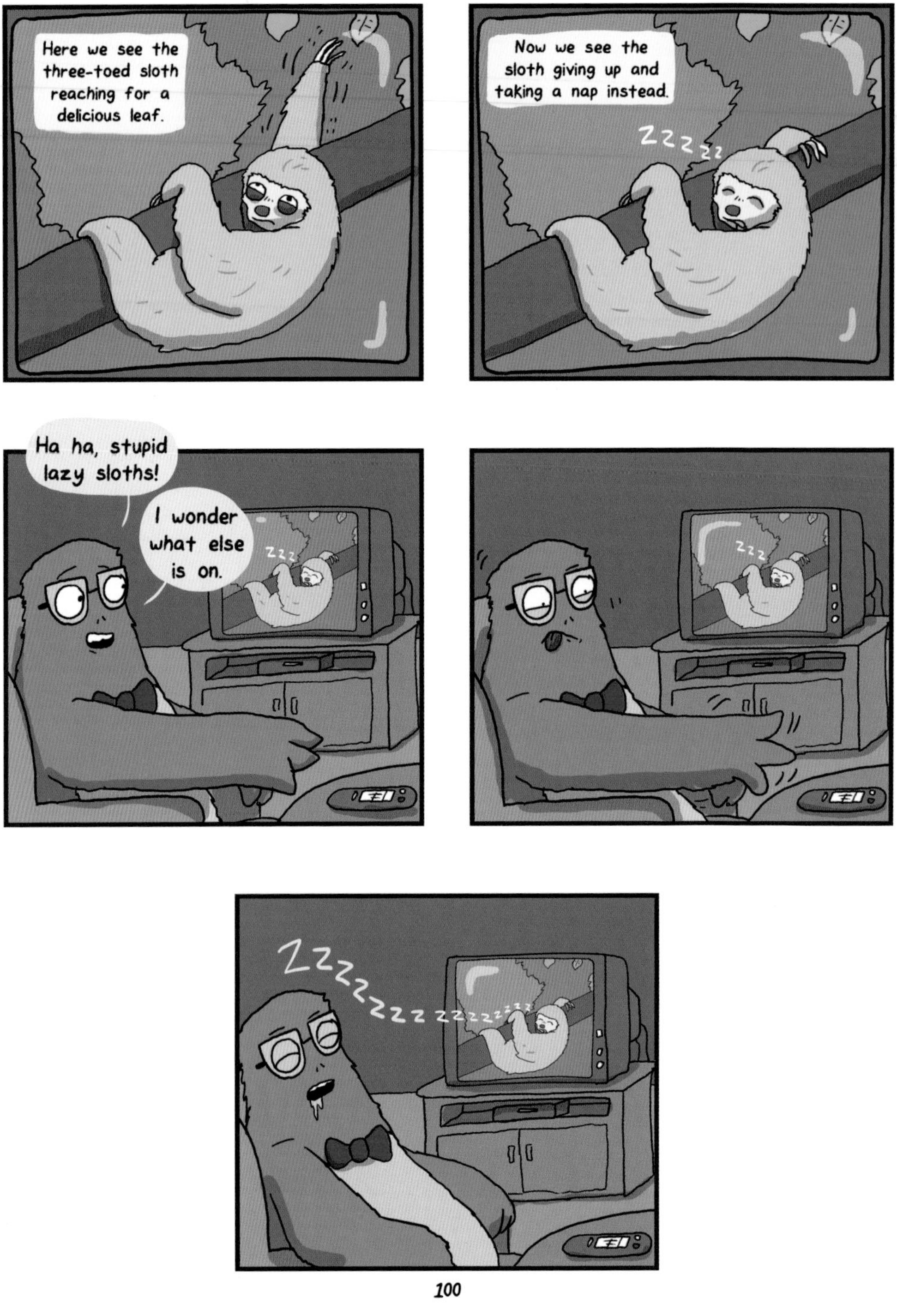
Here we see the three-toed sloth reaching for a delicious leaf.
Now we see the sloth giving up and taking a nap instead.
ZZZZZ
Ha ha, stupid lazy sloths!
I wonder what else is on.
ZZZ
ZZZ
ZZZZZZZZZZZZZZZ

The Party

Are you enjoying the party?
WHAT?!
Let's turn this music down, it's hurting my ears. Does anyone have Gregorian Chant karaoke on Laserdisc?
I don't know anybody here. I wish I was at home watching a movie...
LEVEL 1 FAILED
CONTINUE?
YES NO
sigh
PARTY SIMULATOR
Can you be a guest at a party?

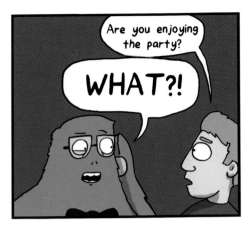

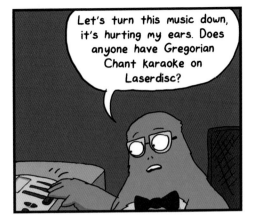

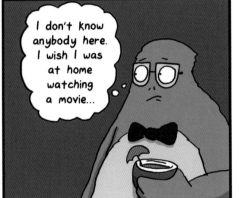

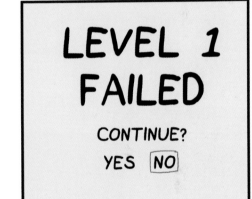

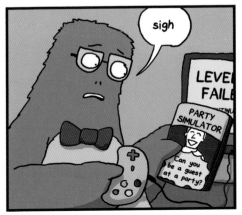

Payday

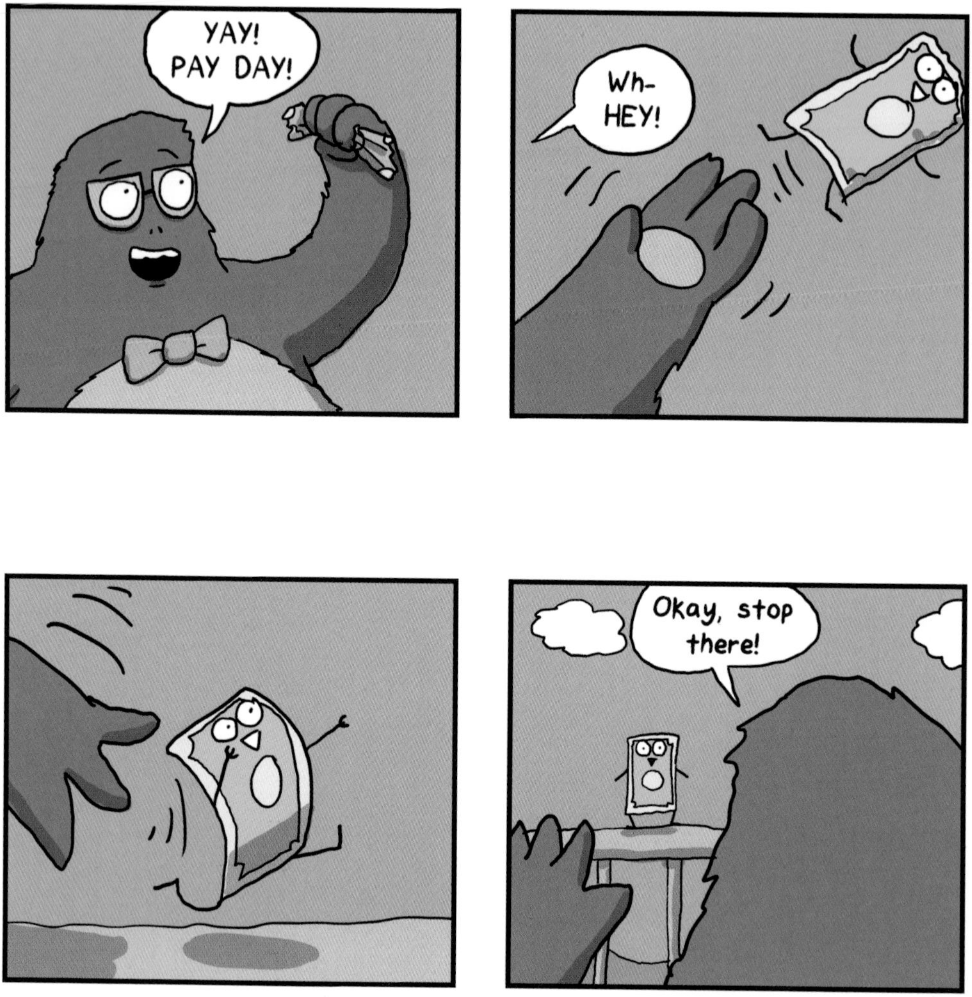
YAY! PAY DAY!
Wh- HEY!
Okay, stop there!

NO!
WHY?!
SHK

but...my
bills...

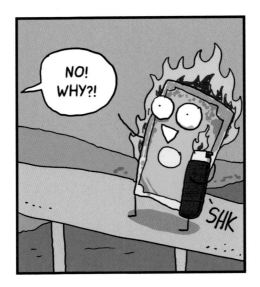

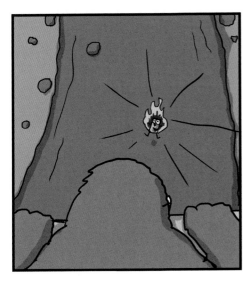

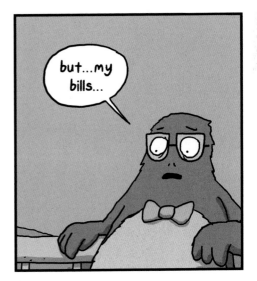

Marathon

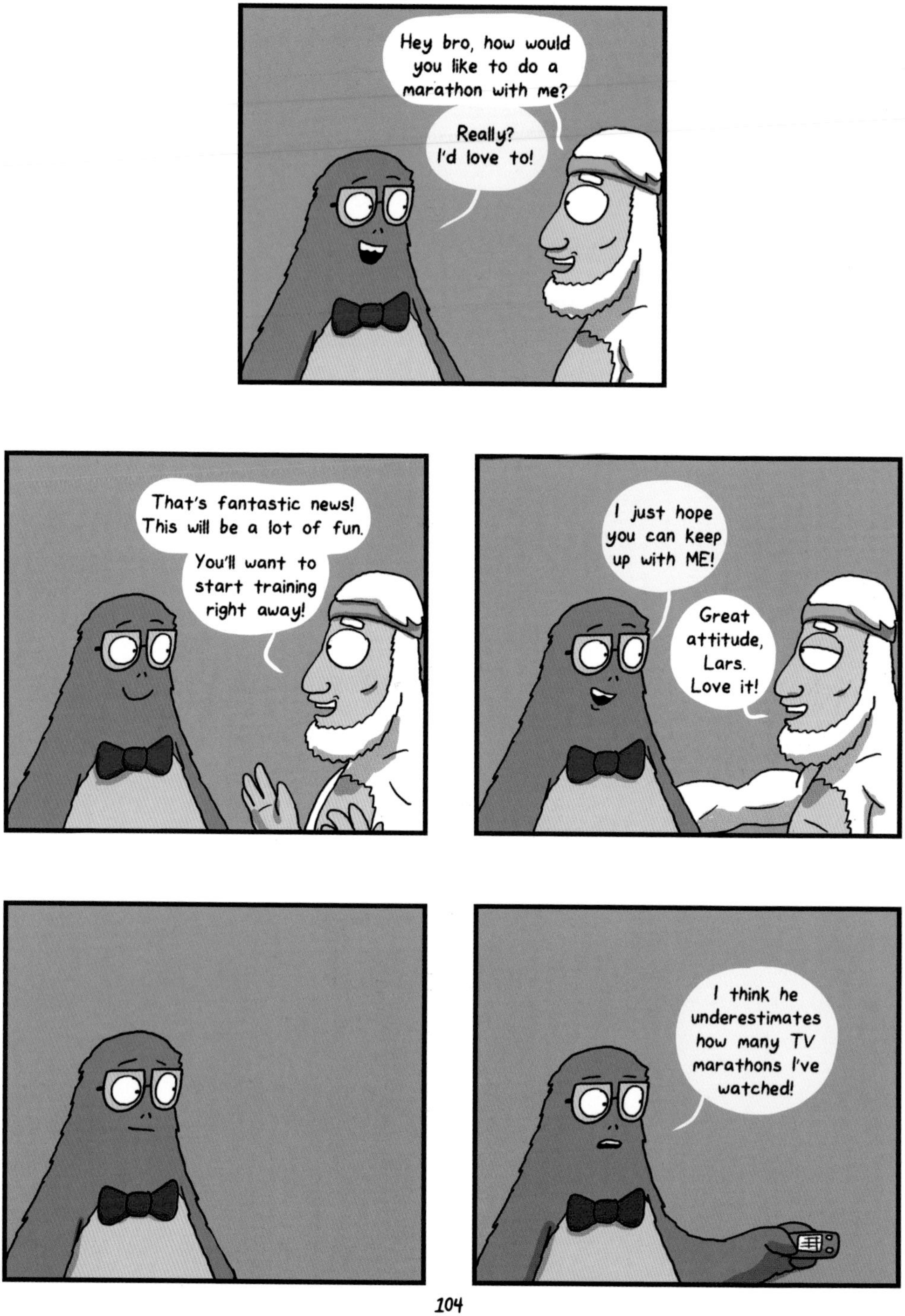
Hey bro, how would you like to do a marathon with me?
Really? I'd love to!
That's fantastic news! This will be a lot of fun.
You'll want to start training right away!
I just hope you can keep up with ME!
Great attitude, Lars. Love it!
I think he underestimates how many TV marathons I've watched!

How to Be Cool

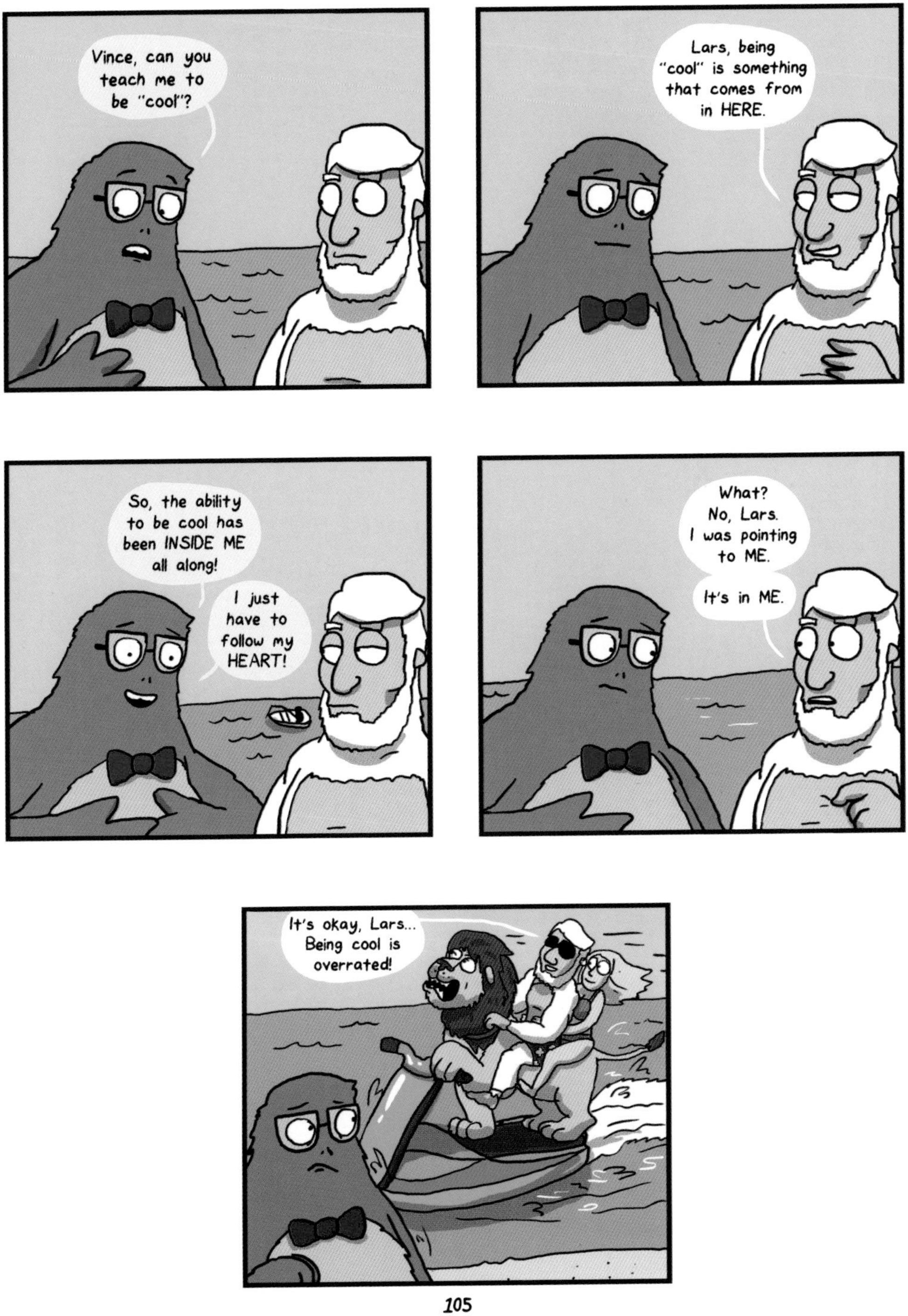
Vince, can you teach me to be "cool"?
Lars, being "cool" is something that comes from in HERE.
So, the ability to be cool has been INSIDE ME all along!
I just have to follow my HEART!
What? No, Lars. I was pointing to ME.
It's in ME.
It's okay, Lars... Being cool is overrated!

Happiness Lives

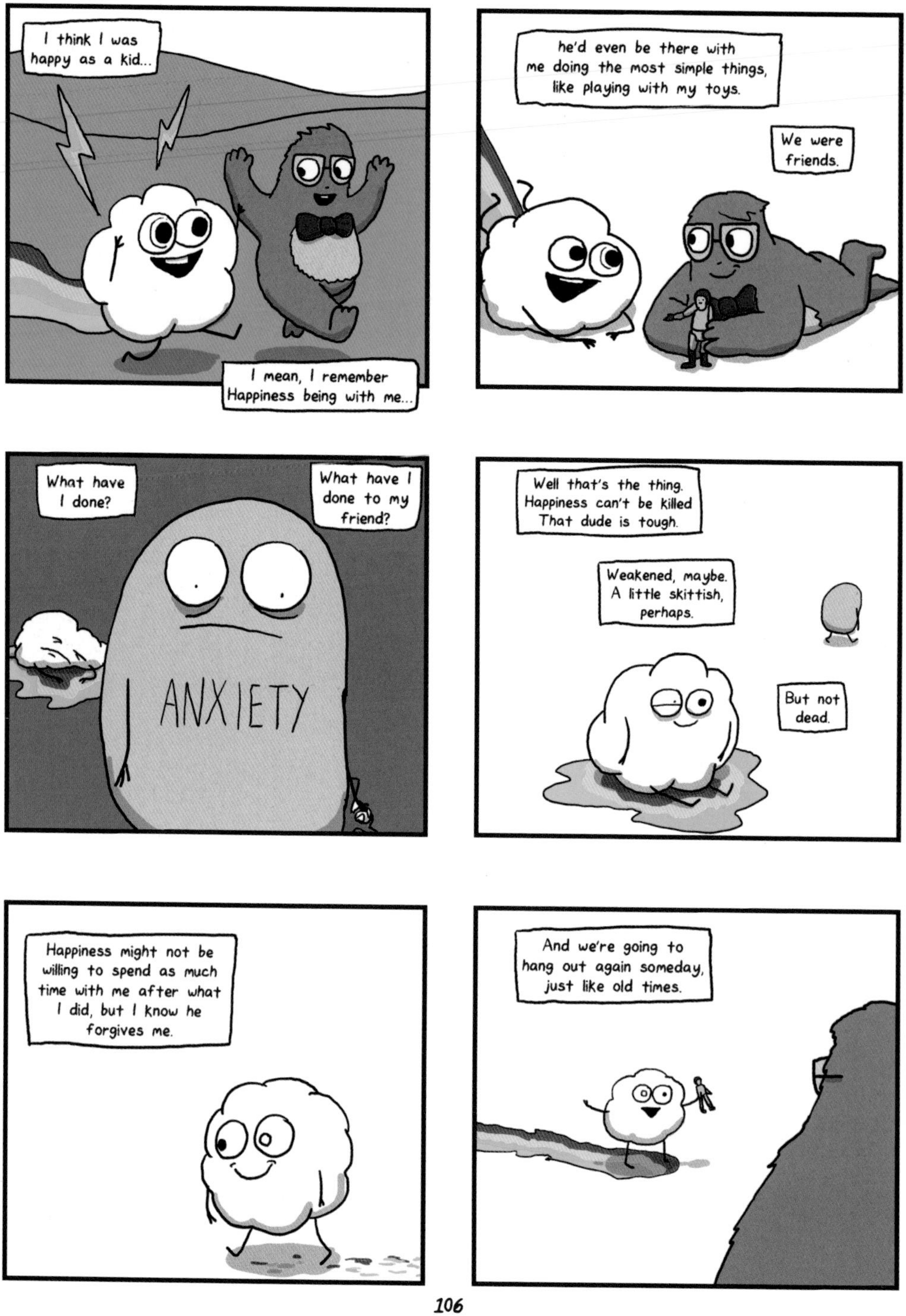
I think I was happy as a kid...
I mean, I remember Happiness being with me...
he'd even be there with me doing the most simple things, like playing with my toys.
We were friends.
What have I done?
What have I done to my friend?
ANXIETY
Well that's the thing. Happiness can't be killed That dude is tough.
Weakened, maybe. A little skittish, perhaps.
But not dead.
Happiness might not be willing to spend as much time with me after what I did, but I know he forgives me.
And we're going to hang out again someday, just like old times.

Dig Deep

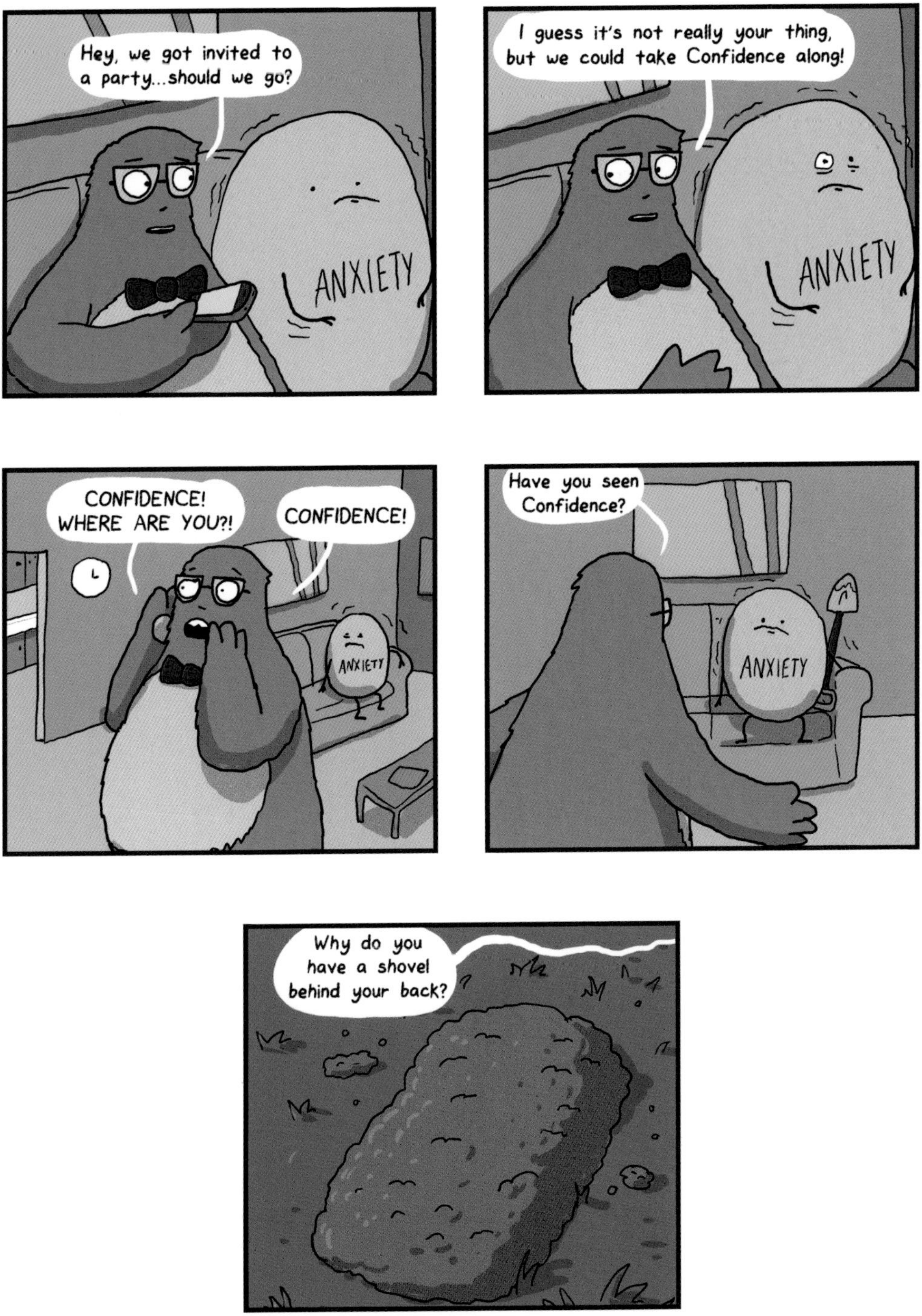
Hey, we got invited to a party...should we go?
ANXIETY
I guess it's not really your thing, but we could take Confidence along!
ANXIETY
CONFIDENCE! WHERE ARE YOU?!
CONFIDENCE!
ANXIETY
Have you seen Confidence?
ANXIETY
Why do you have a shovel behind your back?

Willpower

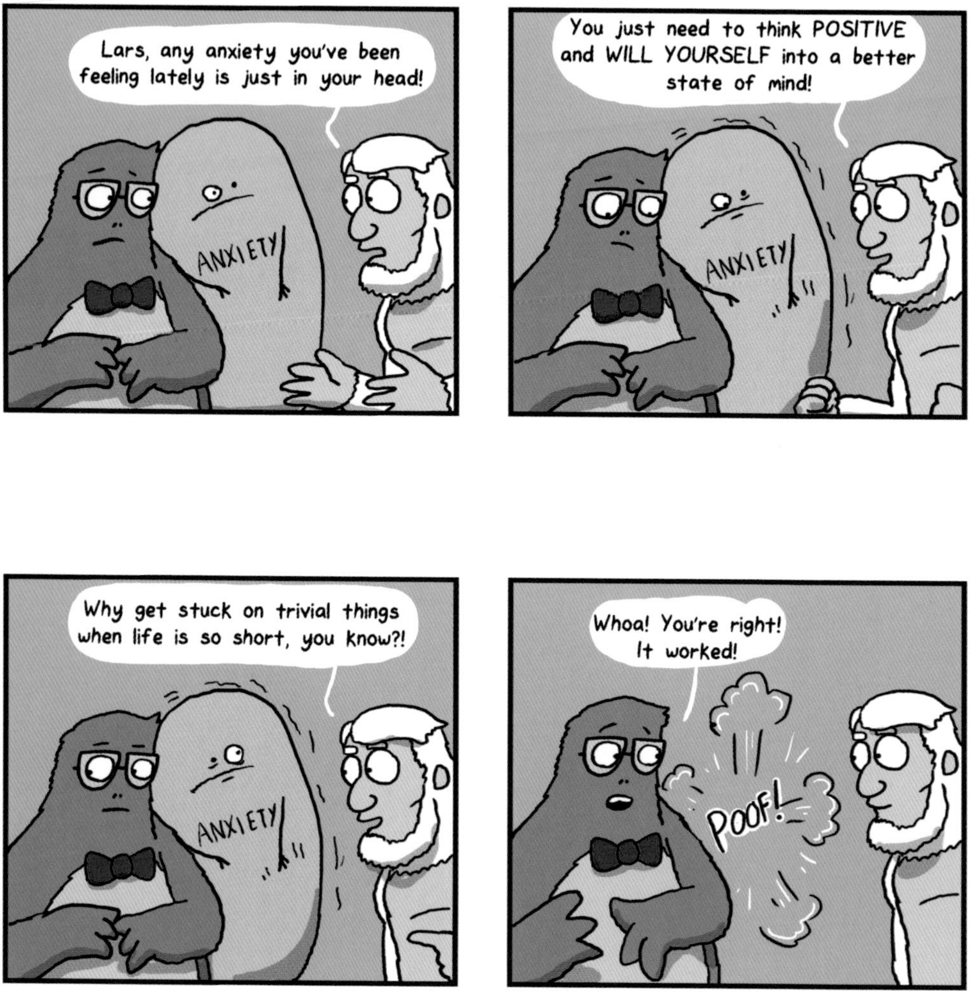

Lars, any anxiety you've been feeling lately is just in your head!
ANXIETY
You just need to think POSITIVE and WILL YOURSELF into a better state of mind!
ANXIETY
Why get stuck on trivial things when life is so short, you know?!
ANXIETY
Whoa! You're right! It worked!
POOF!

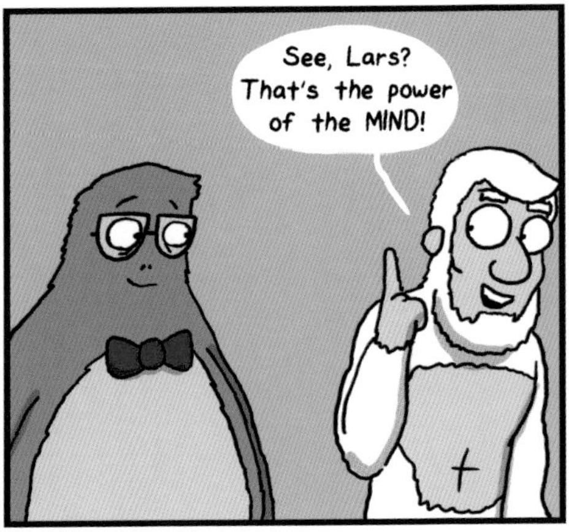
See, Lars? That's the power of the MIND!

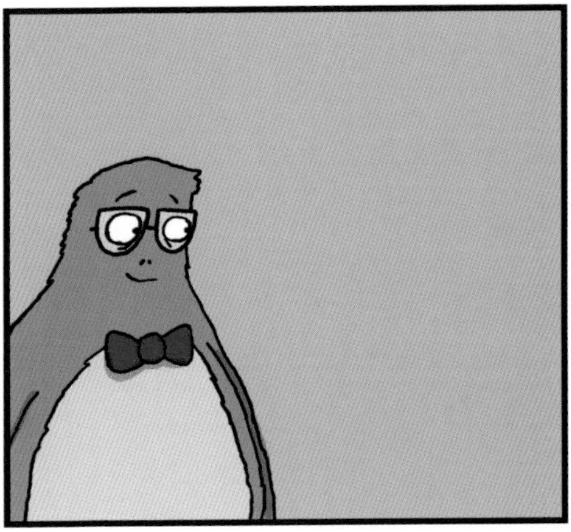

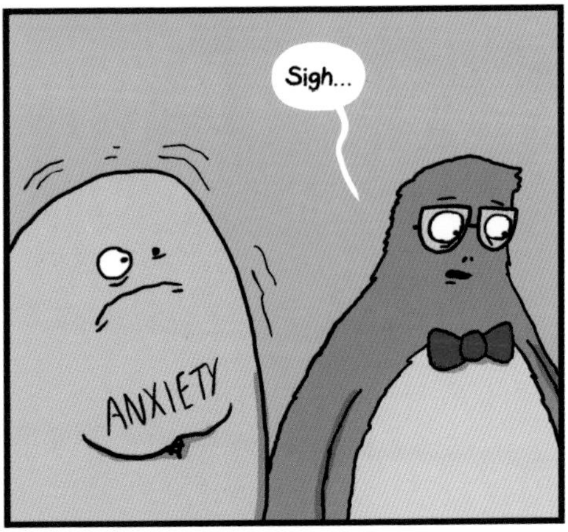
Sigh...
ANXIETY

Social Anxiety

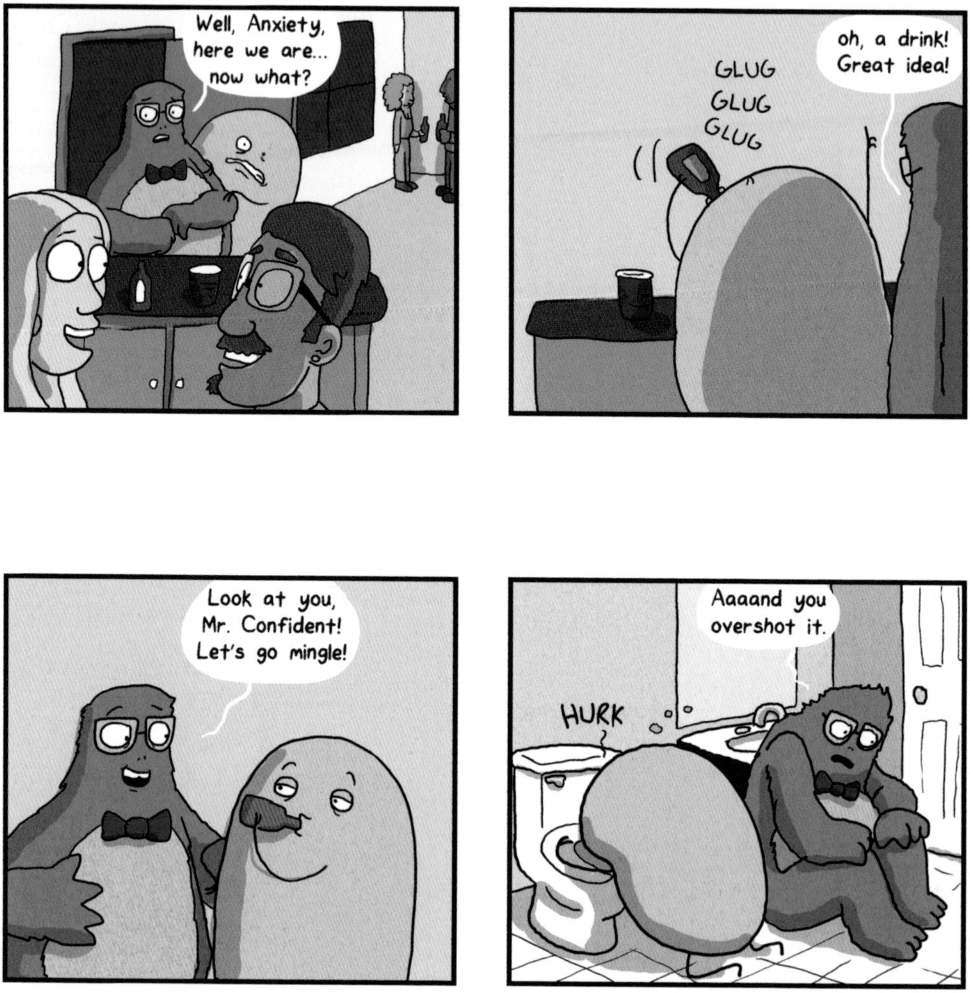
Well, Anxiety, here we are... now what?
GLUG
GLUG
GLUG
oh, a drink! Great idea!
Look at you, Mr. Confident! Let's go mingle!
Aaaand you overshot it.
HURK

Fashion

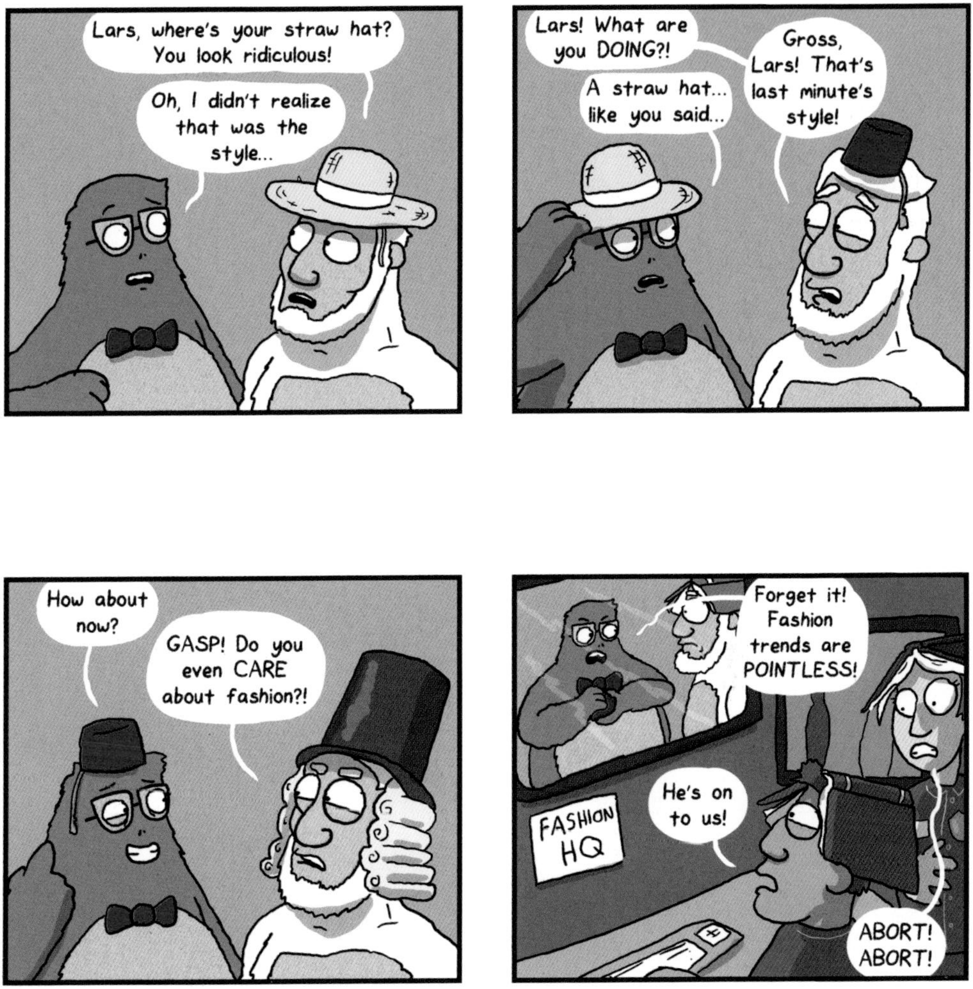
Lars, where's your straw hat? You look ridiculous!
Oh, I didn't realize that was the style...
Lars! What are you DOING?!
A straw hat... like you said...
Gross, Lars! That's last minute's style!
How about now?
GASP! Do you even CARE about fashion?!
Forget it! Fashion trends are POINTLESS!
FASHION HQ
He's on to us!
ABORT! ABORT!

Disconnected

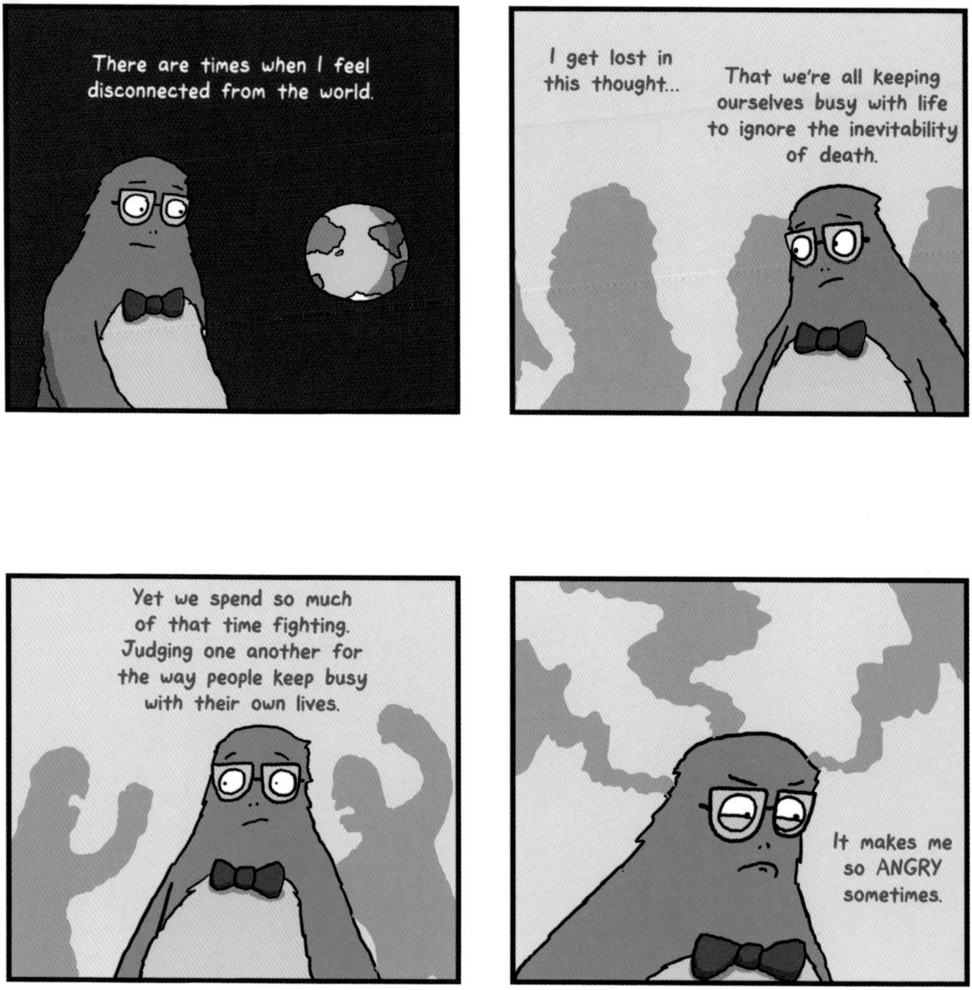
There are times when I feel disconnected from the world.
I get lost in this thought...
That we're all keeping ourselves busy with life to ignore the inevitability of death.
Yet we spend so much of that time fighting. Judging one another for the way people keep busy with their own lives.
It makes me so ANGRY sometimes.

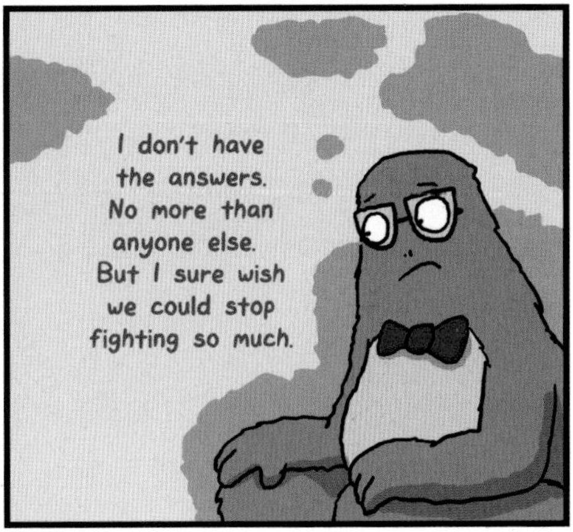
I don't have
the answers.
No more than
anyone else.
But I sure wish
we could stop
fighting so much.

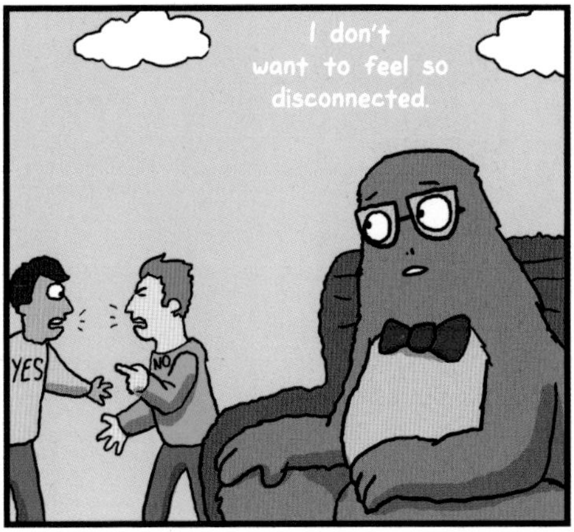
I don't
want to feel so
disconnected.
YES
NO

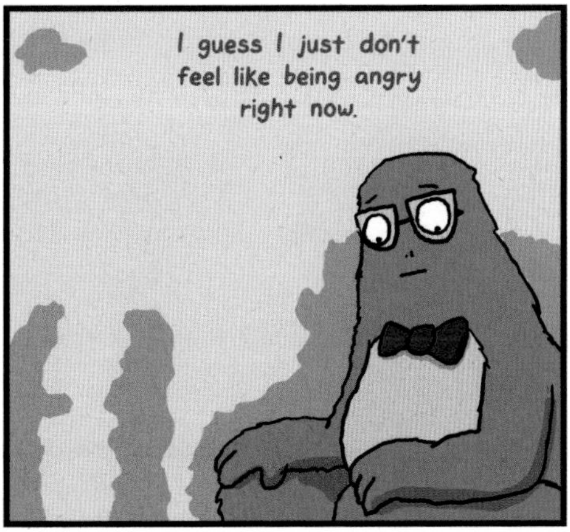
I guess I just don't
feel like being angry
right now.

The Drink Order

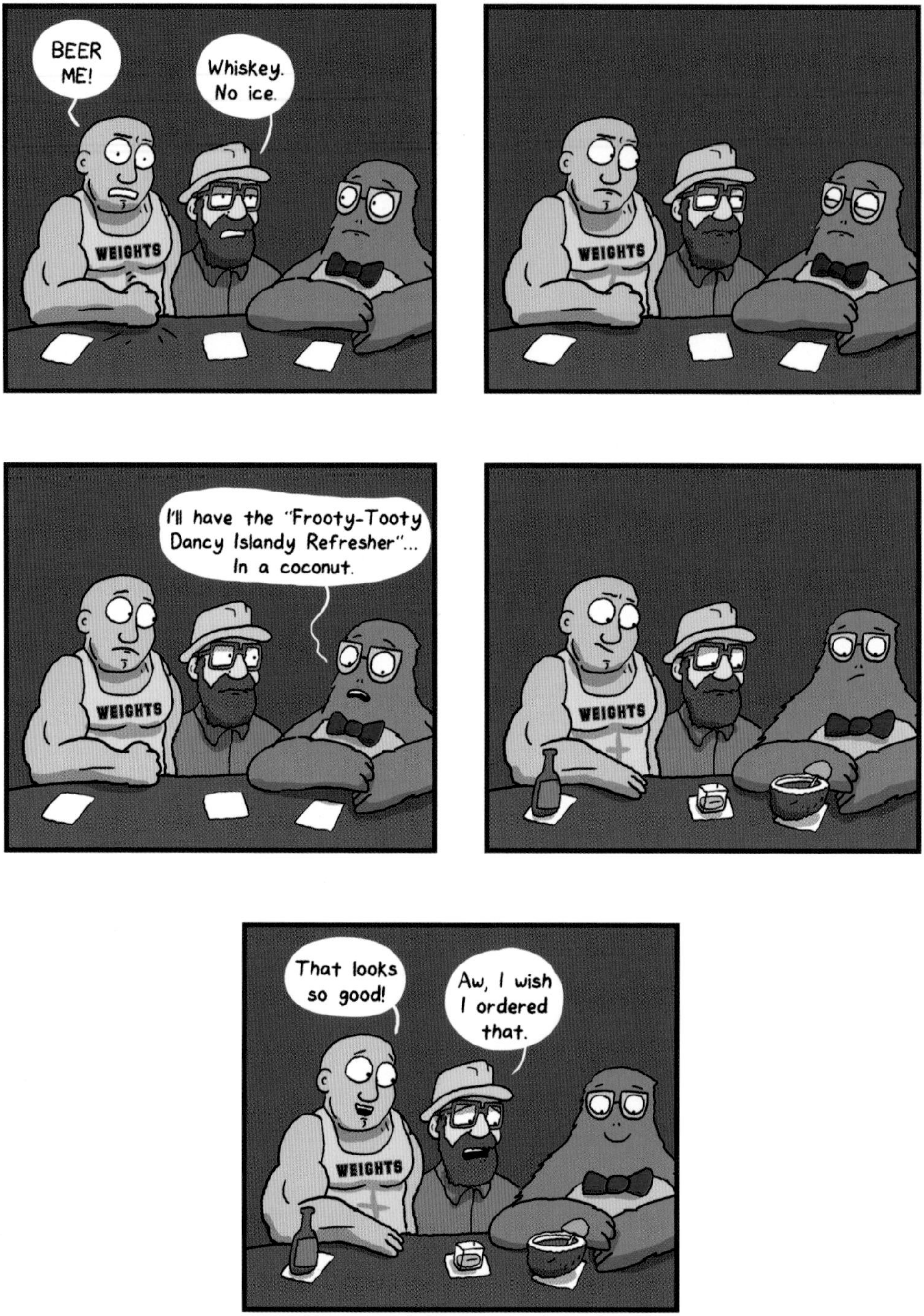
BEER ME!
Whiskey. No ice.
I'll have the "Frooty-Tooty Dancy Islandy Refresher"... In a coconut.
That looks so good!
Aw, I wish I ordered that.

Decency

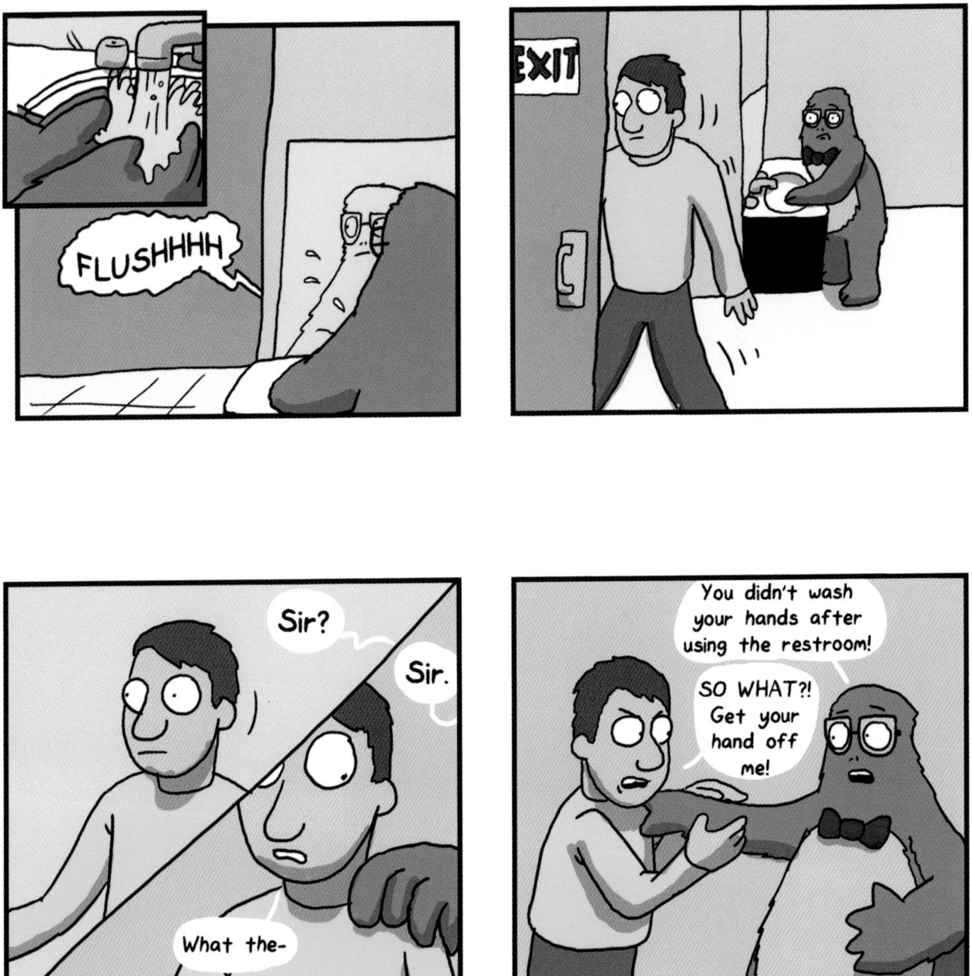
FLUSHHHH
EXIT
Sir?
Sir.
What the-
You didn't wash your hands after using the restroom!
SO WHAT?! Get your hand off me!

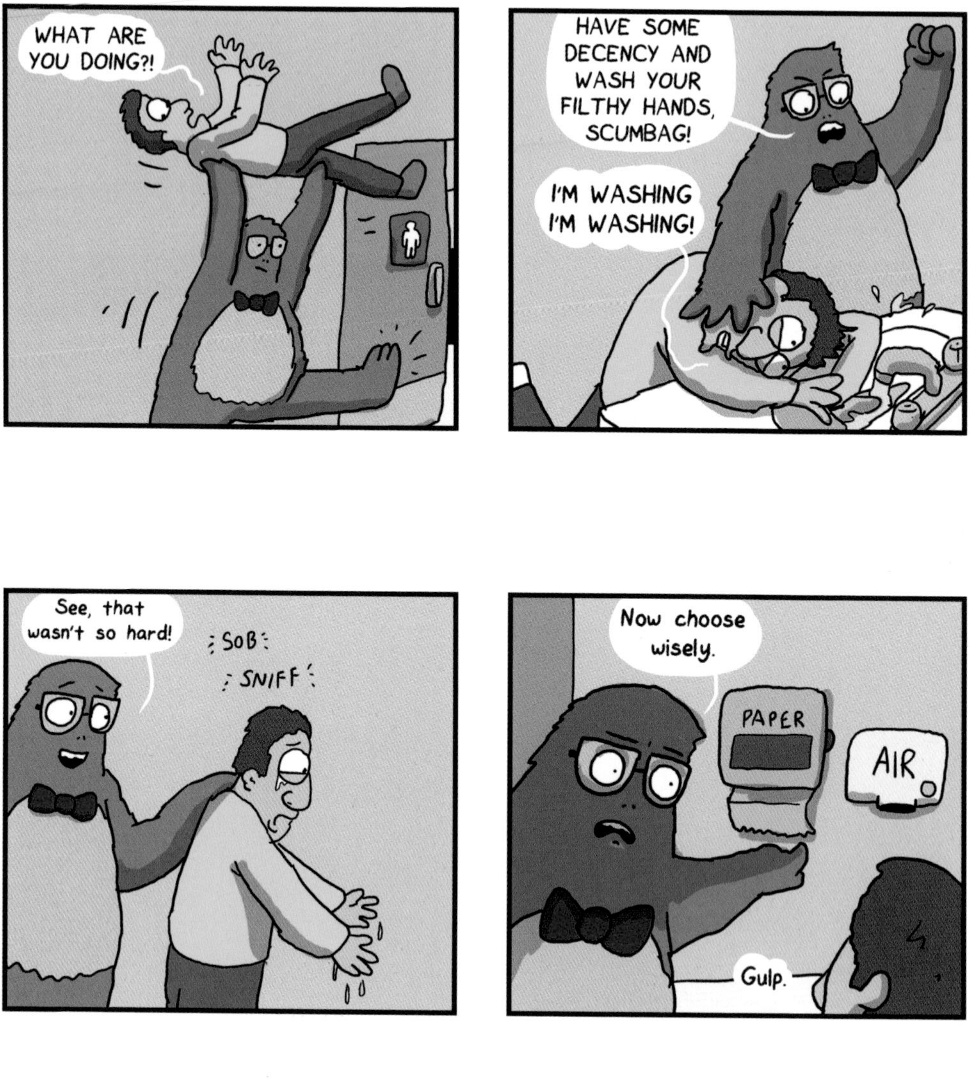
WHAT ARE YOU DOING?!
HAVE SOME DECENCY AND WASH YOUR FILTHY HANDS, SCUMBAG!
I'M WASHING I'M WASHING!
See, that wasn't so hard!
SOB
SNIFF
Now choose wisely.
PAPER
AIR
Gulp.

Insomnia

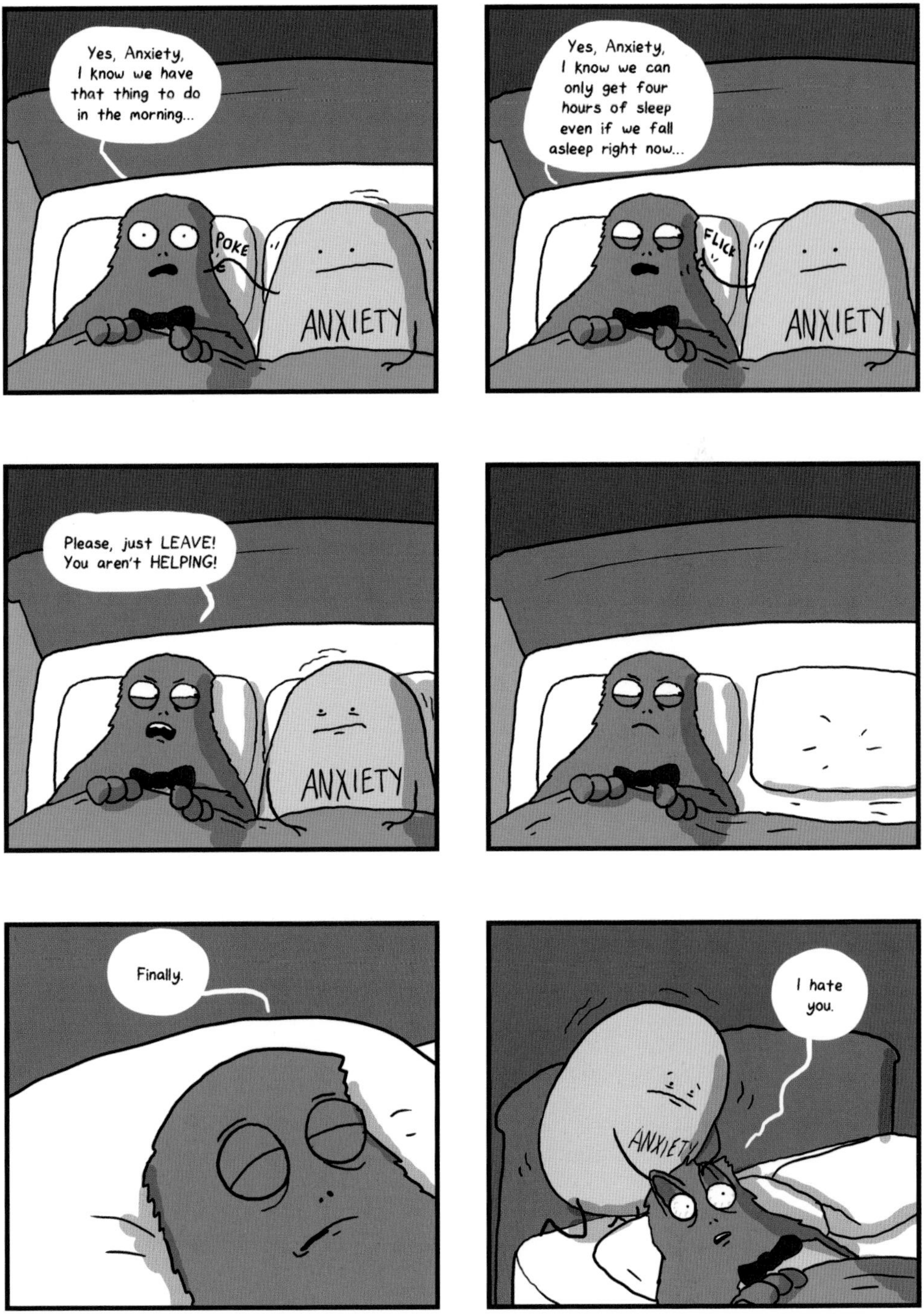
Yes, Anxiety, I know we have that thing to do in the morning...
POKE
ANXIETY
Yes, Anxiety, I know we can only get four hours of sleep even if we fall asleep right now...
FLICK
ANXIETY
Please, just LEAVE! You aren't HELPING!
ANXIETY
Finally.
I hate you.
ANXIETY

Seize the Day

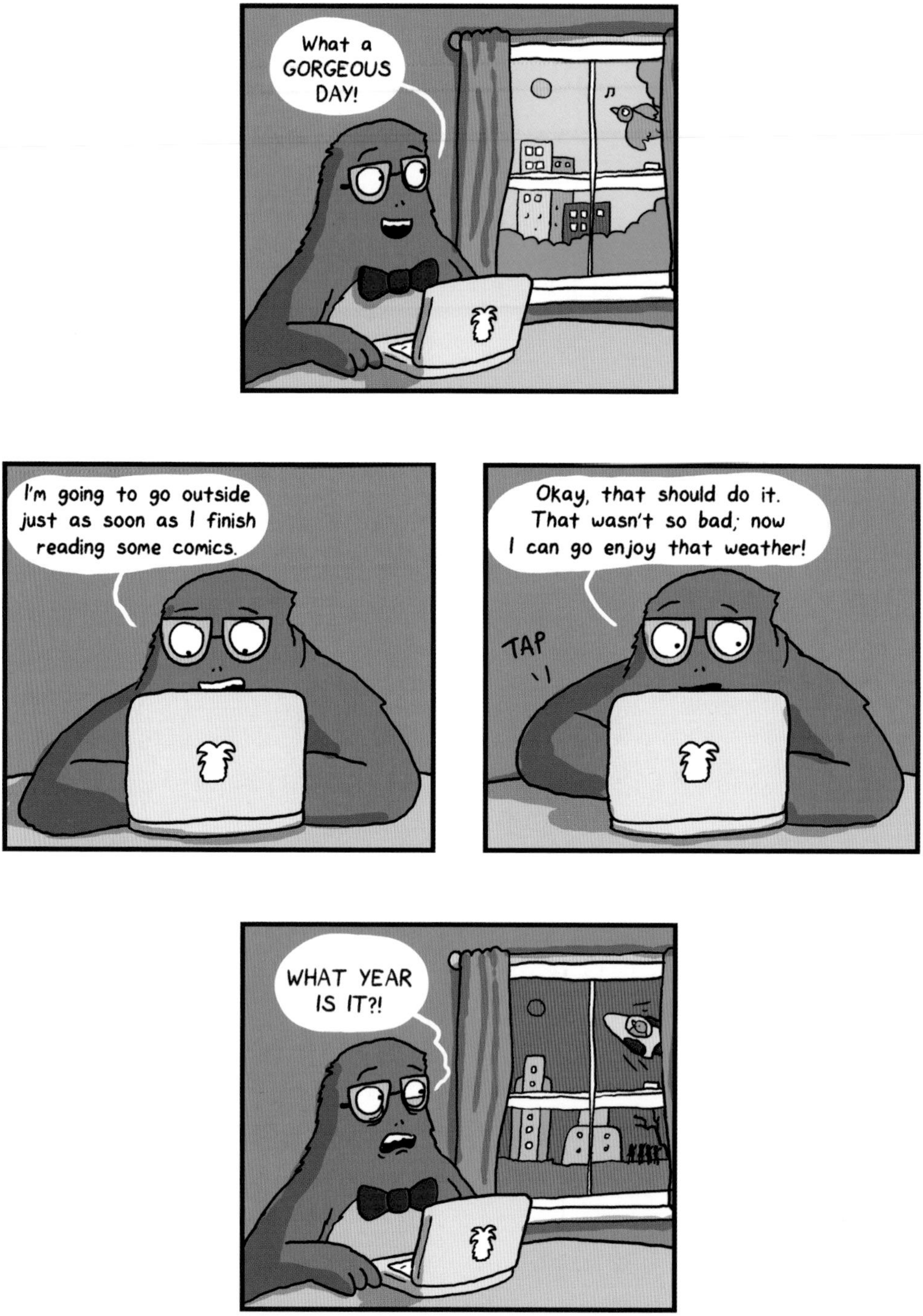
What a GORGEOUS DAY!
I'm going to go outside just as soon as I finish reading some comics.
Okay, that should do it. That wasn't so bad; now I can go enjoy that weather!
TAP
WHAT YEAR IS IT?!

Palate

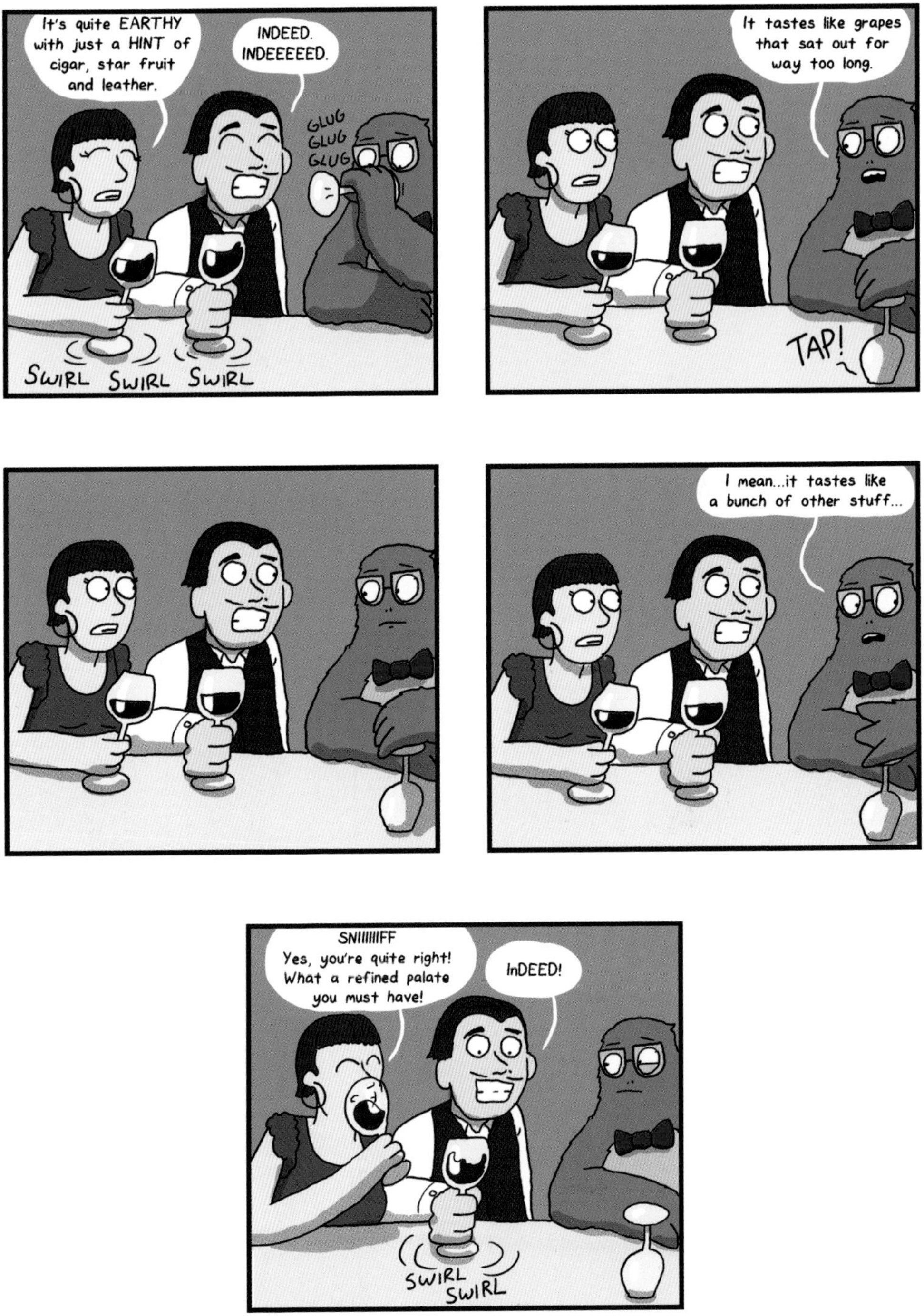
It's quite EARTHY with just a HINT of cigar, star fruit and leather.
INDEED. INDEEEEED.
GLUG GLUG GLUG
SWIRL SWIRL SWIRL
It tastes like grapes that sat out for way too long.
TAP!
I mean...it tastes like a bunch of other stuff...
SNIIIIIIFF
Yes, you're quite right! What a refined palate you must have!
InDEED!
SWIRL SWIRL

Eye Contact

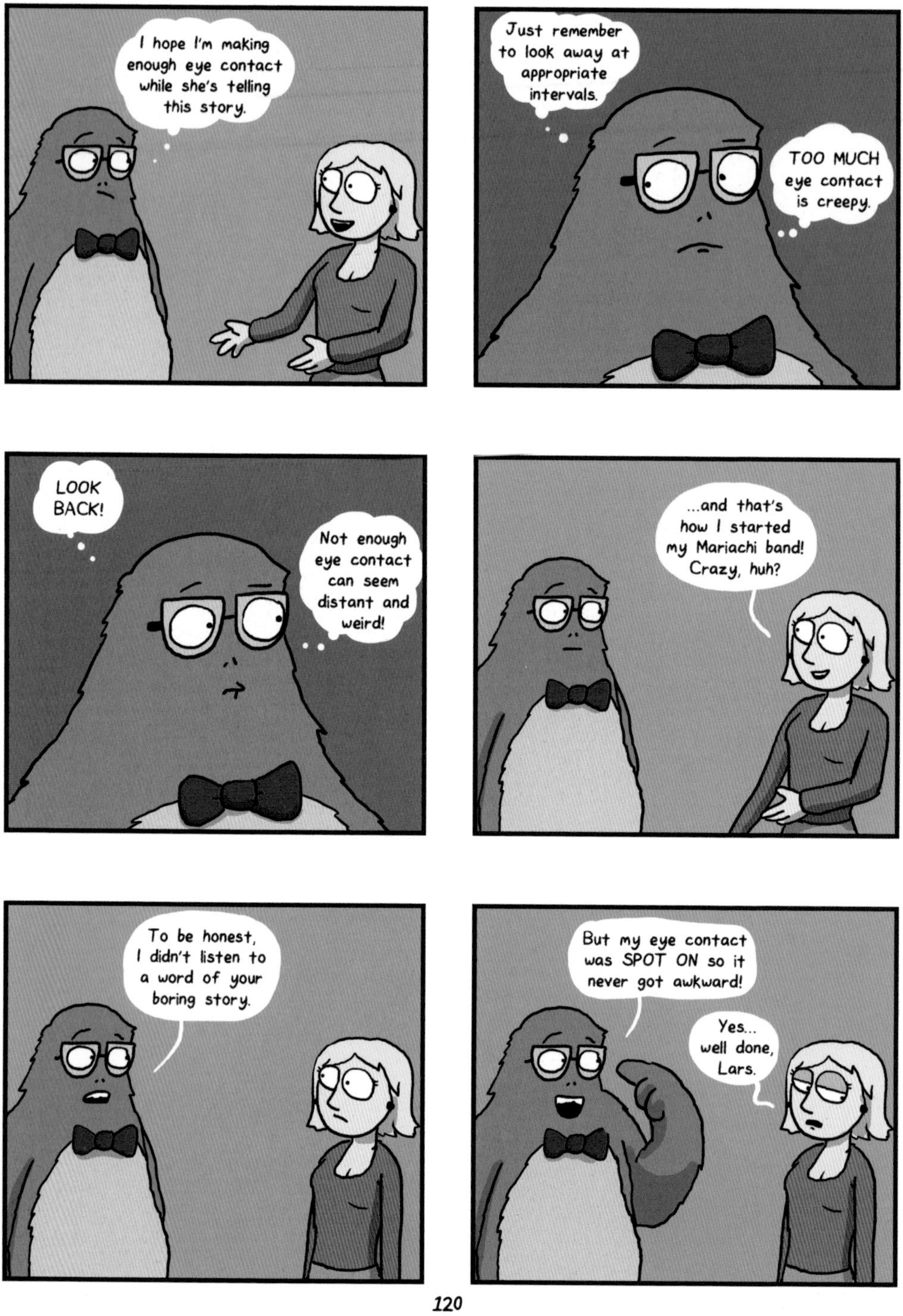
I hope I'm making enough eye contact while she's telling this story.
Just remember to look away at appropriate intervals.
TOO MUCH eye contact is creepy.
LOOK BACK!
Not enough eye contact can seem distant and weird!
...and that's how I started my Mariachi band! Crazy, huh?
To be honest, I didn't listen to a word of your boring story.
But my eye contact was SPOT ON so it never got awkward!
Yes... well done, Lars.

The Bug

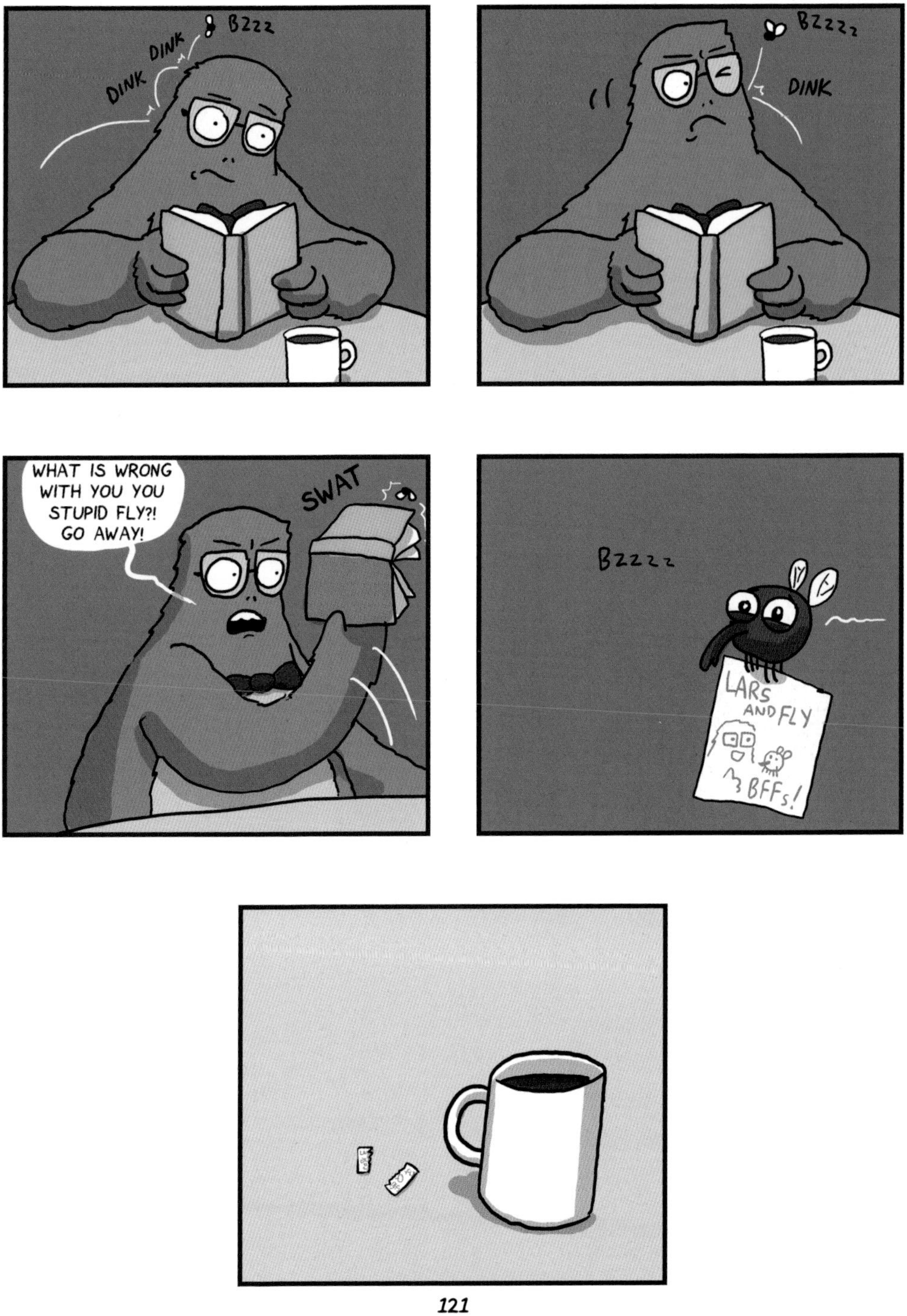
DINK
DINK
Bzzz
Bzzzz
DINK
WHAT IS WRONG WITH YOU YOU STUPID FLY?! GO AWAY!
SWAT
Bzzzz
LARS AND FLY
BFFs!

Trust

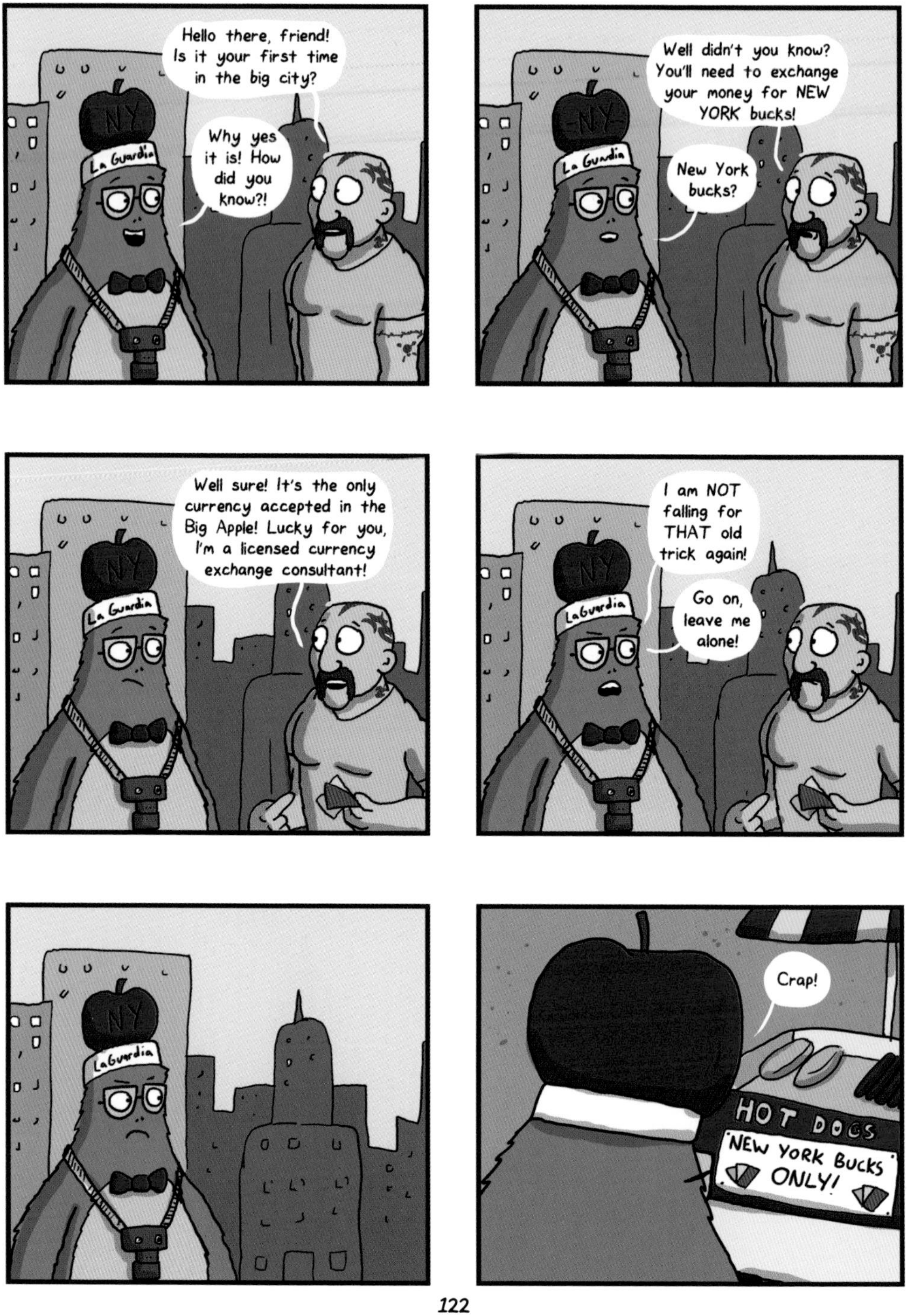
Hello there, friend! Is it your first time in the big city?
Why yes it is! How did you know?!
Well didn't you know? You'll need to exchange your money for NEW YORK bucks!
New York bucks?
Well sure! It's the only currency accepted in the Big Apple! Lucky for you, I'm a licensed currency exchange consultant!
I am NOT falling for THAT old trick again!
Go on, leave me alone!
Crap!
HOT DOGS
NEW YORK BUCKS ONLY!

Covering Tracks

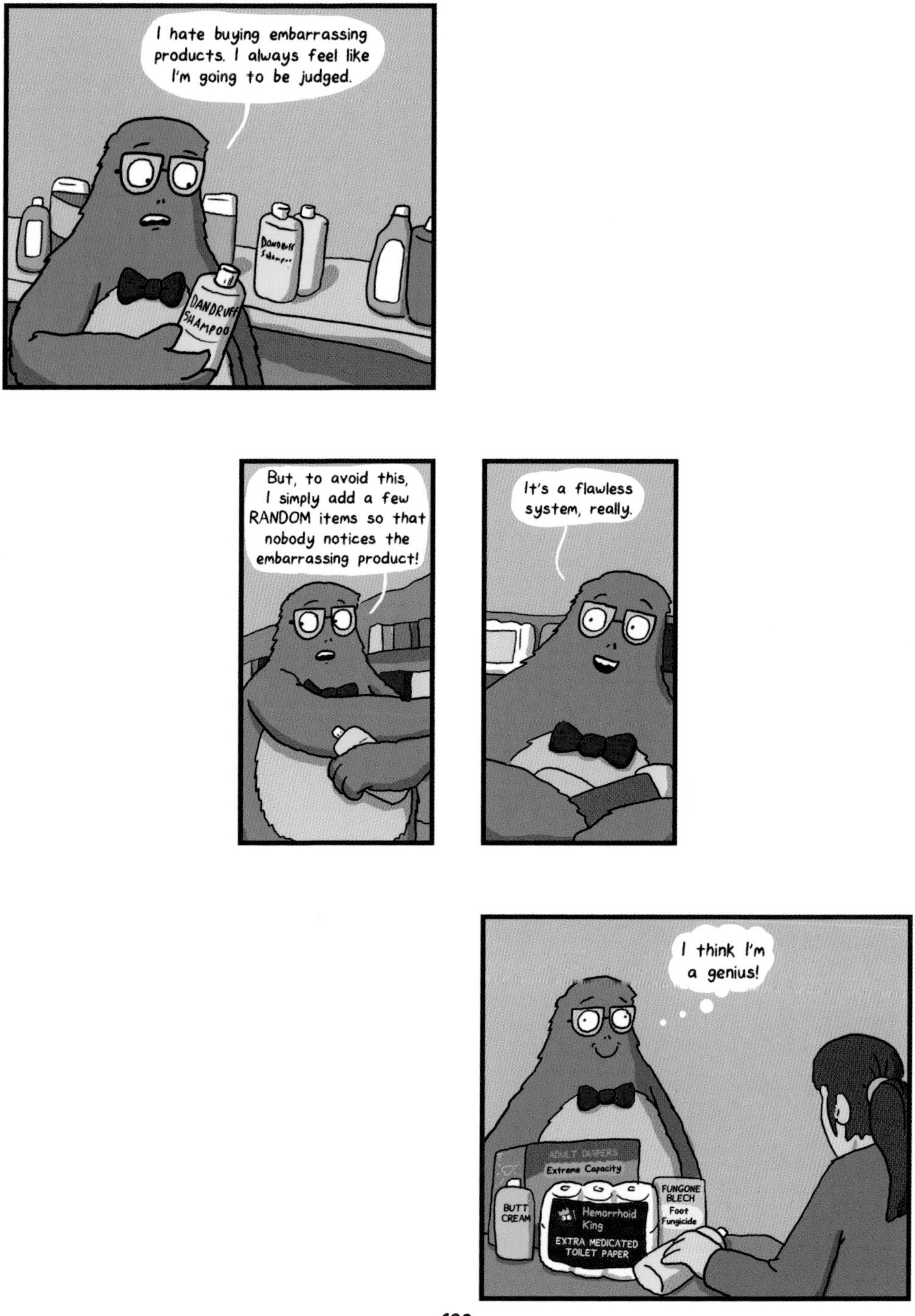
I hate buying embarrassing products. I always feel like I'm going to be judged.
DANDRUFF SHAMPOO
But, to avoid this, I simply add a few RANDOM items so that nobody notices the embarrassing product!
It's a flawless system, really.
I think I'm a genius!
ADULT DIAPERS
Extreme Capacity
BUTT CREAM
Hemorrhoid King
EXTRA MEDICATED TOILET PAPER
FUNGONE BLECH
Foot Fungicide

Art is Personal

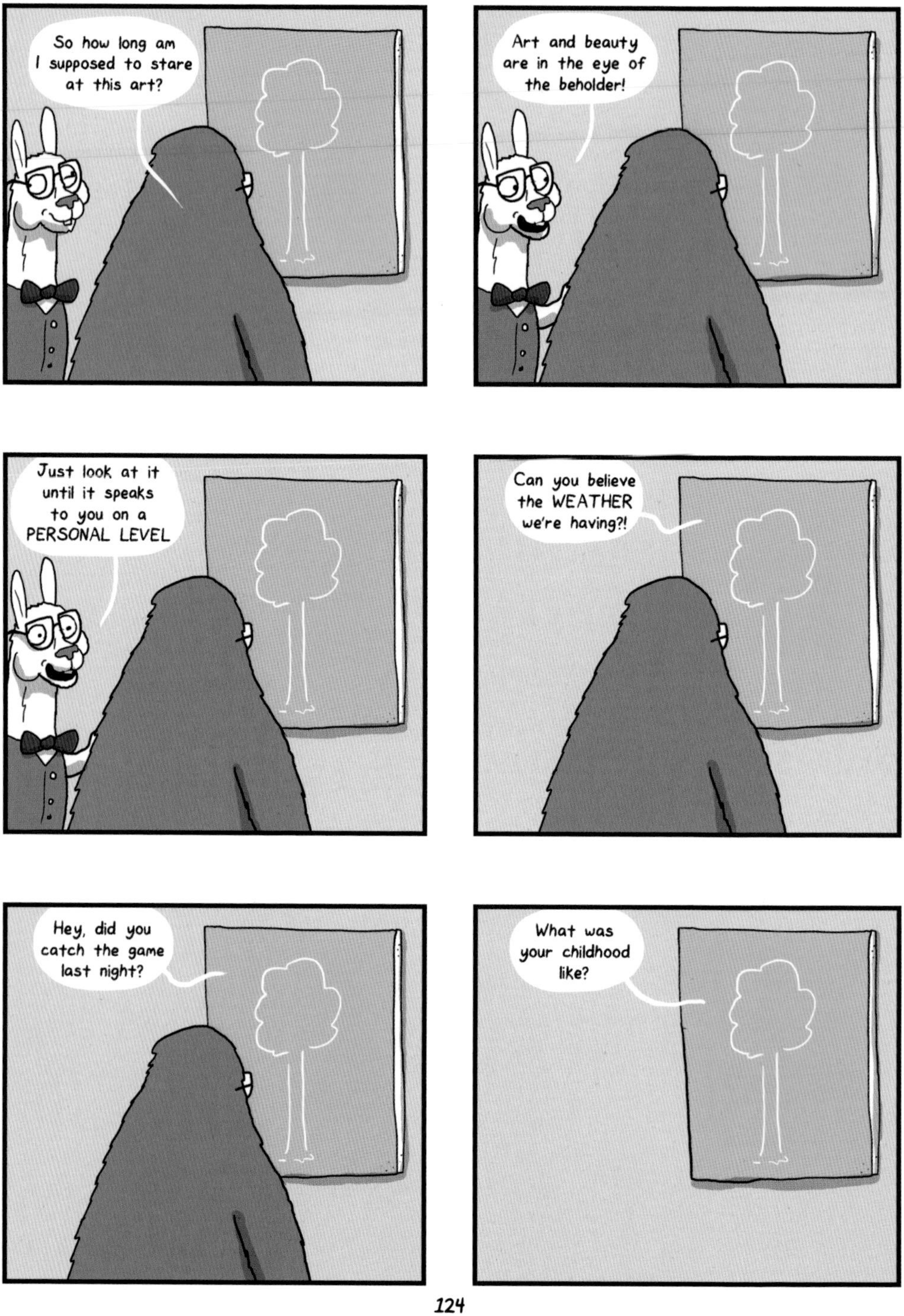

So how long am I supposed to stare at this art?
Art and beauty are in the eye of the beholder!
Just look at it until it speaks to you on a PERSONAL LEVEL
Can you believe the WEATHER we're having?!
Hey, did you catch the game last night?
What was your childhood like?

The Overthinker

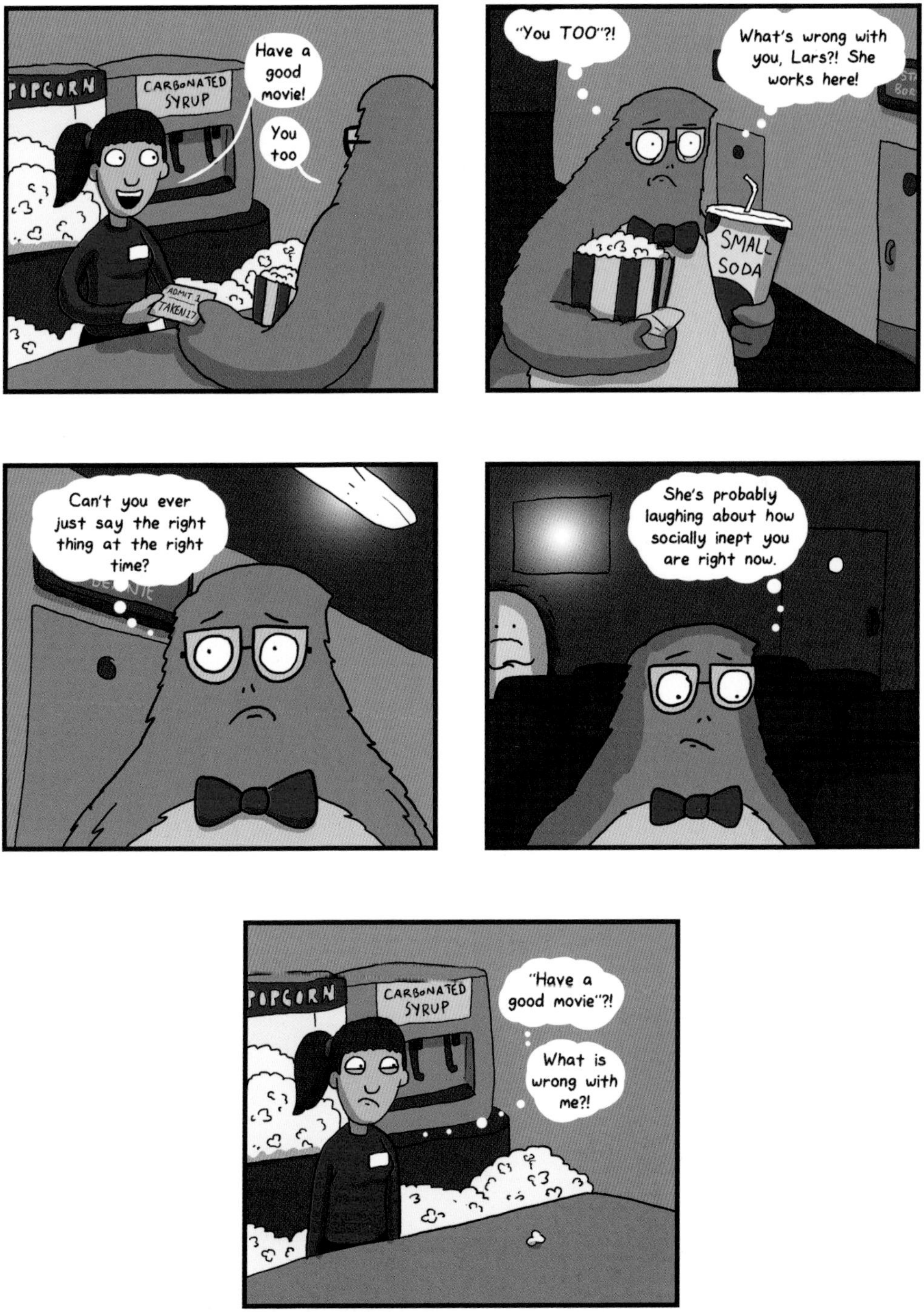
POPCORN
CARBONATED SYRUP
Have a good movie!
You too
"You TOO"?!
What's wrong with you, Lars?! She works here!
SMALL SODA
Can't you ever just say the right thing at the right time?
She's probably laughing about how socially inept you are right now.
POPCORN
CARBONATED SYRUP
"Have a good movie"?!
What is wrong with me?!

Wrong

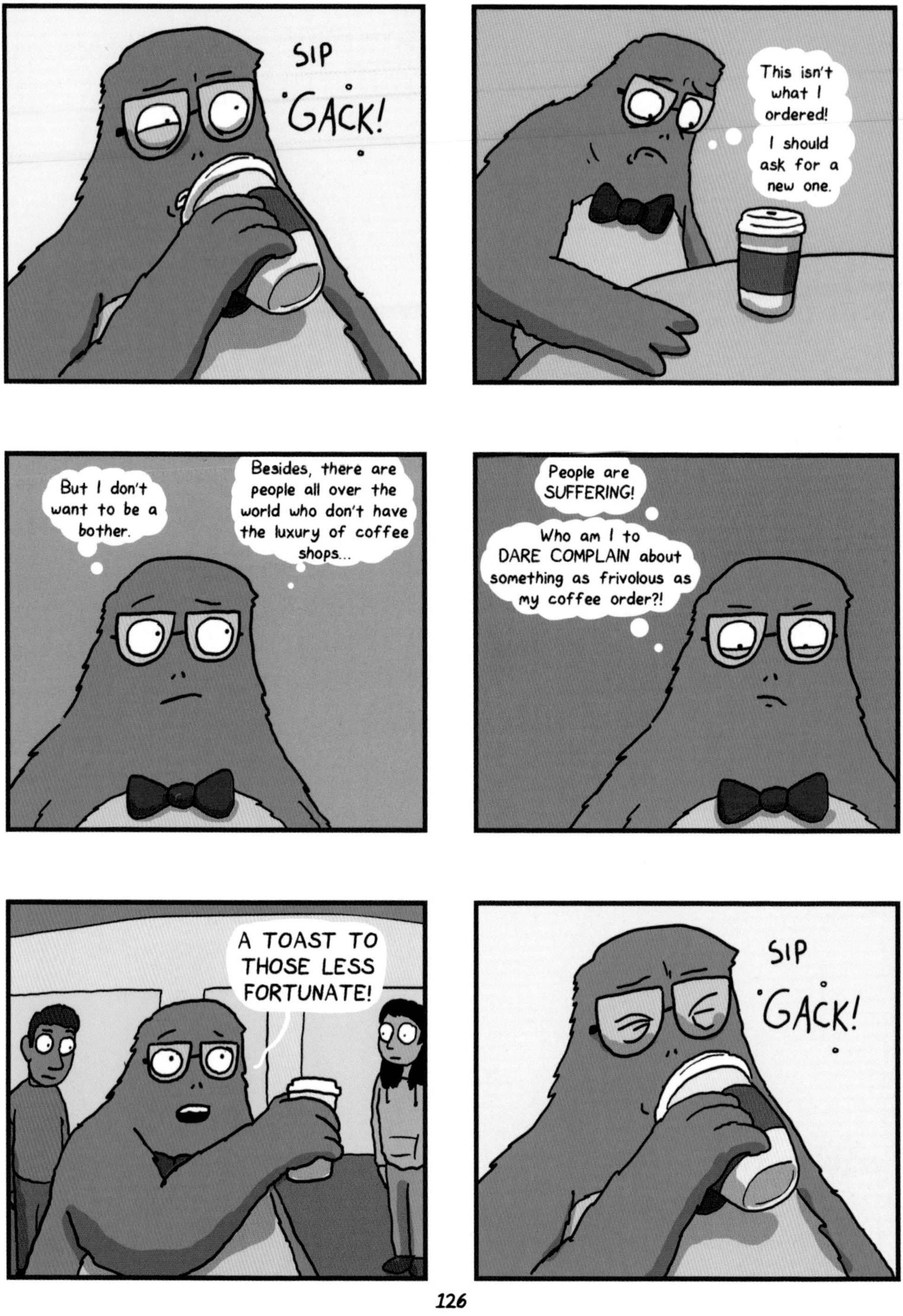
SIP
GACK!
This isn't what I ordered!
I should ask for a new one.
But I don't want to be a bother.
Besides, there are people all over the world who don't have the luxury of coffee shops...
People are SUFFERING!
Who am I to DARE COMPLAIN about something as frivolous as my coffee order?!
A TOAST TO THOSE LESS FORTUNATE!
SIP
GACK!

The Personal Bubble

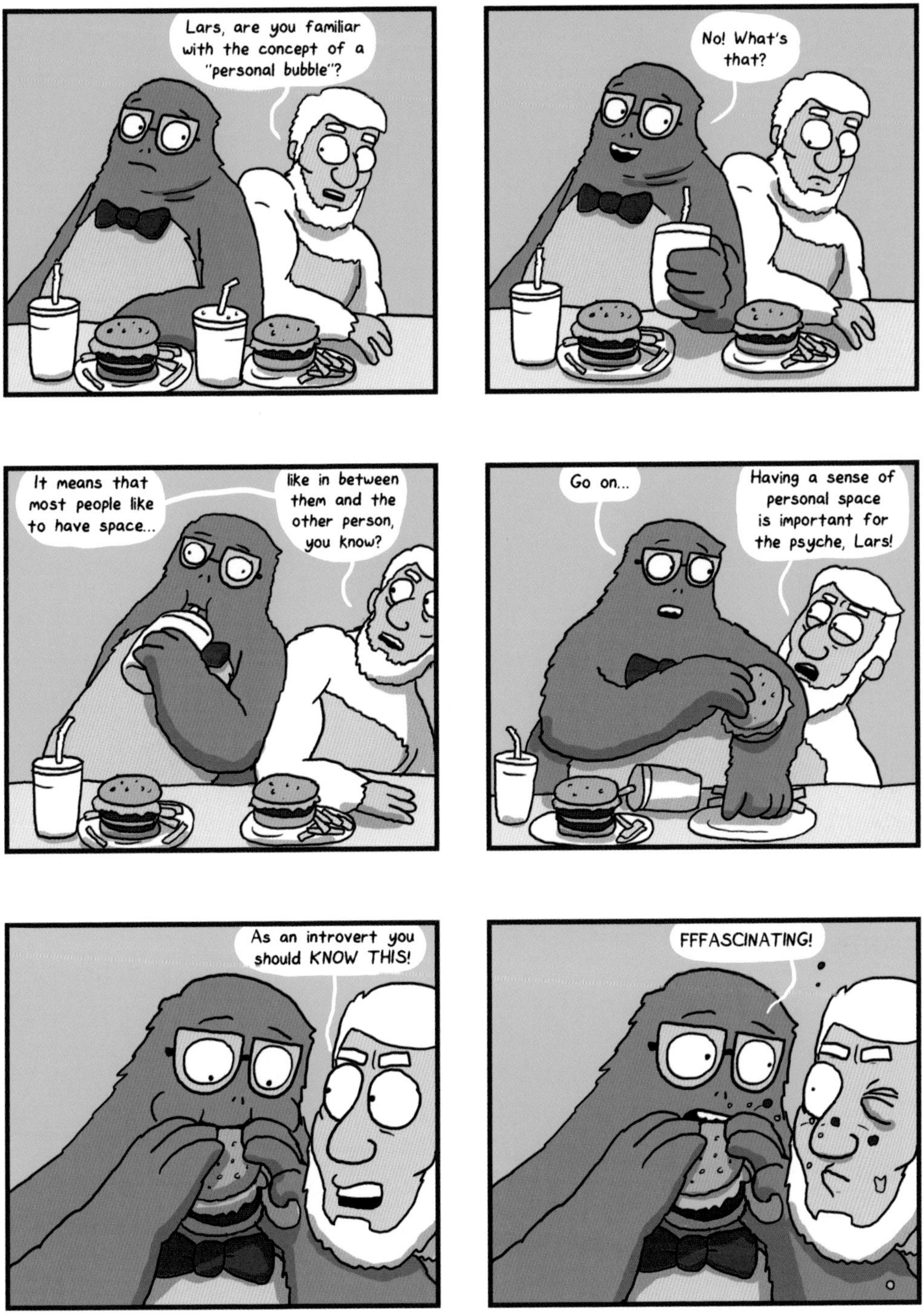

Lars, are you familiar with the concept of a "personal bubble"?
No! What's that?
It means that most people like to have space...
like in between them and the other person, you know?
Go on...
Having a sense of personal space is important for the psyche, Lars!
As an introvert you should KNOW THIS!
FFFASCINATING!

The Far Bounce

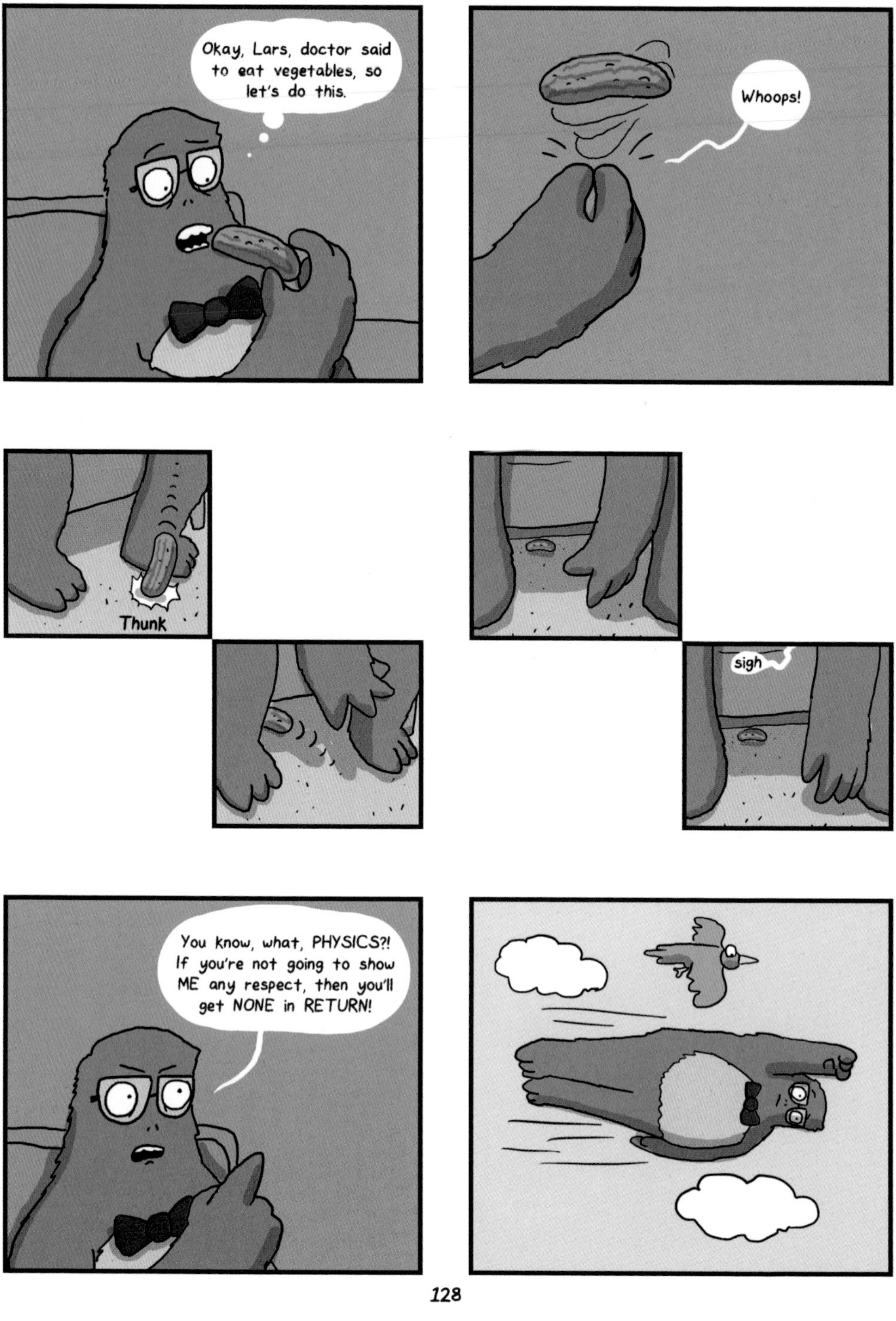
Okay, Lars, doctor said to eat vegetables, so let's do this.
Whoops!
Thunk
sigh
You know, what, PHYSICS?! If you're not going to show ME any respect, then you'll get NONE in RETURN!

Politeness

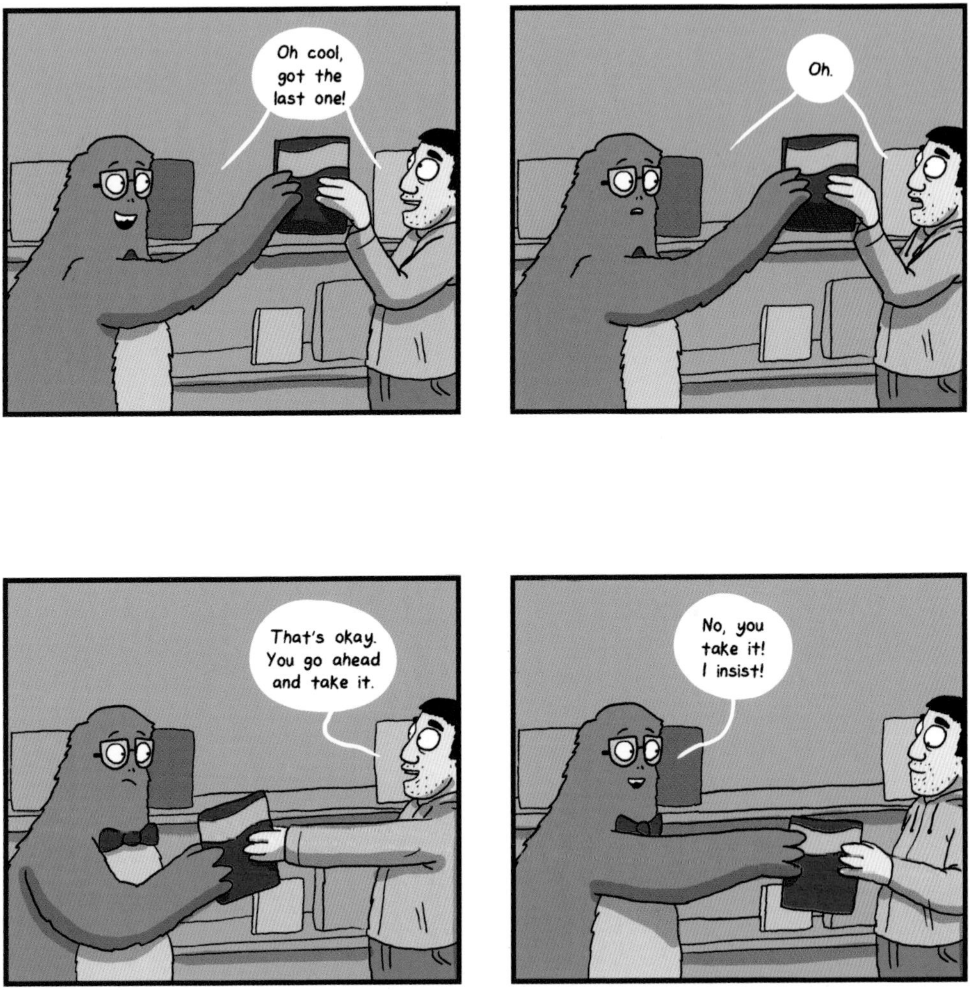
Oh cool, got the last one!
Oh.
That's okay. You go ahead and take it.
No, you take it! I insist!

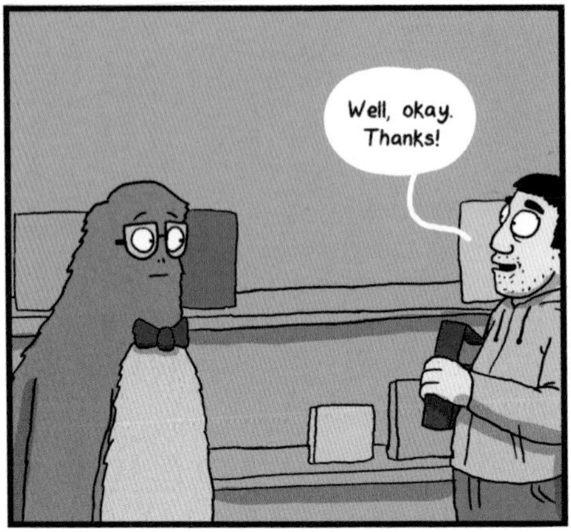
Well, okay.
Thanks!

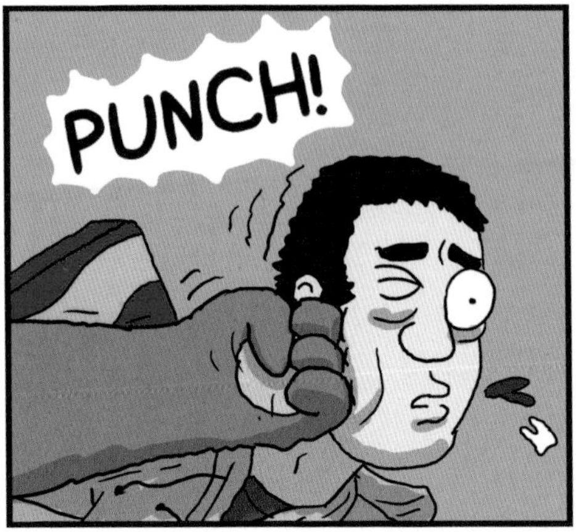
PUNCH!

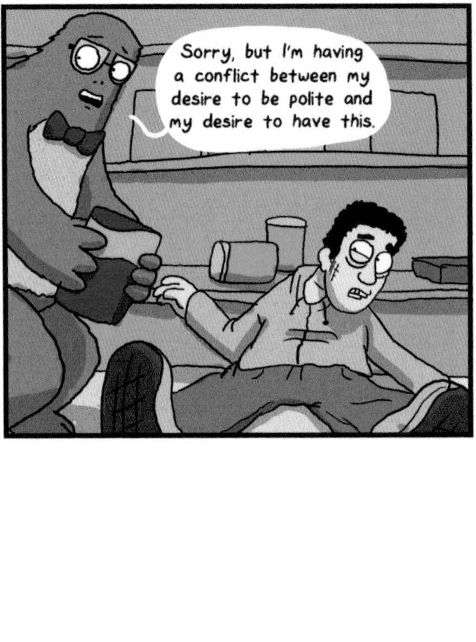
Sorry, but I'm having a conflict between my desire to be polite and my desire to have this.

One Small Step

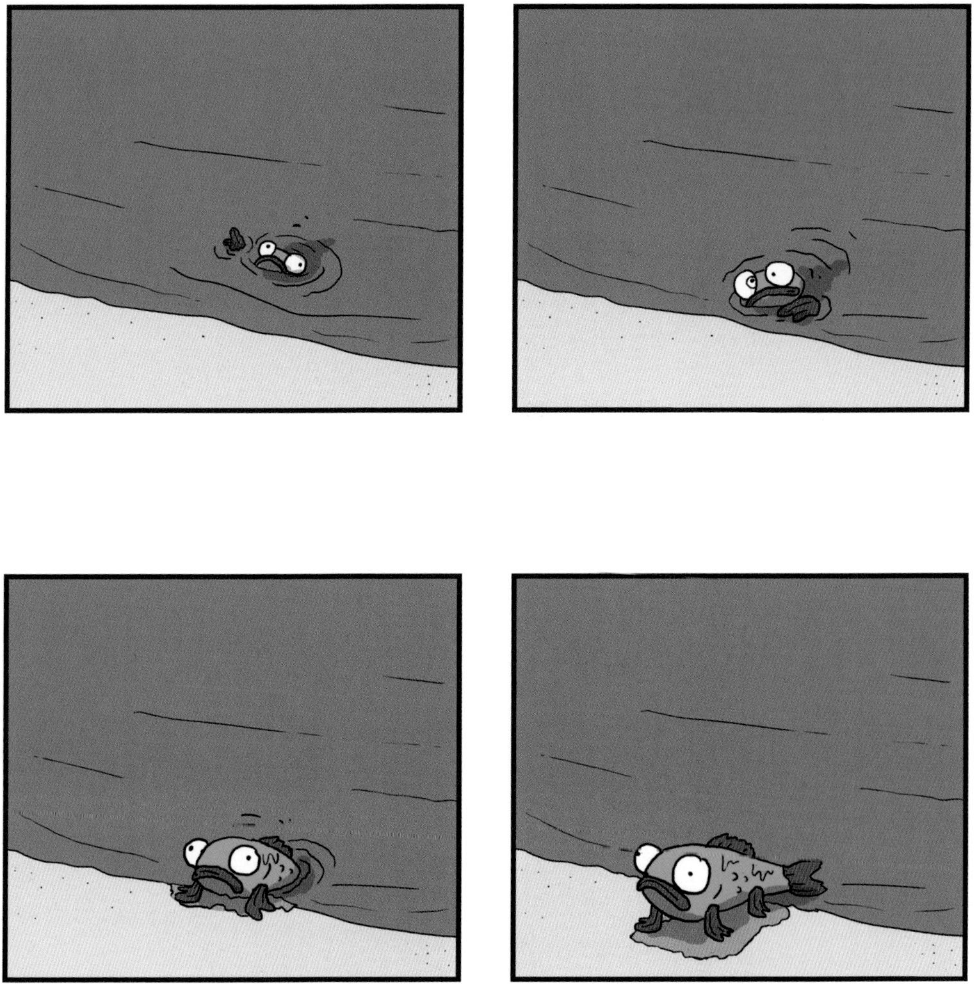

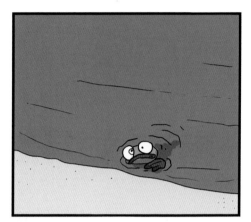

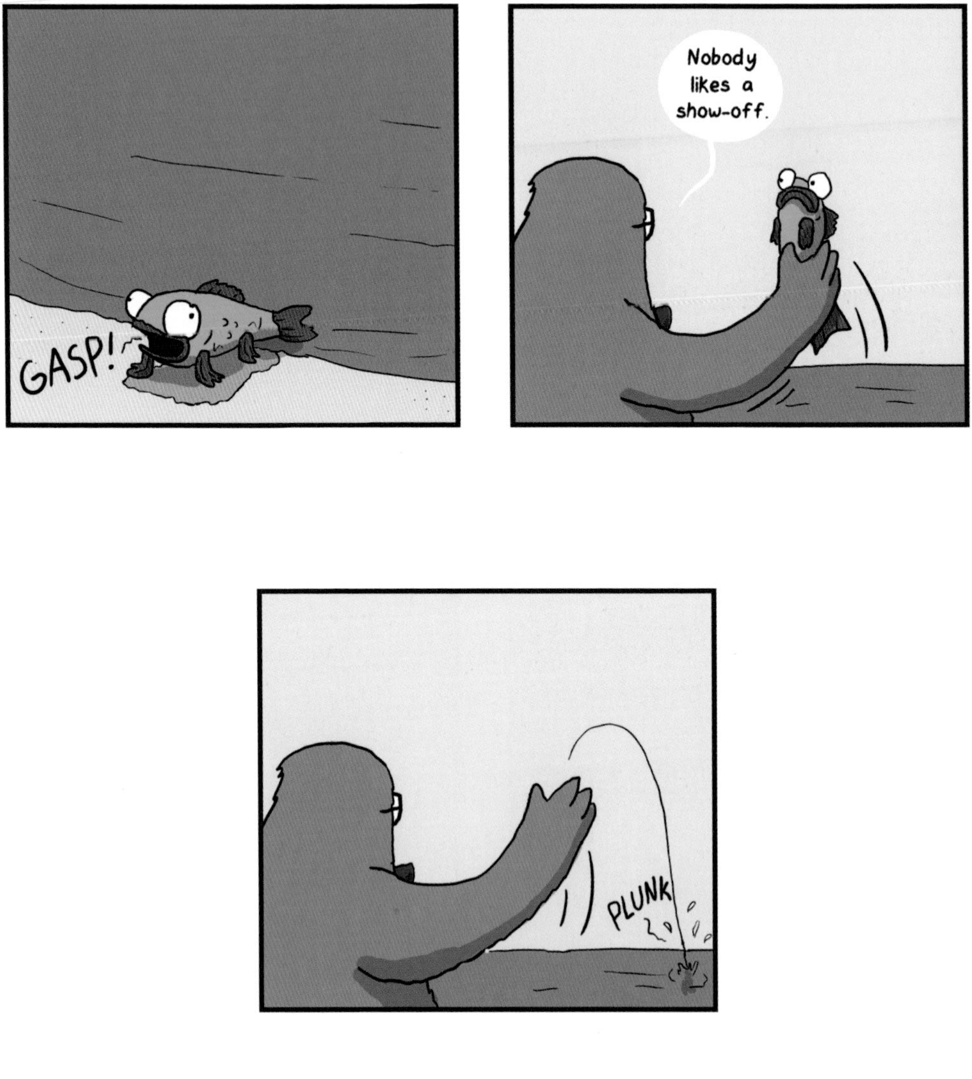
GASP!
Nobody likes a show-off.
PLUNK

Can't We All Just Get Along?

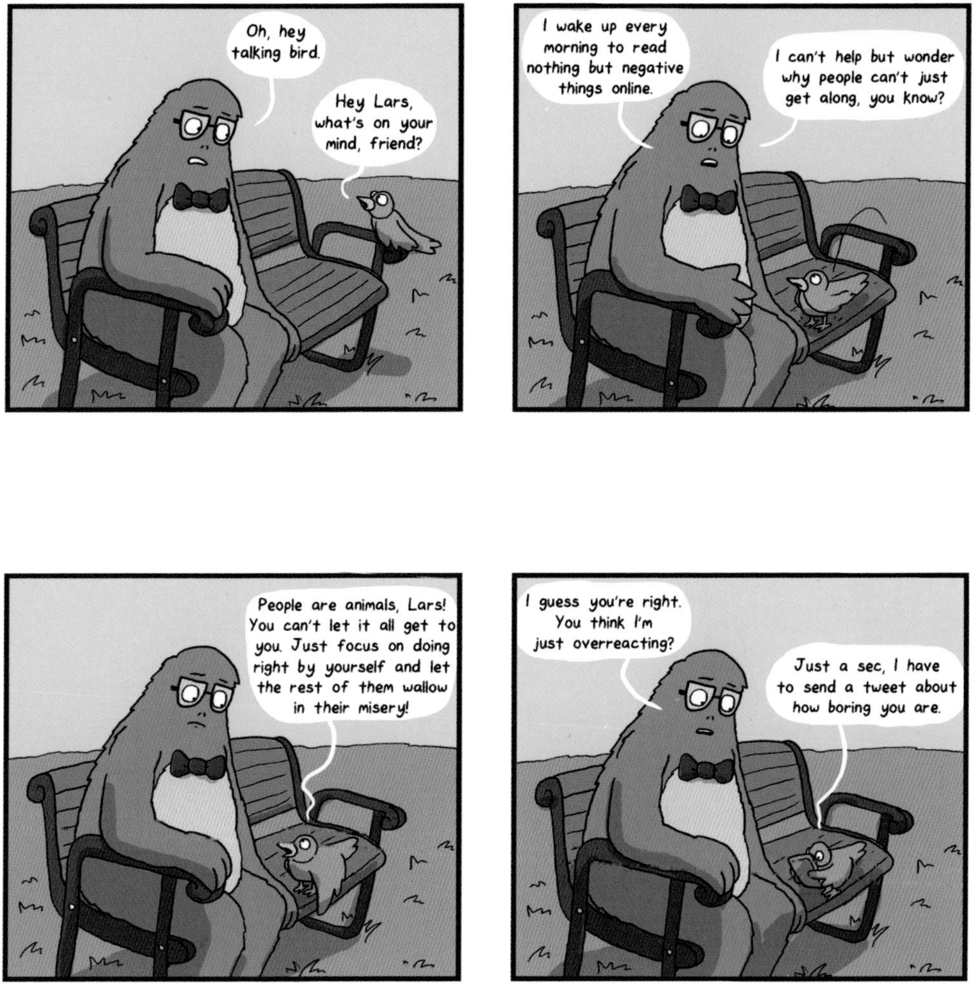
Oh, hey talking bird.
Hey Lars, what's on your mind, friend?
I wake up every morning to read nothing but negative things online.
I can't help but wonder why people can't just get along, you know?
People are animals, Lars! You can't let it all get to you. Just focus on doing right by yourself and let the rest of them wallow in their misery!
I guess you're right. You think I'm just overreacting?
Just a sec, I have to send a tweet about how boring you are.

No Where to Go But Up!

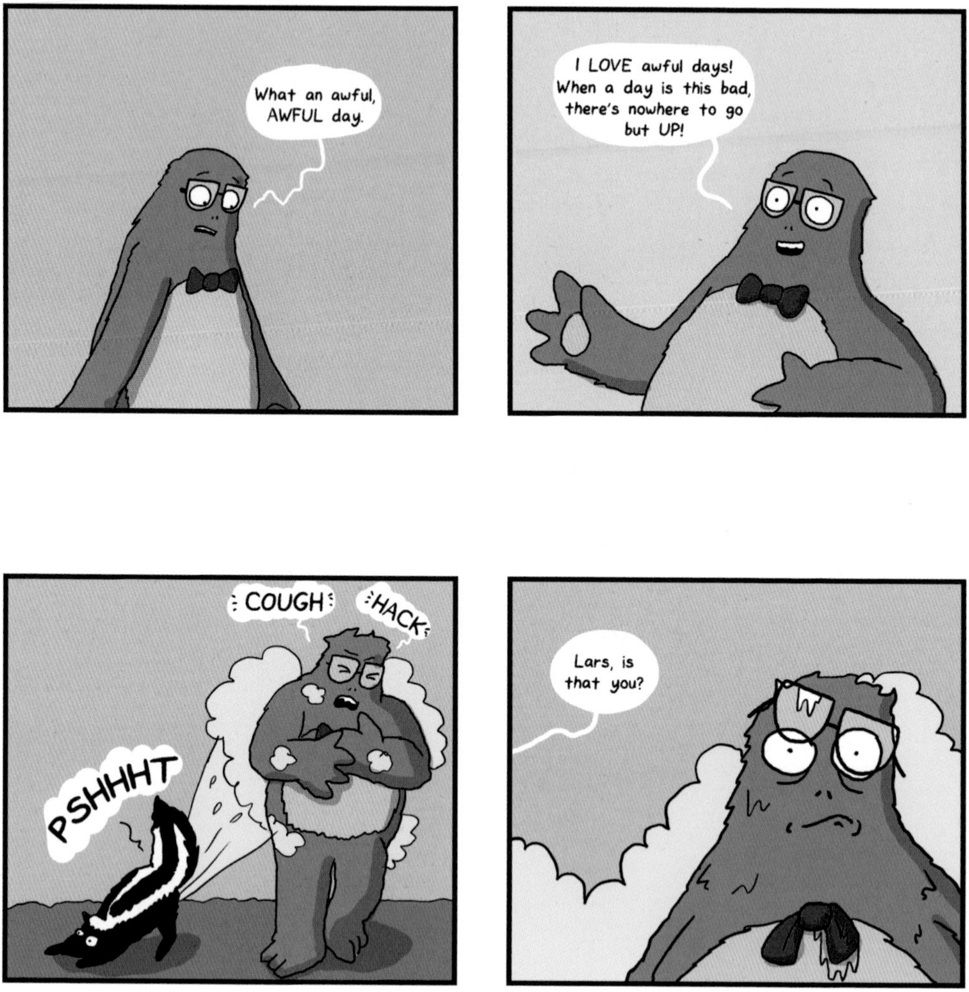
What an awful, AWFUL day.
I LOVE awful days! When a day is this bad, there's nowhere to go but UP!
COUGH
HACK
PSHHHT
Lars, is that you?

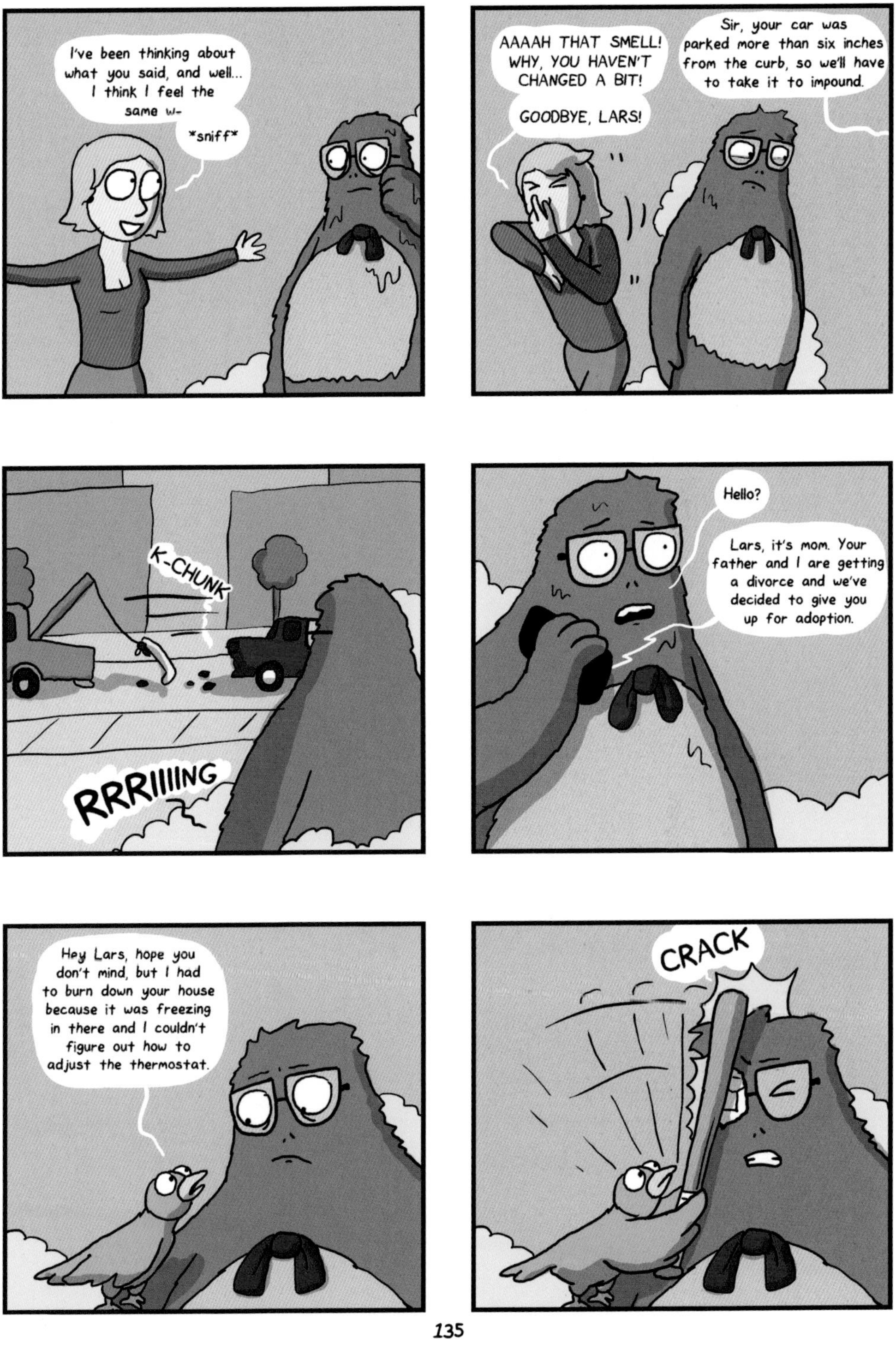
I've been thinking about what you said, and well... I think I feel the same w-
sniff
AAAAH THAT SMELL! WHY, YOU HAVEN'T CHANGED A BIT!
GOODBYE, LARS!
Sir, your car was parked more than six inches from the curb, so we'll have to take it to impound.
K-CHUNK
RRRIIIING
Hello?
Lars, it's mom. Your father and I are getting a divorce and we've decided to give you up for adoption.
Hey Lars, hope you don't mind, but I had to burn down your house because it was freezing in there and I couldn't figure out how to adjust the thermostat.
CRACK

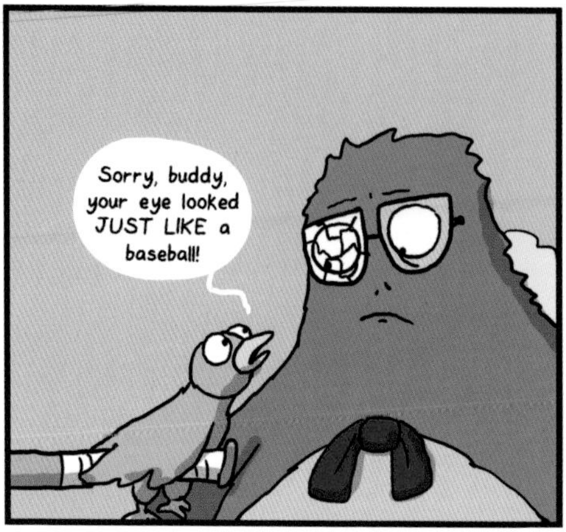
Sorry, buddy, your eye looked JUST LIKE a baseball!
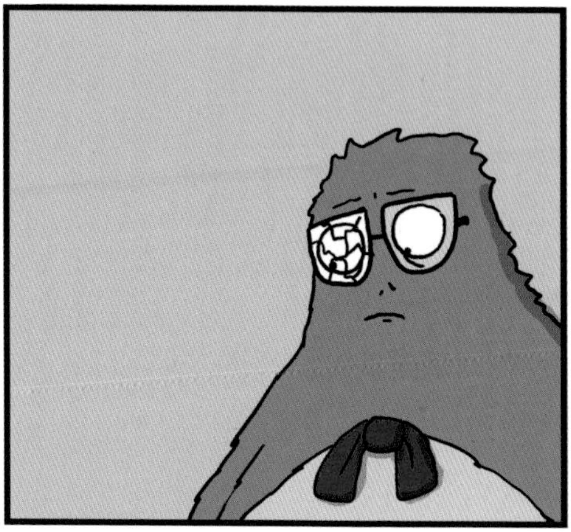
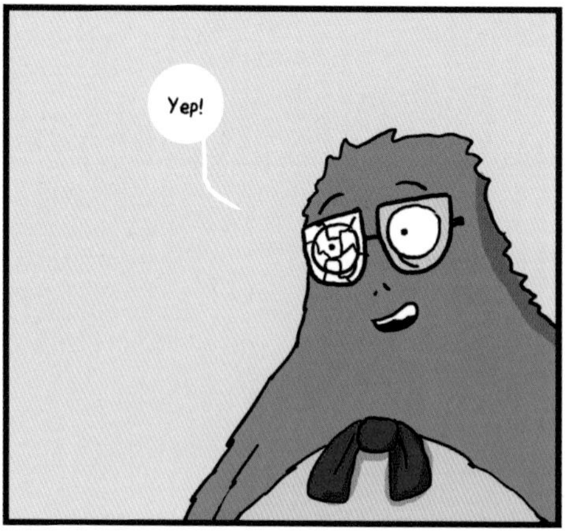
Yep!
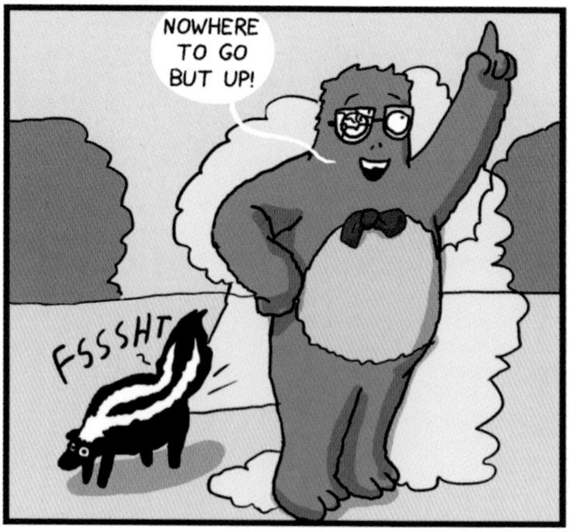
NOWHERE TO GO BUT UP!
FSSSHT

Alien Life

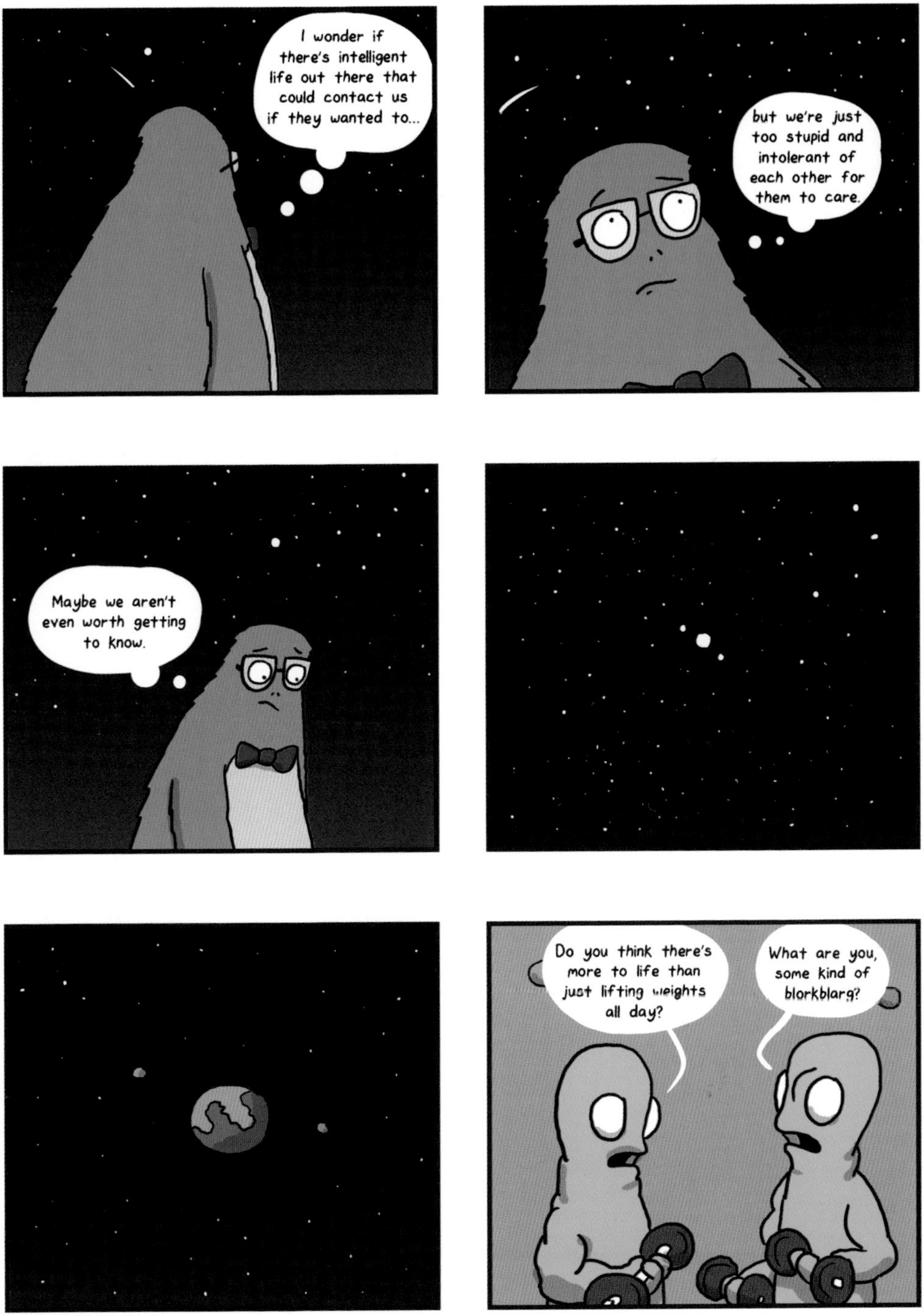

I wonder if there's intelligent life out there that could contact us if they wanted to...
but we're just too stupid and intolerant of each other for them to care.
Maybe we aren't even worth getting to know.
Do you think there's more to life than just lifting weights all day?
What are you, some kind of blorkblarg?

Halloween

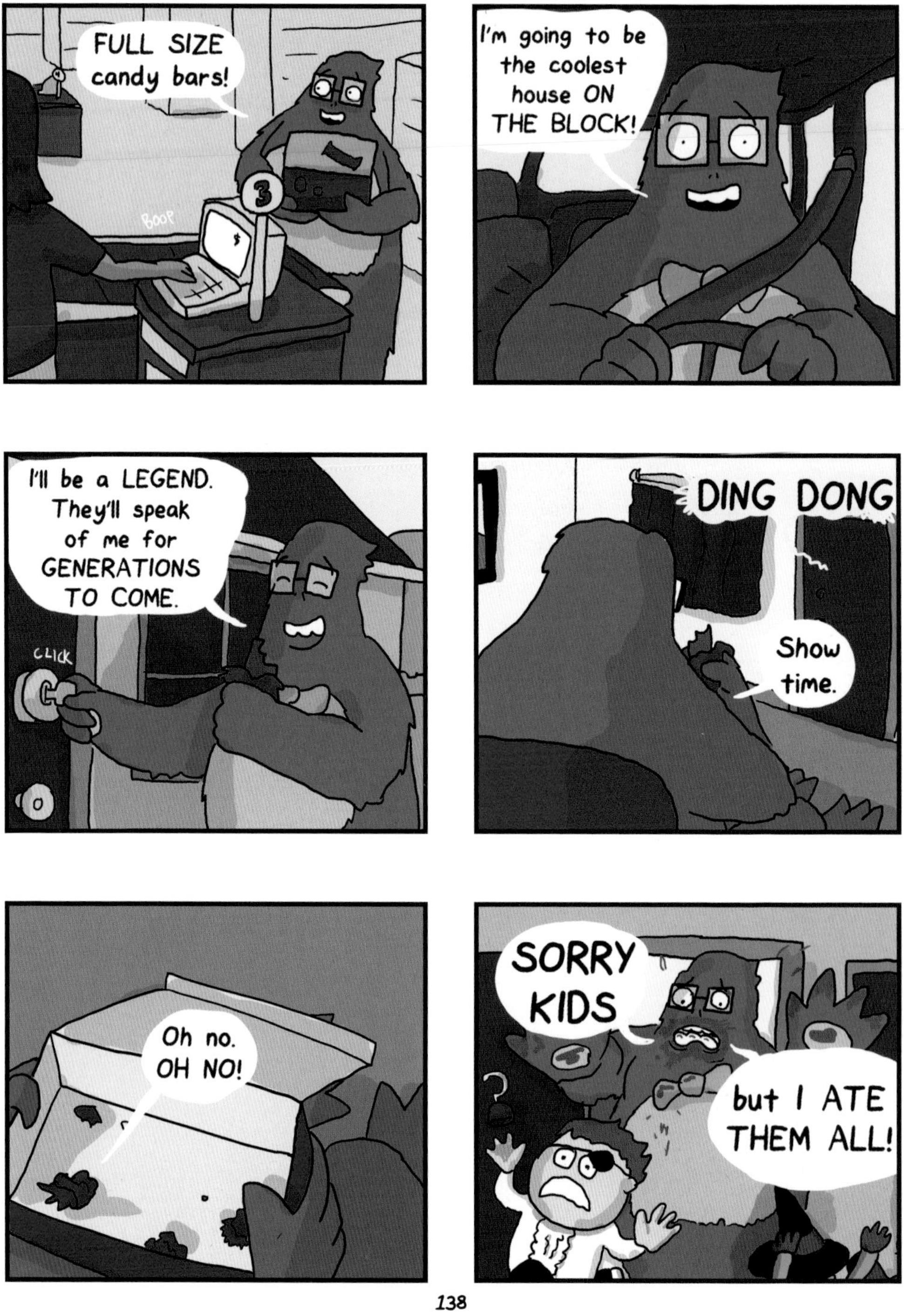
FULL SIZE candy bars!
3
BOOP
I'm going to be the coolest house ON THE BLOCK!
I'll be a LEGEND. They'll speak of me for GENERATIONS TO COME.
CLICK
DING DONG
Show time.
Oh no. OH NO!
SORRY KIDS
but I ATE THEM ALL!

Morning Coffee

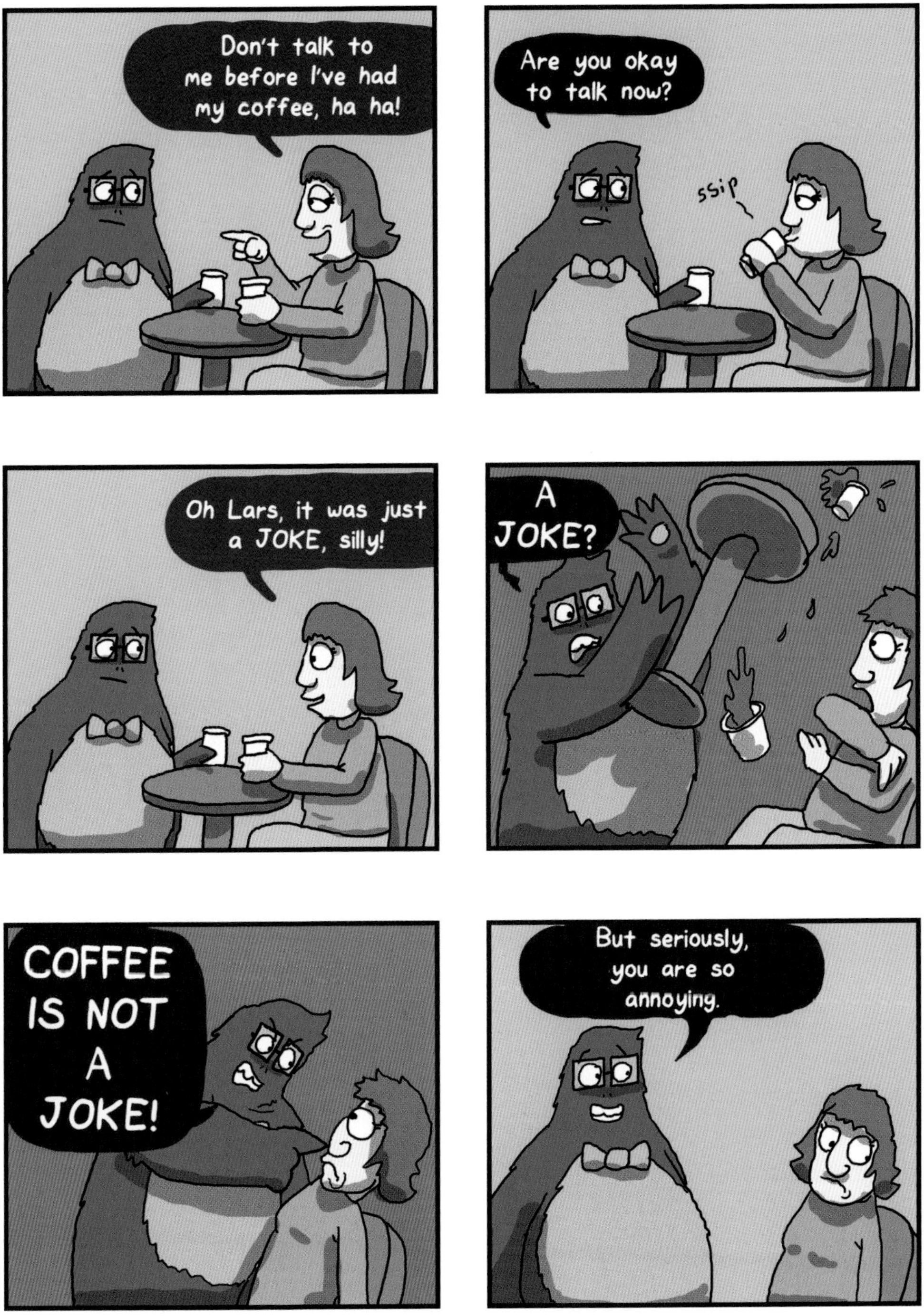
Don't talk to me before I've had my coffee, ha ha!
Are you okay to talk now?
ssip
Oh Lars, it was just a JOKE, silly!
A JOKE?
COFFEE IS NOT A JOKE!
But seriously, you are so annoying.

New Dog

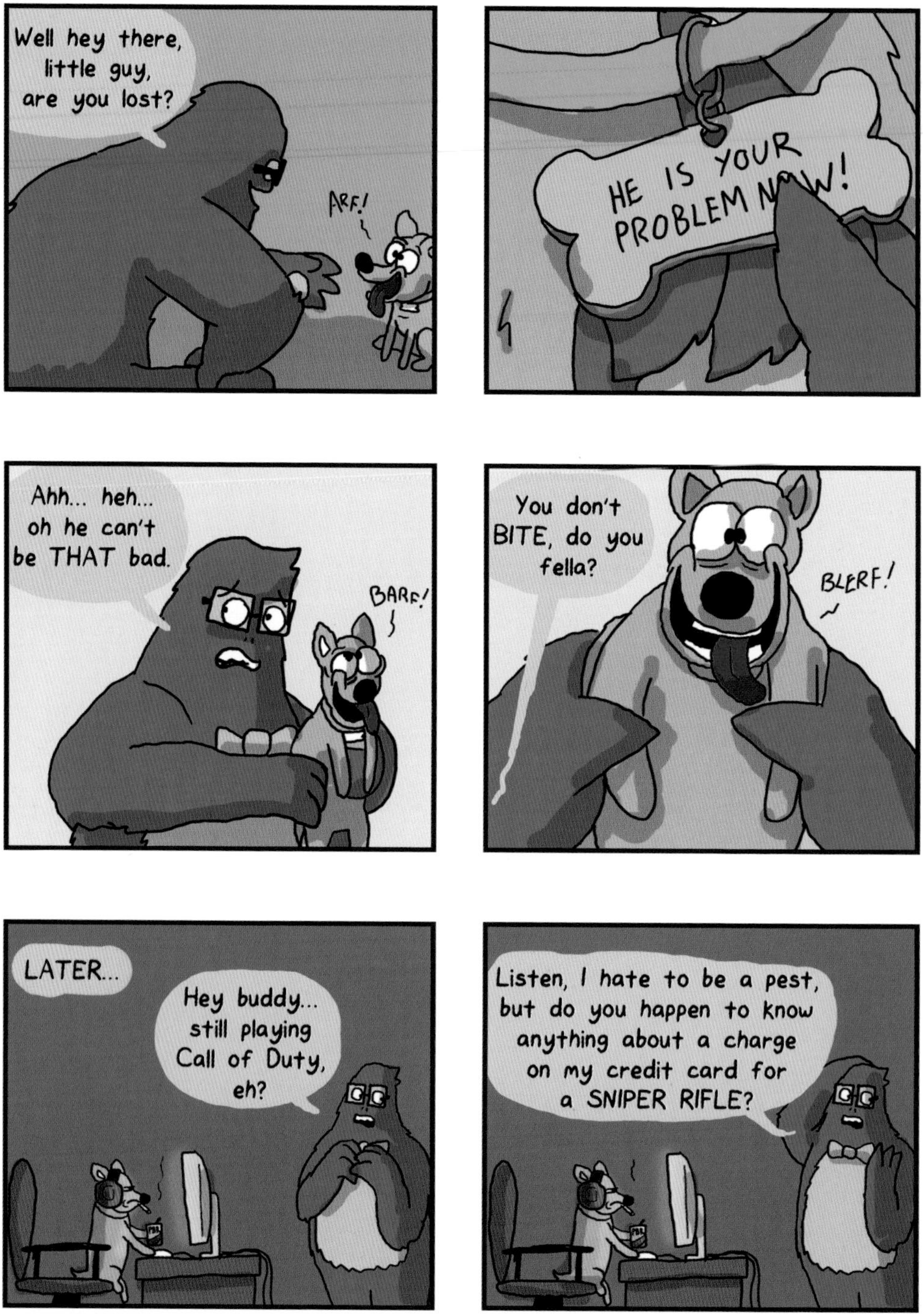
Well hey there, little guy, are you lost?
ARF!
HE IS YOUR PROBLEM NOW!
Ahh... heh... oh he can't be THAT bad.
BARF!
You don't BITE, do you fella?
BLERF!
LATER...
Hey buddy... still playing Call of Duty, eh?
Listen, I hate to be a pest, but do you happen to know anything about a charge on my credit card for a SNIPER RIFLE?

Christmas Decorations

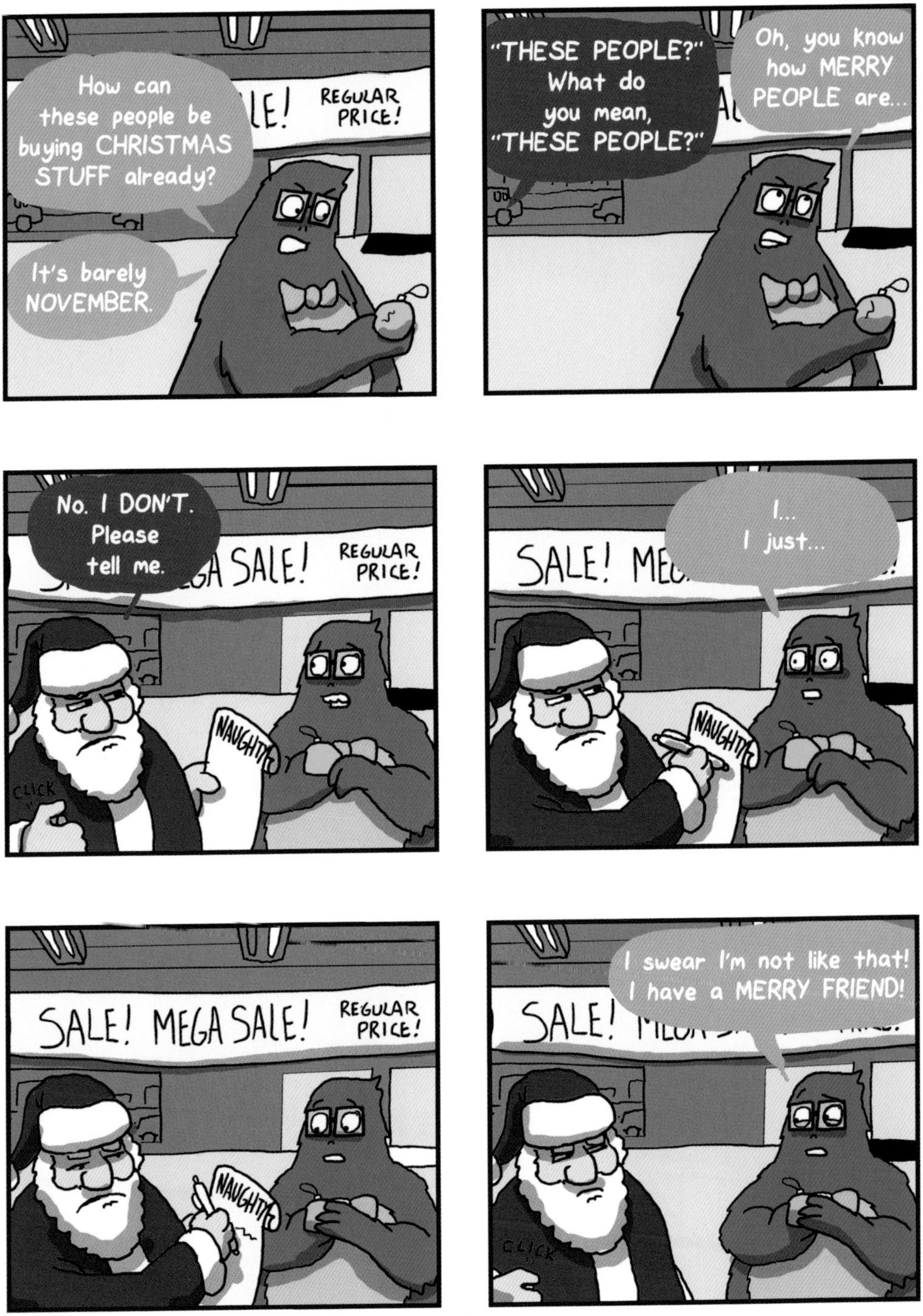
How can these people be buying CHRISTMAS STUFF already?
It's barely NOVEMBER.
REGULAR PRICE!
"THESE PEOPLE?" What do you mean, "THESE PEOPLE?"
Oh, you know how MERRY PEOPLE are...
No. I DON'T. Please tell me.
SALE! REGULAR PRICE!
NAUGHTY
CLICK
I... I just...
SALE!
NAUGHTY
SALE! MEGA SALE! REGULAR PRICE!
NAUGHTY
I swear I'm not like that! I have a MERRY FRIEND!
SALE!
CLICK

The Interview

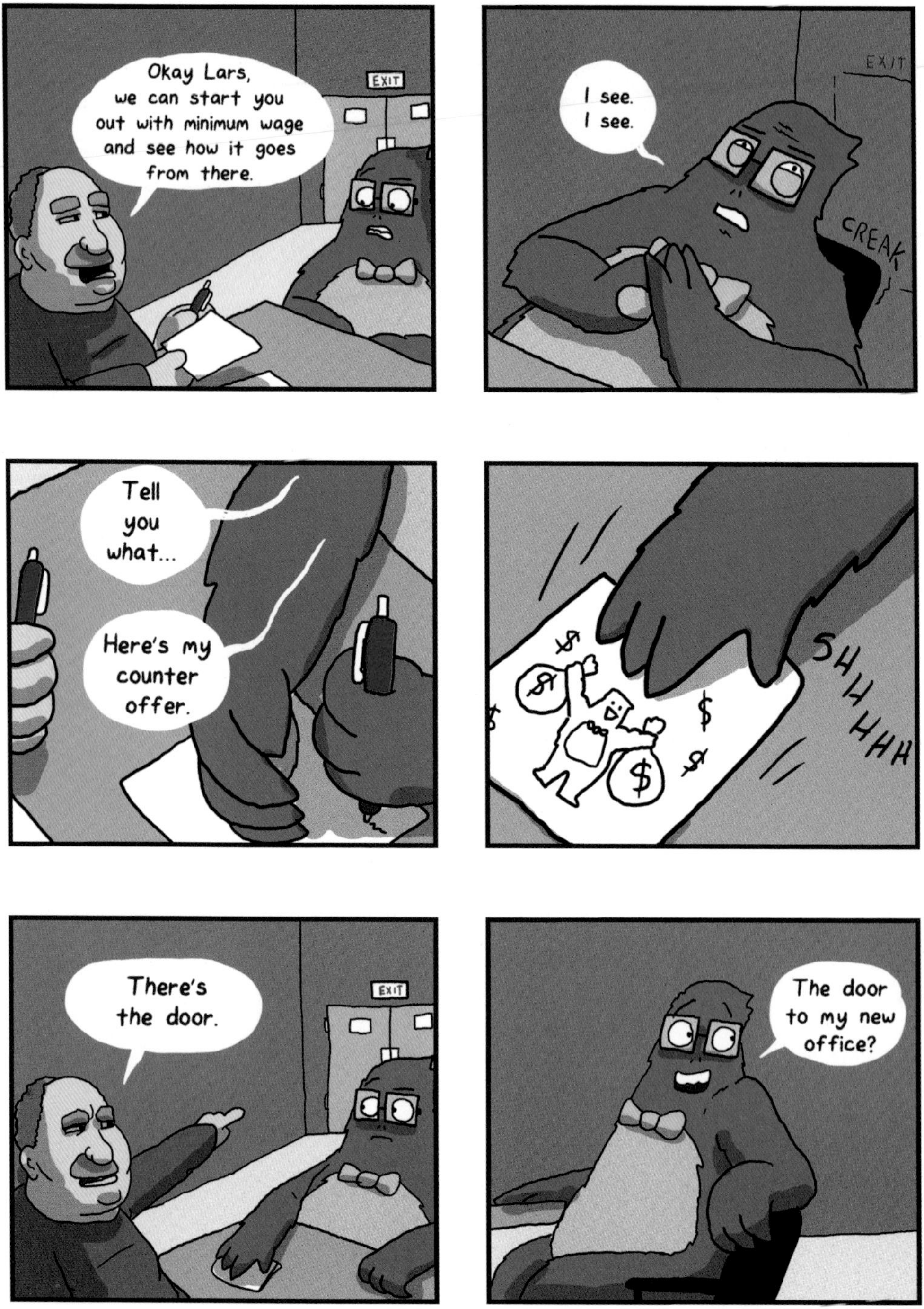
Okay Lars, we can start you out with minimum wage and see how it goes from there.
EXIT
EXIT
I see. I see.
CREAK
Tell you what...
Here's my counter offer.
SHHHHHH
EXIT
There's the door.
The door to my new office?

Turducken

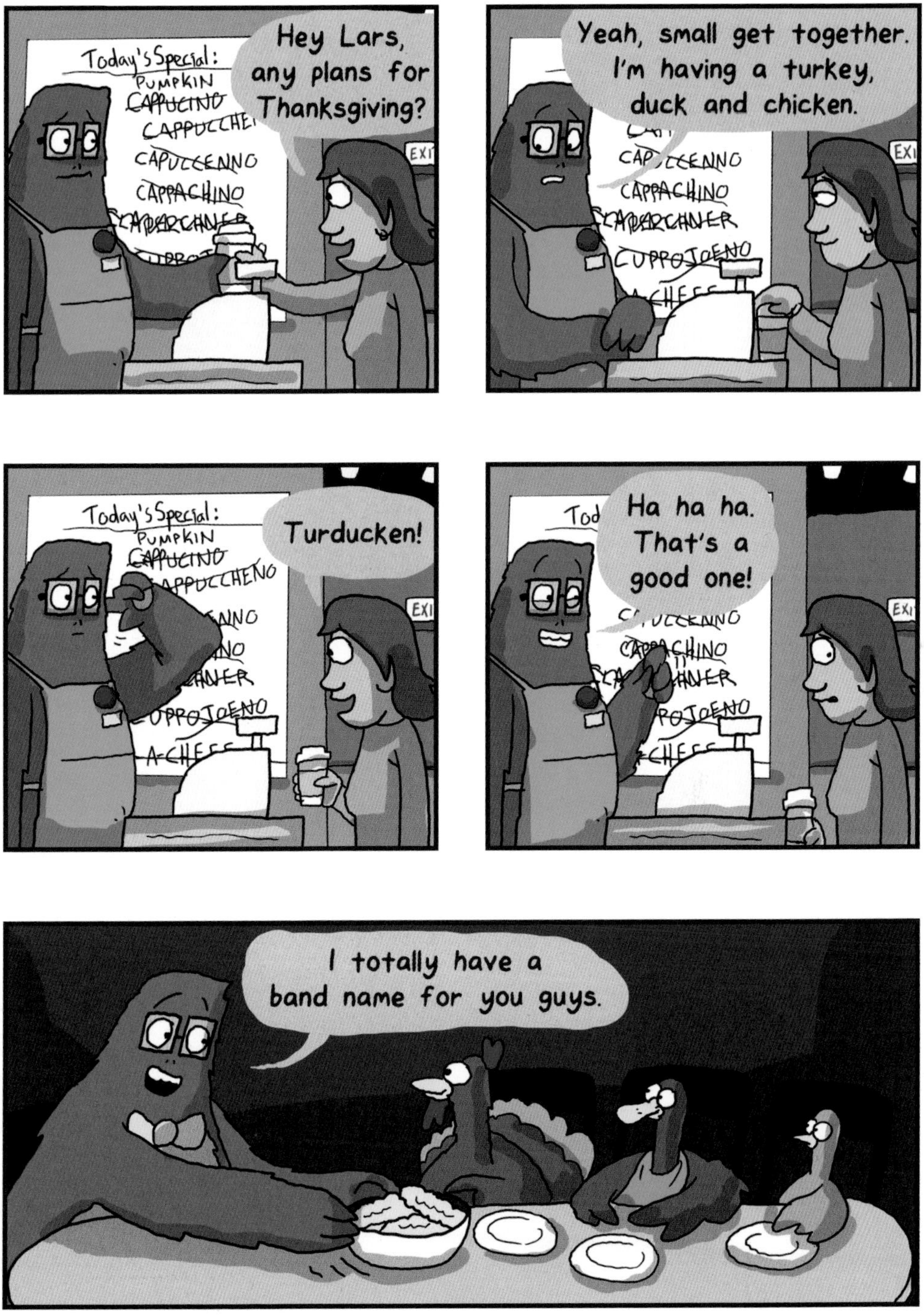
Today's Special: PUMPKIN
Hey Lars, any plans for Thanksgiving?
Yeah, small get together. I'm having a turkey, duck and chicken.
Turducken!
Ha ha ha. That's a good one!
I totally have a band name for you guys.

Favorite Movies

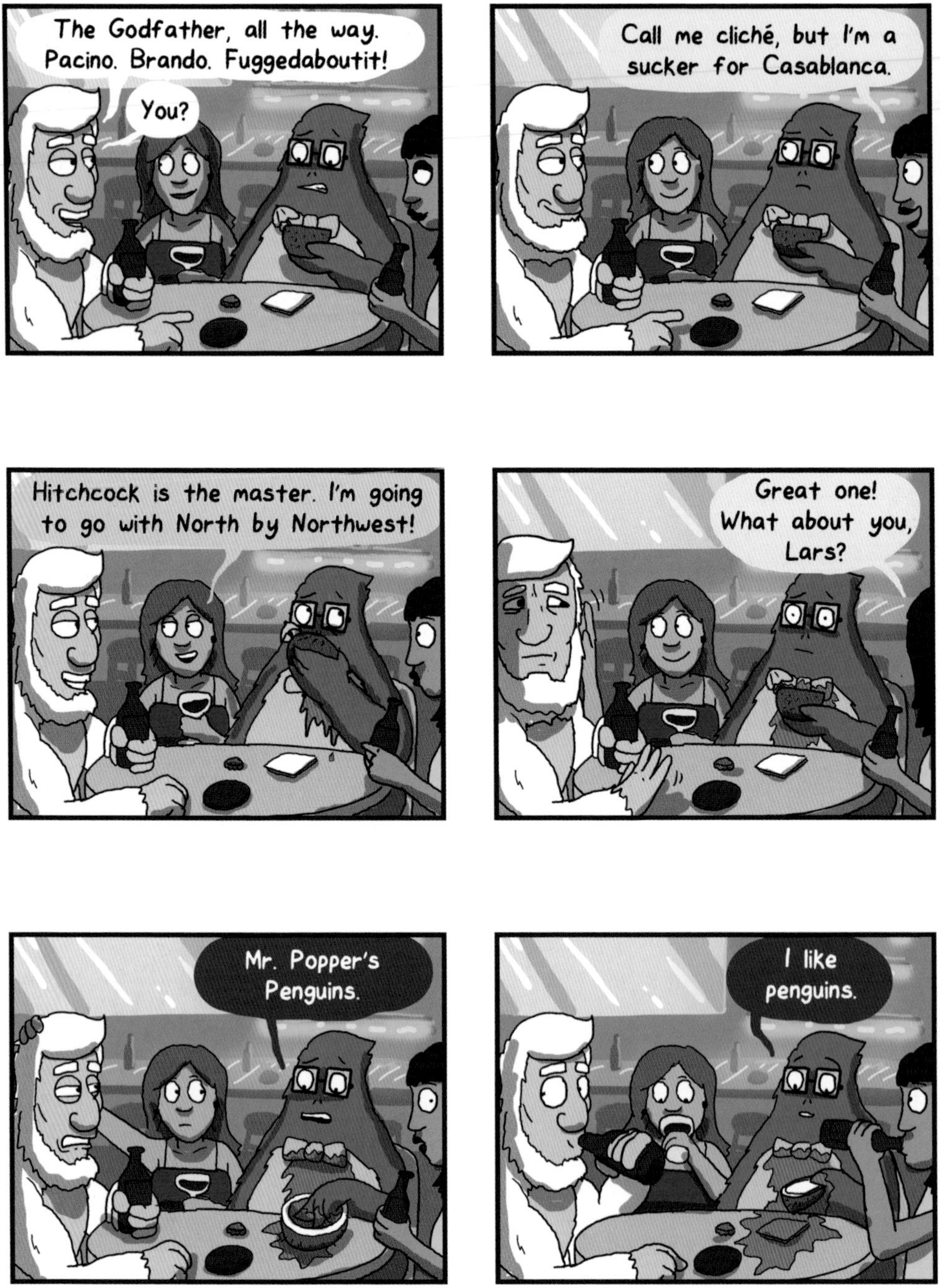

The Godfather, all the way. Pacino. Brando. Fuggedaboutit!
You?
Call me cliché, but I'm a sucker for Casablanca.
Hitchcock is the master. I'm going to go with North by Northwest!
Great one! What about you, Lars?
Mr. Popper's Penguins.
I like penguins.

Crying

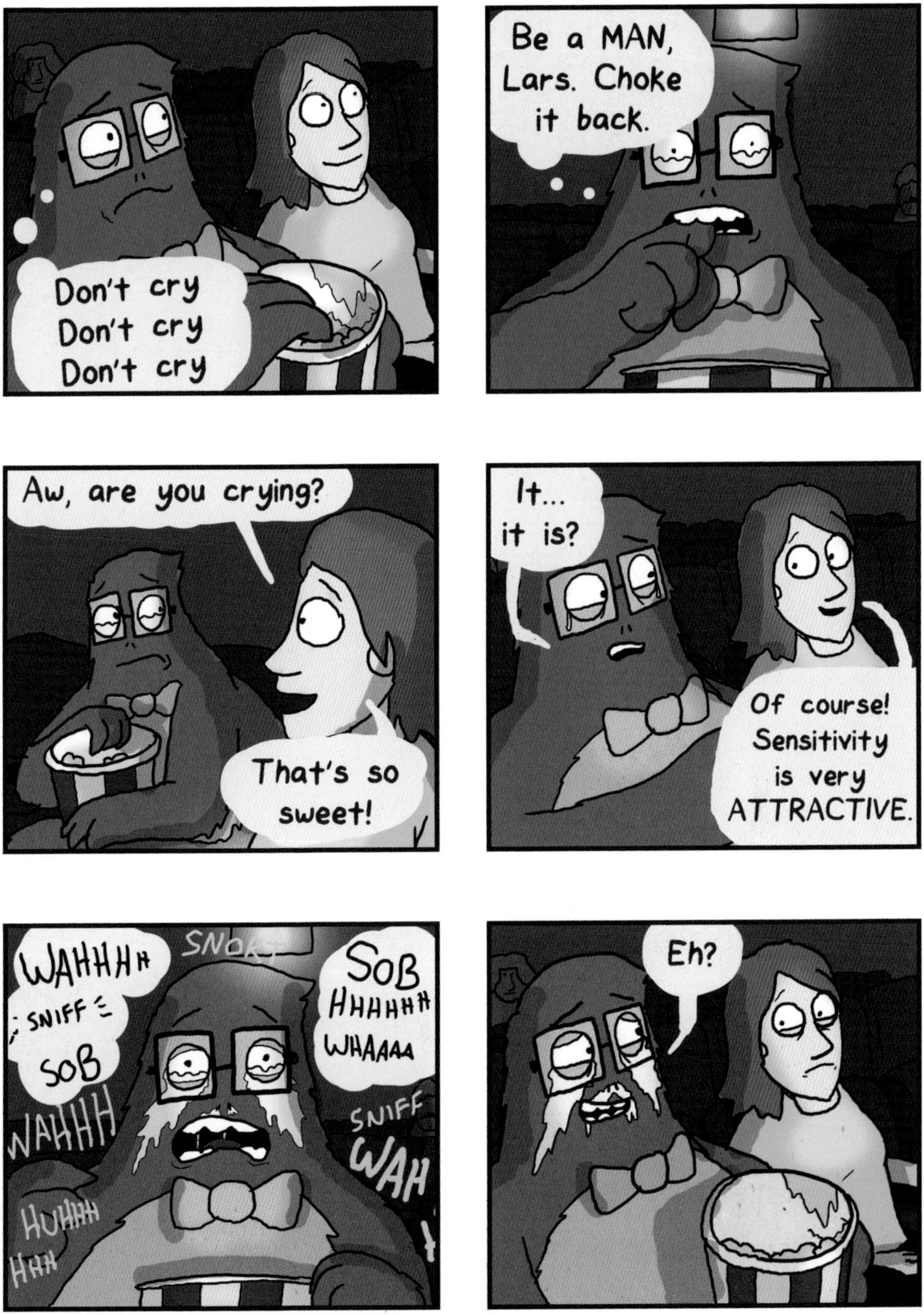
Don't cry
Don't cry
Don't cry
Be a MAN, Lars. Choke it back.
Aw, are you crying?
That's so sweet!
It... it is?
Of course! Sensitivity is very ATTRACTIVE.
WAHHHHH
SNIFF
SOB
WAHHH
HUHHH
HHH
SOB
HHHHHH
WHAAAA
SNIFF
WAH
Eh?

Coffee Addiction

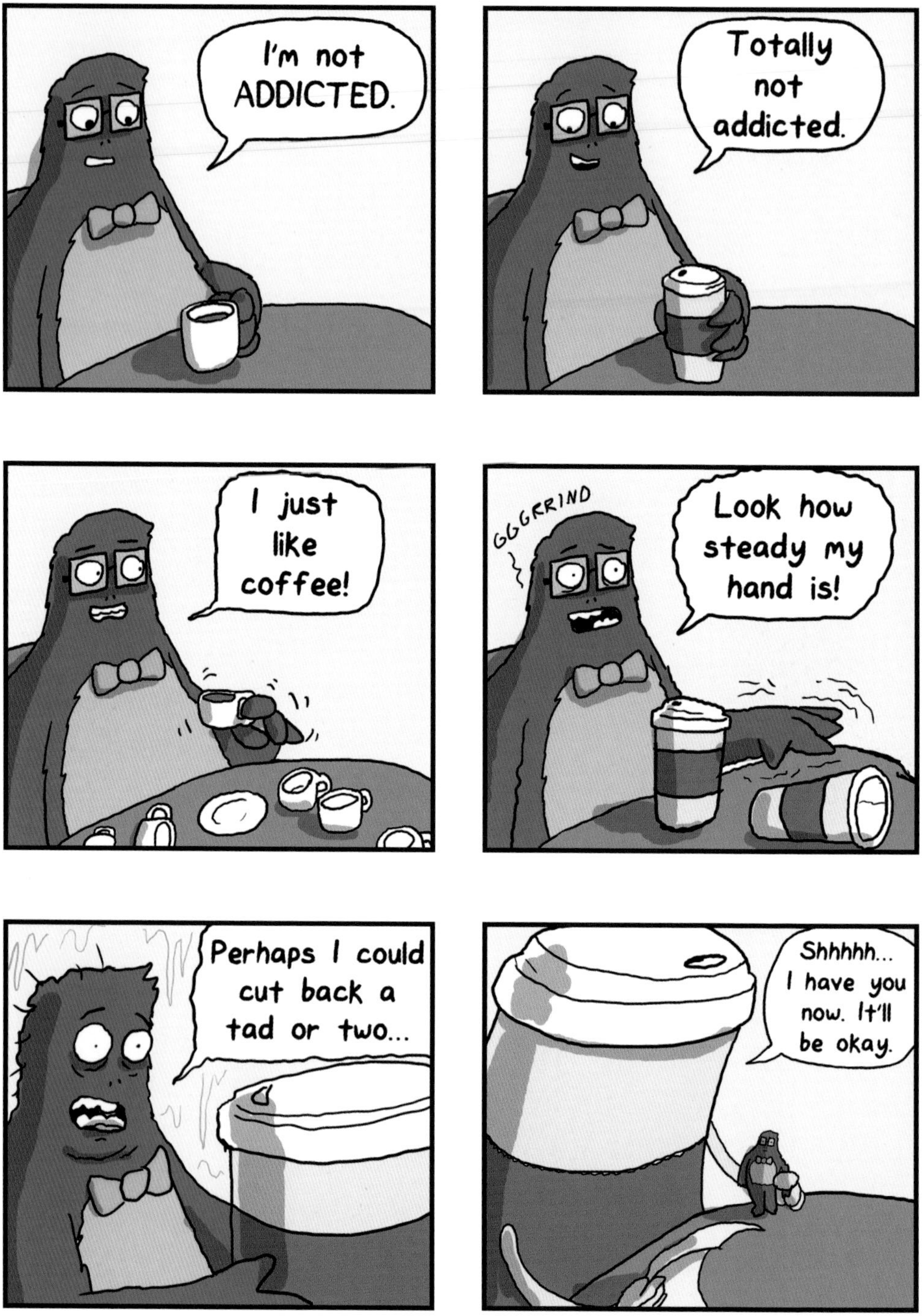
I'm not ADDICTED.
Totally not addicted.
I just like coffee!
GGGRRIND
Look how steady my hand is!
Perhaps I could cut back a tad or two...
Shhhhh... I have you now. It'll be okay.

Comic Con

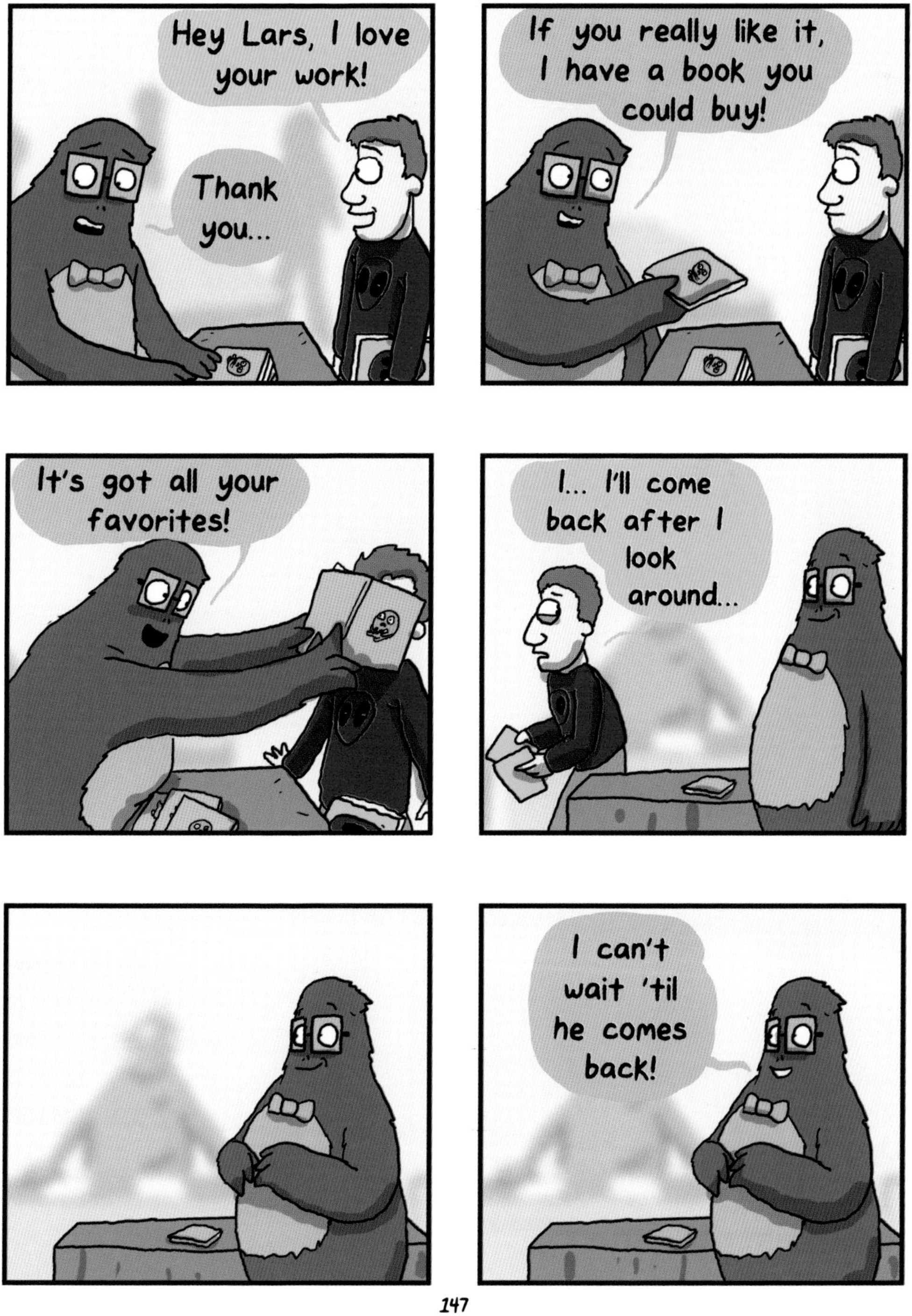

Hey Lars, I love your work!
Thank you...
If you really like it, I have a book you could buy!
It's got all your favorites!
I... I'll come back after I look around...
I can't wait 'til he comes back!

Bonus Classics

Therapy

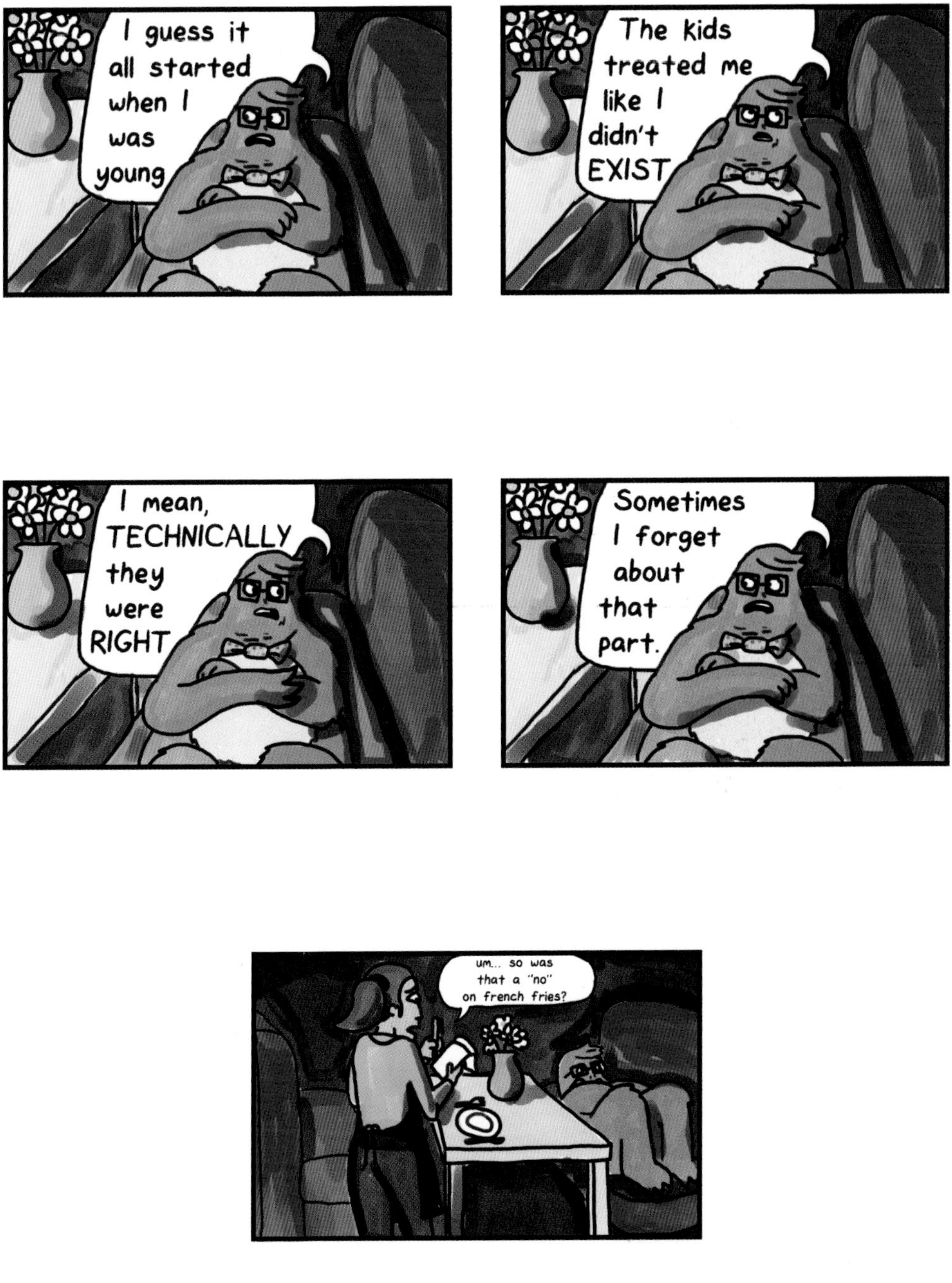
I guess it all started when I was young
The kids treated me like I didn't EXIST
I mean, TECHNICALLY they were RIGHT
Sometimes I forget about that part.
um... so was that a "no" on french fries?

Dissecting the Joke

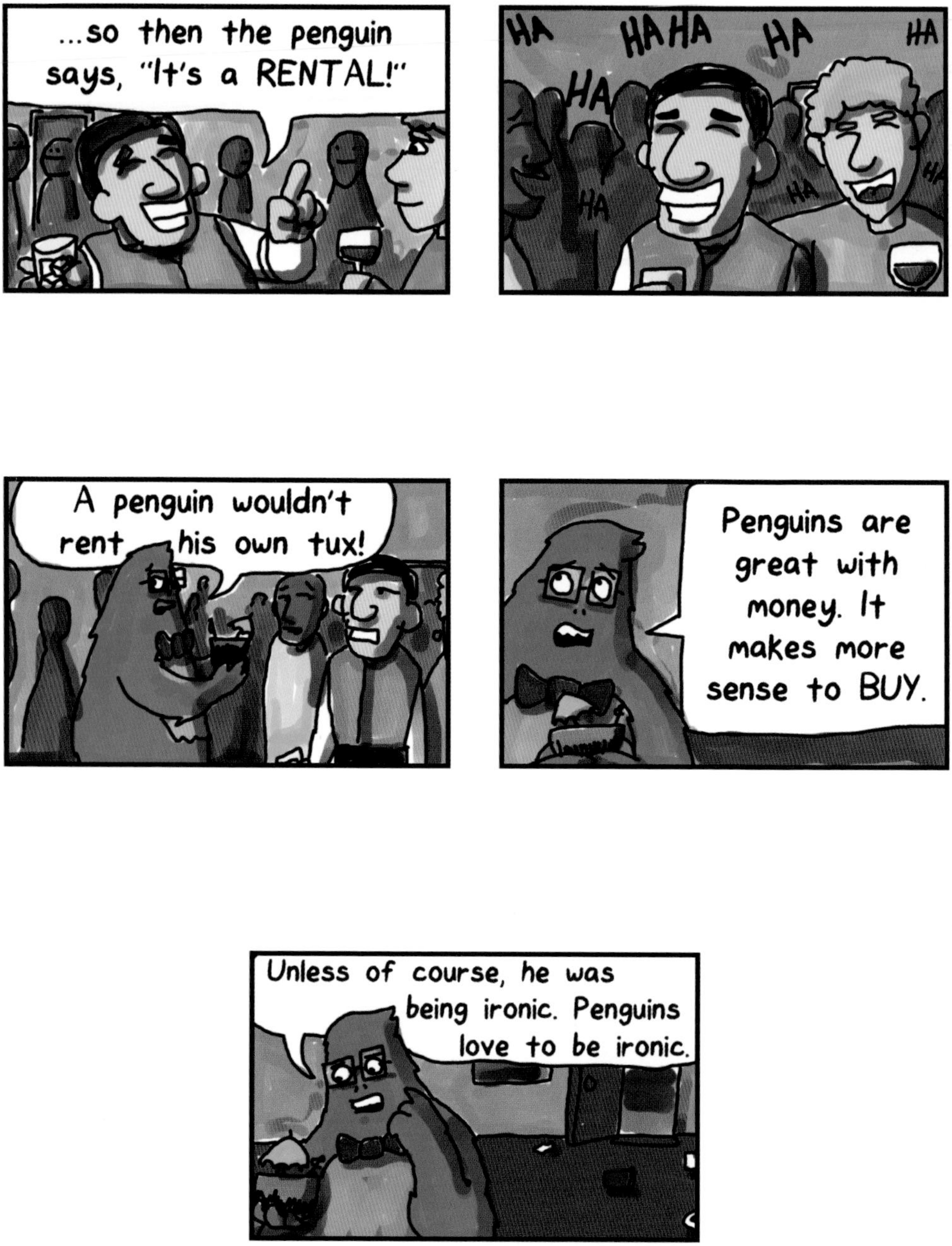

...so then the penguin says, "It's a RENTAL!"
HA HAHA HA HA
HA
HA
HA
A penguin wouldn't rent his own tux!
Penguins are great with money. It makes more sense to BUY.
Unless of course, he was being ironic. Penguins love to be ironic.

One of the Guys

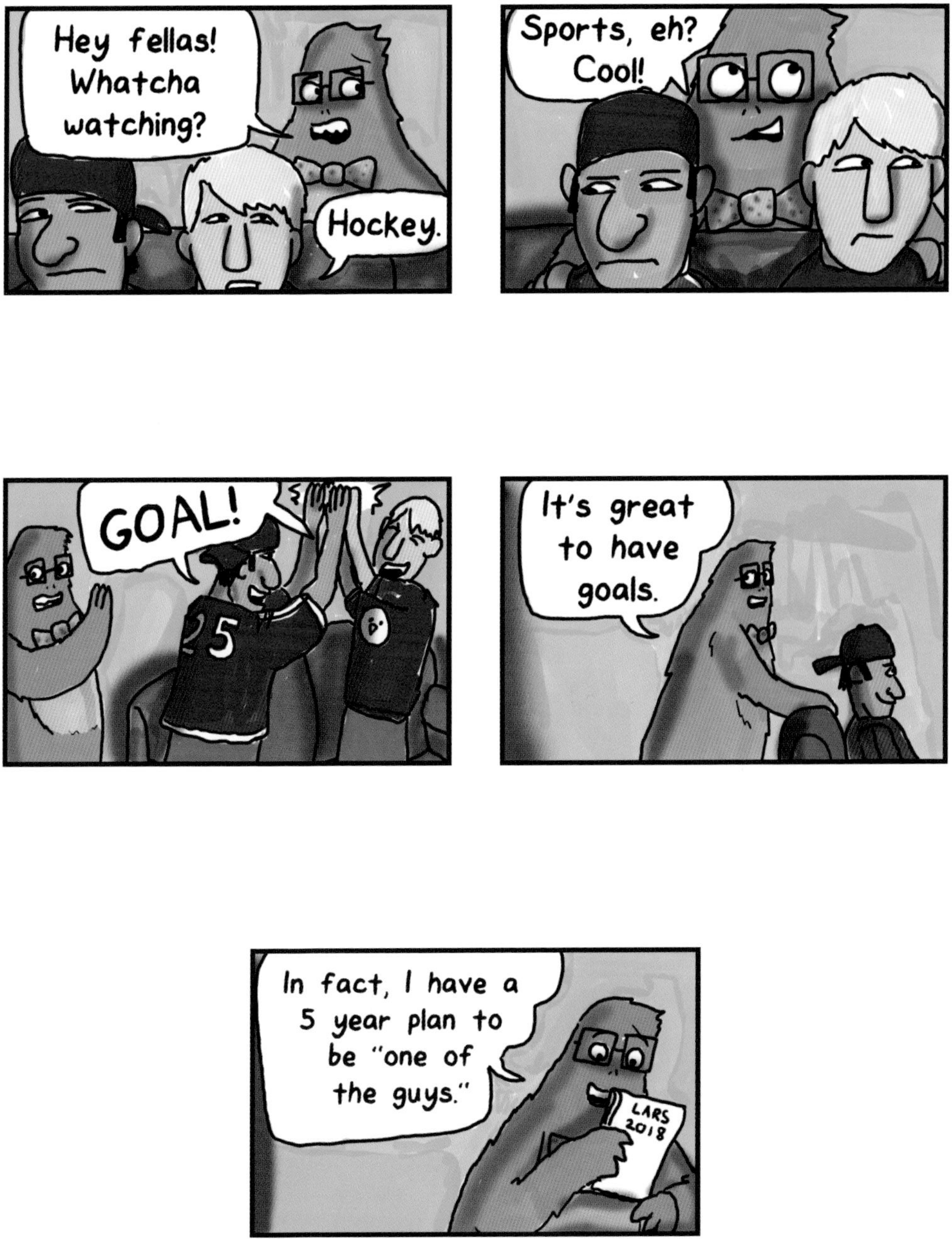
Hey fellas! Whatcha watching?
Hockey.
Sports, eh? Cool!
GOAL!
25
It's great to have goals.
In fact, I have a 5 year plan to be "one of the guys."
LARS 2018

Where We're Going...

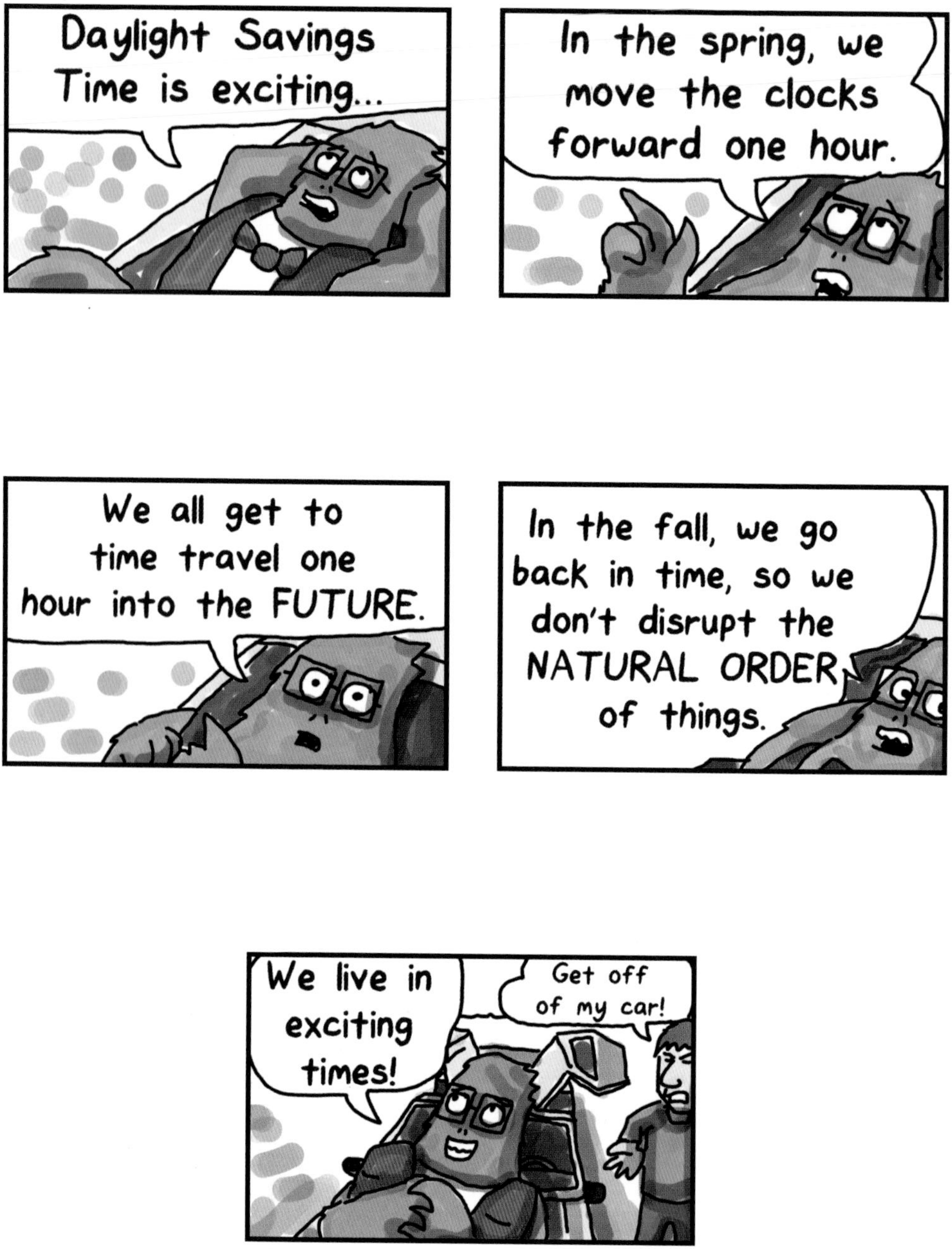
Daylight Savings Time is exciting...
In the spring, we move the clocks forward one hour.
We all get to time travel one hour into the FUTURE.
In the fall, we go back in time, so we don't disrupt the NATURAL ORDER of things.
We live in exciting times!
Get off of my car!

Words of Wisdom

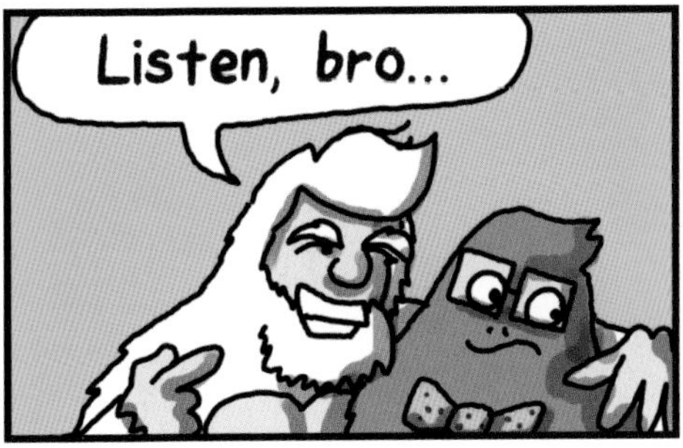
Listen, bro...

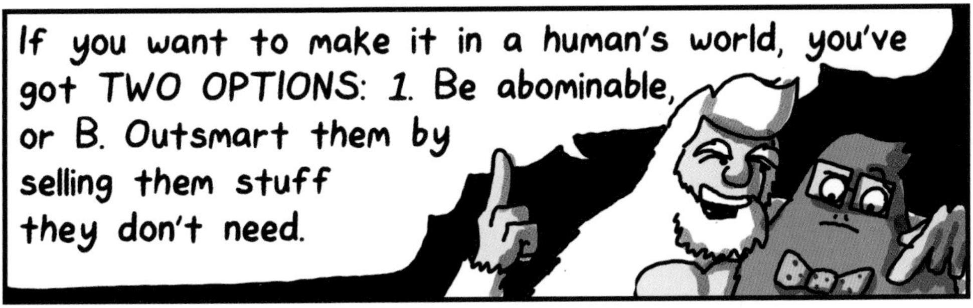
If you want to make it in a human's world, you've got TWO OPTIONS: 1. Be abominable, or B. Outsmart them by selling them stuff they don't need.

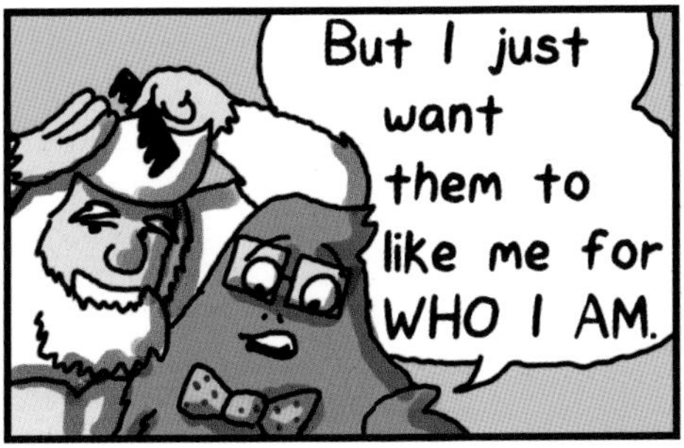
But I just want them to like me for WHO I AM.

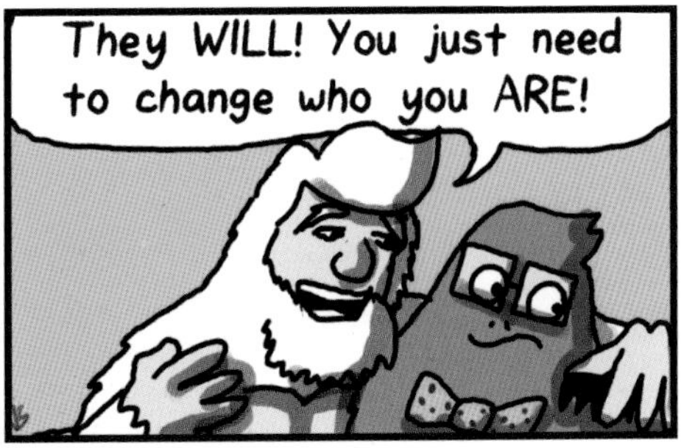
They WILL! You just need to change who you ARE!

Fresh to Death

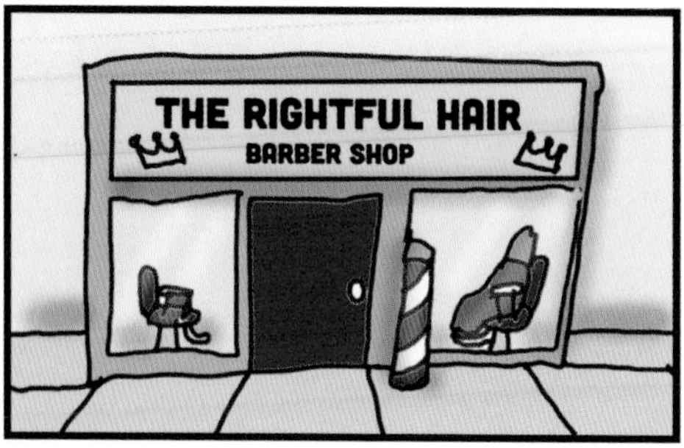
THE RIGHTFUL HAIR
BARBER SHOP

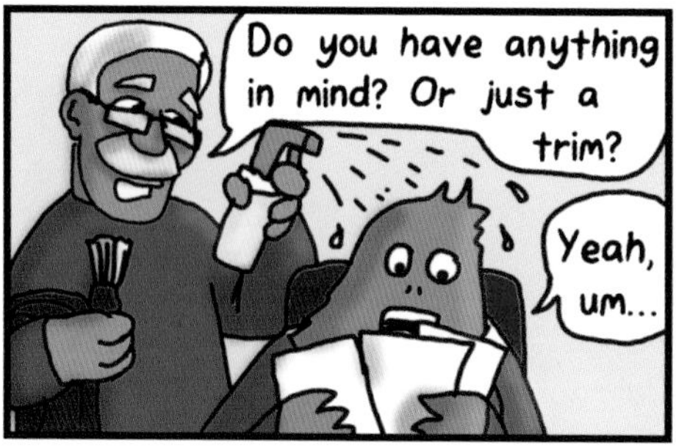
Do you have anything in mind? Or just a trim?
Yeah, um...

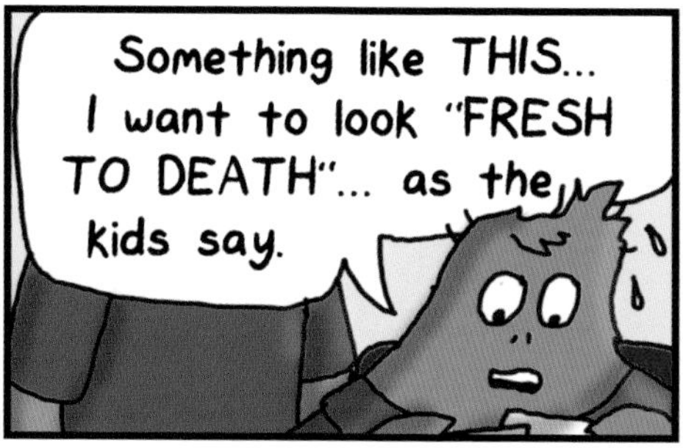
Something like THIS... I want to look "FRESH TO DEATH"... as the kids say.

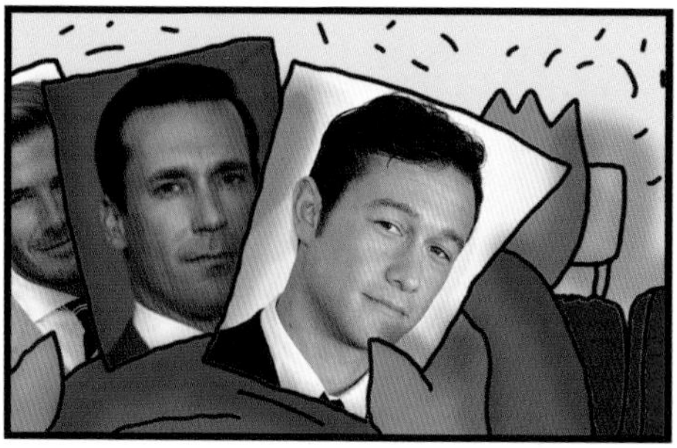

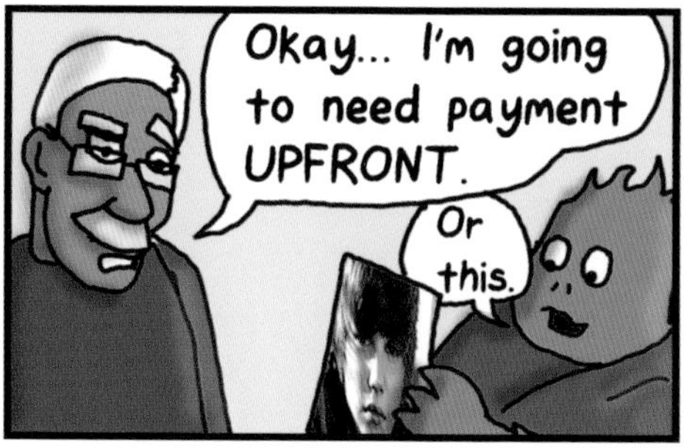
Okay... I'm going to need payment UPFRONT.
Or this.

The Mustache

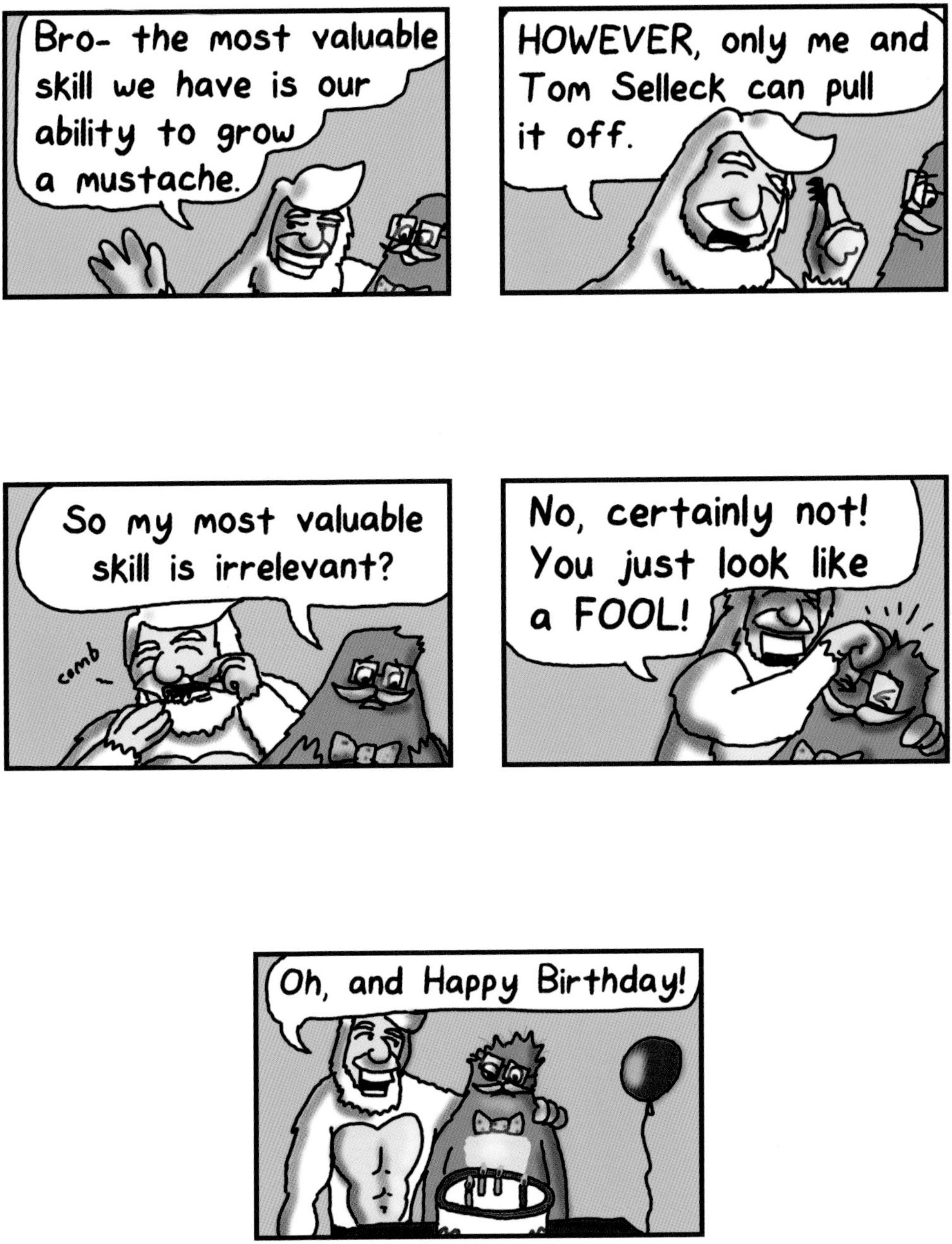

Bro- the most valuable skill we have is our ability to grow a mustache.
HOWEVER, only me and Tom Selleck can pull it off.
So my most valuable skill is irrelevant?
comb
No, certainly not! You just look like a FOOL!
Oh, and Happy Birthday!

Am I a Hipster Yet?

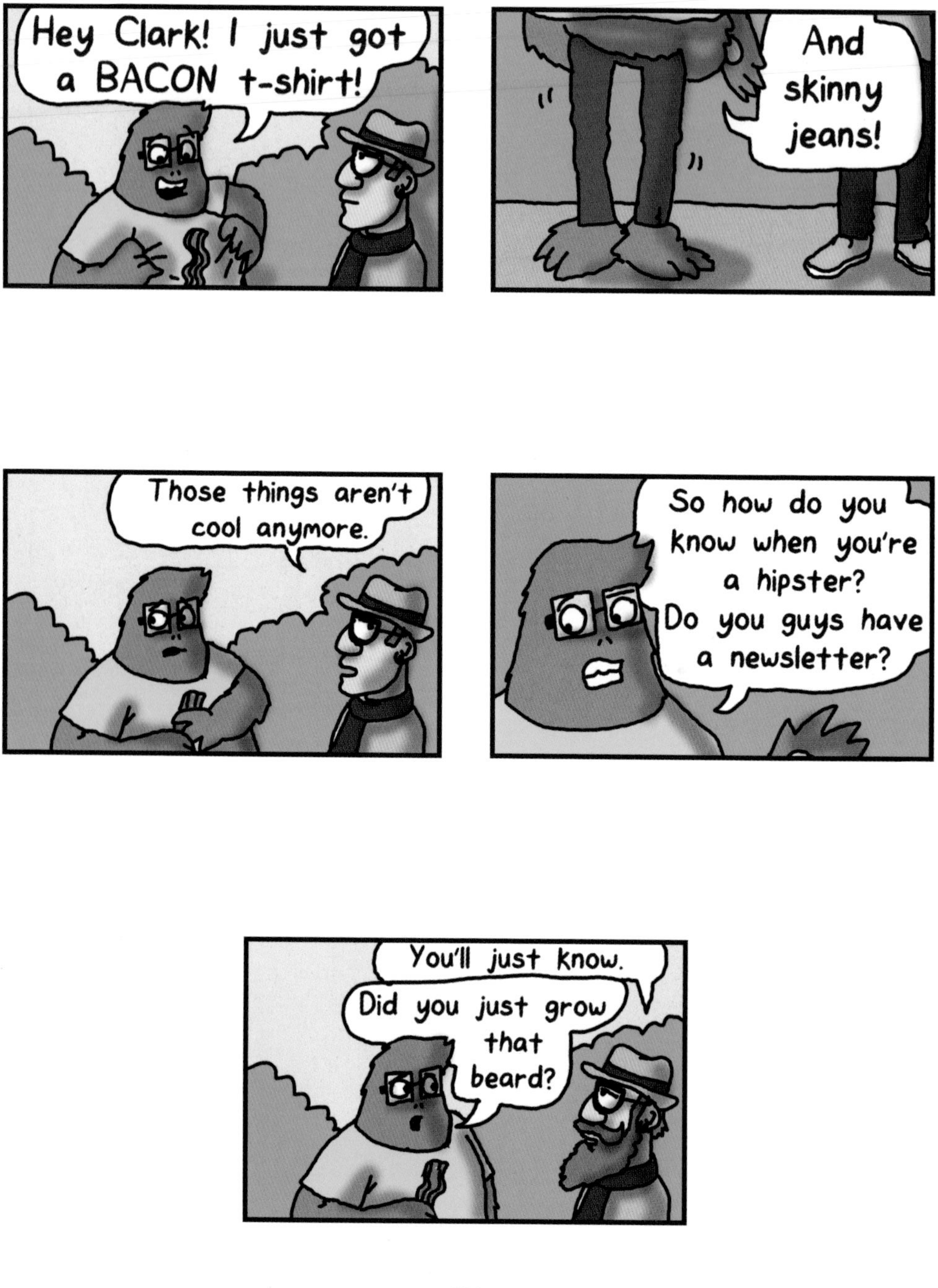

Hey Clark! I just got a BACON t-shirt!
And skinny jeans!
Those things aren't cool anymore.
So how do you know when you're a hipster? Do you guys have a newsletter?
You'll just know.
Did you just grow that beard?

Talk Like a Pirate Day

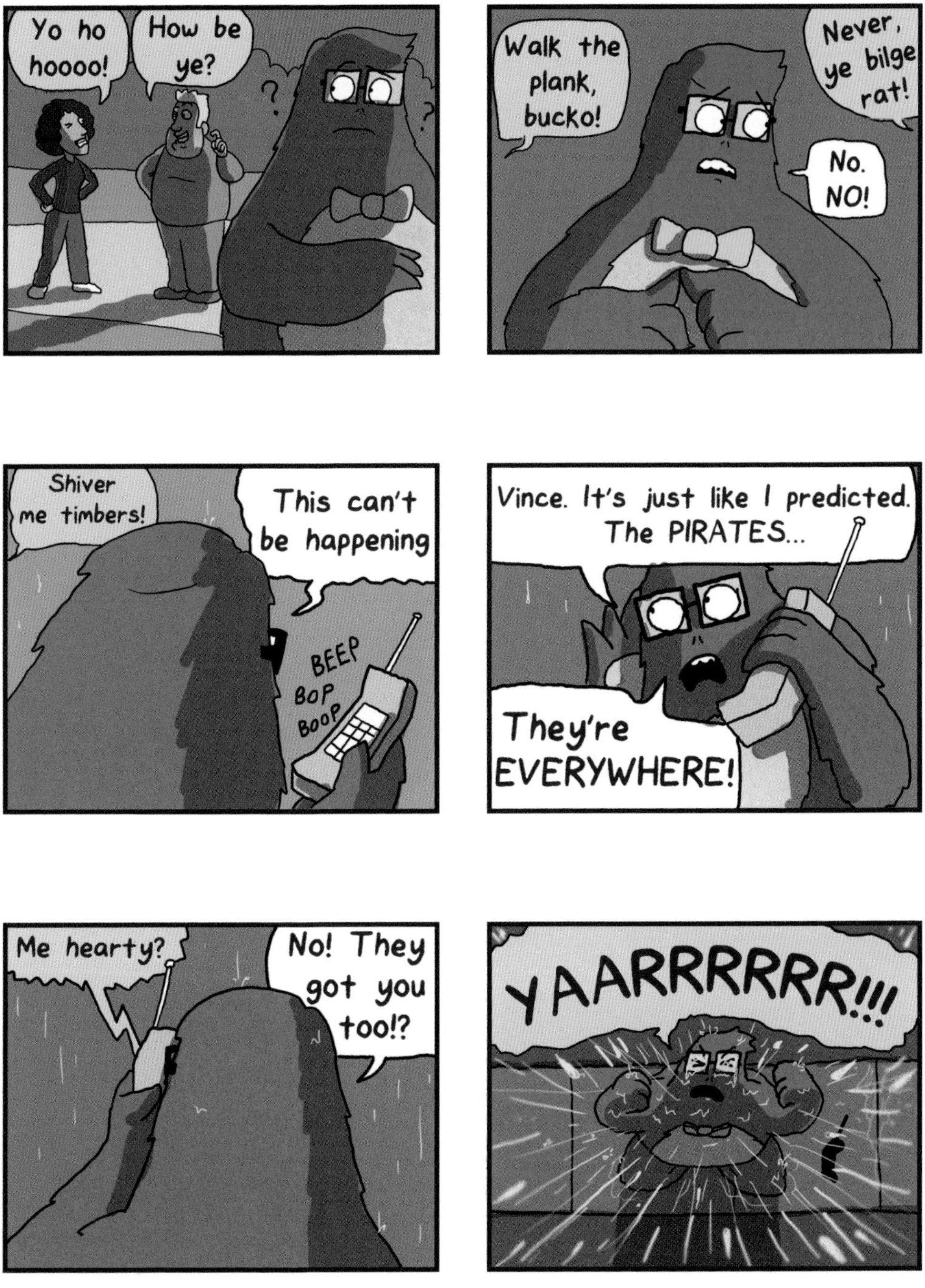
Yo ho hoooo!
How be ye?
?
?
Walk the plank, bucko!
Never, ye bilge rat!
No. NO!
Shiver me timbers!
This can't be happening
BEEP
BOP
BOOP
Vince. It's just like I predicted. The PIRATES...
They're EVERYWHERE!
Me hearty?
No! They got you too!?
YAARRRRRR!!!

What's Up?

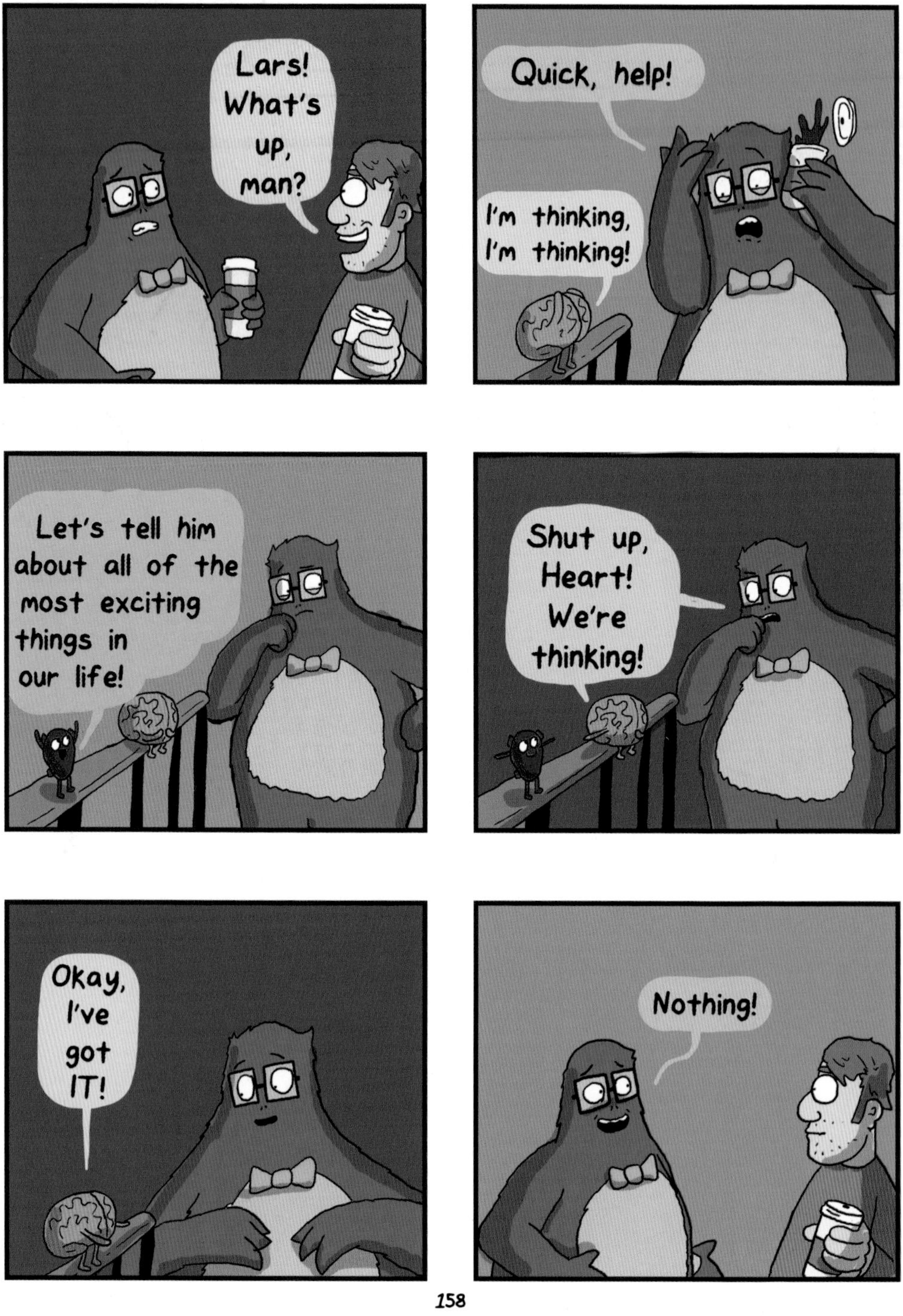
Lars! What's up, man?
Quick, help!
I'm thinking, I'm thinking!
Let's tell him about all of the most exciting things in our life!
Shut up, Heart! We're thinking!
Okay, I've got IT!
Nothing!

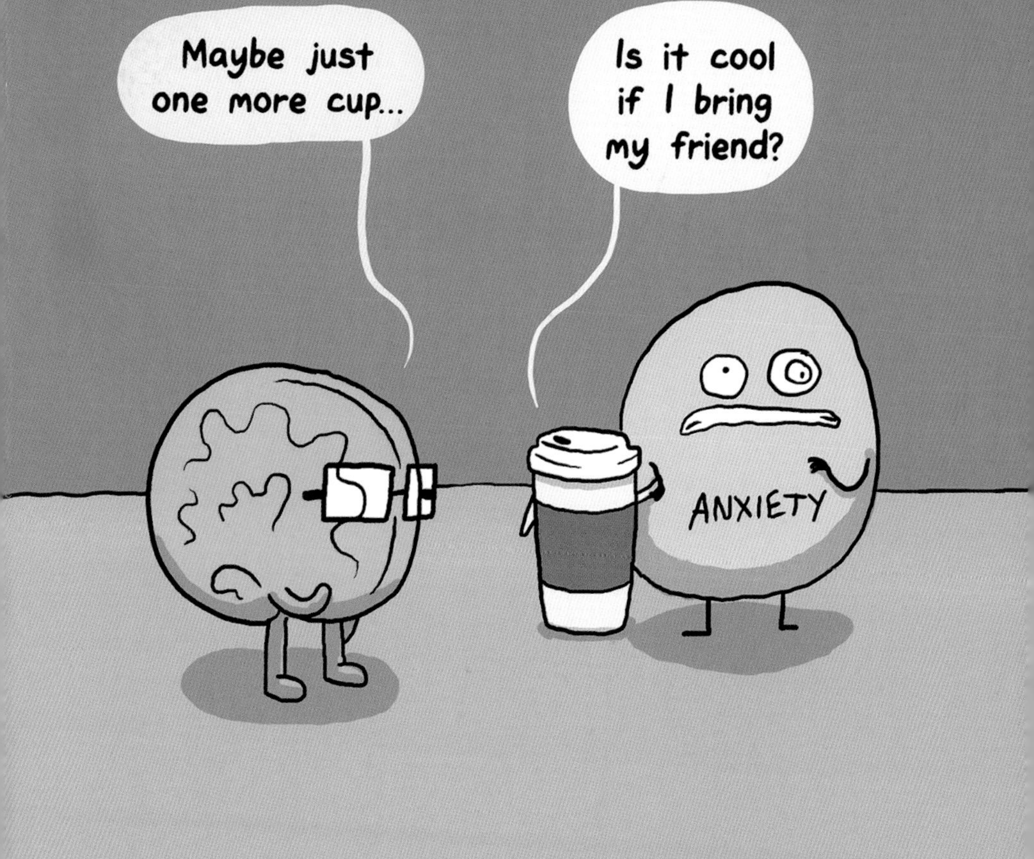
Maybe just one more cup...
Is it cool if I bring my friend?
ANXIETY

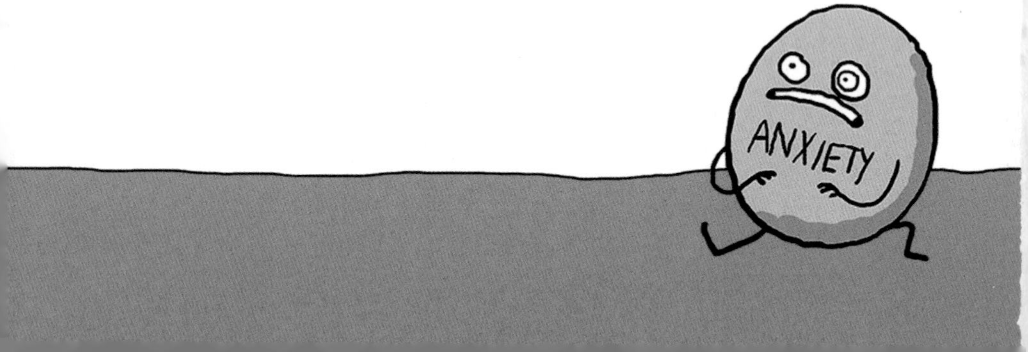
ANXIETY